OXFORD STUDIES IN AFRICAN AFFAIRS

EDUCATIONAL DEVELOPMENT
IN THE SUDAN
1898-1956

EDUCATIONAL DEVELOPMENT
IN THE SUDAN
1898-1956

BY

MOHAMED OMER BESHIR

CLARENDON PRESS·OXFORD
1969

Oxford University Press, Ely House, London W. 1

GLASGOW NEW YORK TORONTO MELBOURNE WELLINGTON
CAPE TOWN SALISBURY IBADAN NAIROBI LUSAKA ADDIS ABABA
BOMBAY CALCUTTA MADRAS KARACHI LAHORE DACCA
KUALA LUMPUR SINGAPORE HONG KONG TOKYO

PRINTED IN GREAT BRITAIN
BY
CAMBRIDGE UNIVERSITY PRESS

CONTENTS

ABBREVIATIONS

EDA   Education Archives, Ministry of Education, Khartoum.

E.D.R.   Annual Reports, Department of Education, Khartoum.

G.G.R.   Annual Reports of H.M.'s Agent and Consul General on the Finances, Administration, and Conditions of Egypt and the Sudan, the Reports by H.M.'s High Commissioner on the Finances, Administration, and Conditions of Egypt and the Sudan and the Reports on the Finances, Administration, and Conditions of the Sudan.

G.M.C.R. Annual Reports and Accounts of the Gordon Memorial College.

MIA   Ministry of Interior Archives, Khartoum.

PRO   Public Records Office, London.

SAD   Sudan Archives, School of Oriental Studies, University of Durham.

SGA   Sudan Government Central Archives, Khartoum.

SP   Papers of the third Marquis of Salisbury deposited at Christ Church, Oxford.

UKA   University of Khartoum Archives, Khartoum.

INTRODUCTION

THE central questions facing the underdeveloped countries today are what makes their economy grow and how to achieve this. Economists are emphasizing the role of education in economic development, and no longer believe that investment in material capital alone will necessarily lead to economic development. The absence of a system of education capable of producing the right attitudes and required skills and professions can easily impede progress and frustrate results expected from capital investment. It is almost impossible to increase the wealth of a nation without at the same time improving the quality and level of its human resources. This shift in focus from physical capital to people represents a fundamental change in economic thinking and the beginning of an era of emphasis on social development. Hence the renewed interest in education by both economists and educationalists, and their increasing effort to find out the relationship between a country's educational effort and its economic, political, and social progress.

The importance of education in political development is likewise recognized. Political progress in a number of underdeveloped countries is hampered by the absence of a national unity.

In almost every aspect of their social structures, the Societies on which the new States must be based are characterized by a 'gap'. It is the gap between the few very rich and the mass of the poor, between the educated and the uneducated, between the townsman and the villager, between the cosmopolitan or national and the local, between the modern and traditional, between the rulers and the ruled.[1]

These gaps, whether real or imaginary, can similarly frustrate the efforts to establish a machinery of government capable of improving economic and educational progress. The dispersion of education can be an effective tool in overcoming these gaps. The attempts to foster national unity through education are often the only alternative to conflict and bloodshed. The political scientist and sociologist are therefore busy finding the relationship between educational quantity and quality and political advancement.

The route may have been signposted but the way ahead is

---

[1] Shils, E., *Political Development in the New States*, Comparative Studies in Society and History, ii (1960), pp. 281–2.

difficult. Very little research has yet been done in the fields of social development—including education. The facts are not at hand and the major task today is to find out the basic facts relating to both the economic and the educational system.

Since Sudanese Independence in 1956 education has been the subject of a number of investigations and inquiries directed towards the development of an educational system which would facilitate economic progress and national unity between its two regions—the north and the south. In 1958 a Committee of eleven Sudanese educationalists was appointed under the chairmanship of Dr. Akrawi, a Unesco expert, to study the aims of education in the Sudan and to recommend the steps necessary for reorientation to the needs of the country.[1] The report of the Committee submitted in 1959 set out a number of new aims for Sudan education to achieve. On the role of education in economic development it stated that 'education can be a powerful aid and stimulant to economic development, to the rise of national income, and to the improvement of the standard of living.'[2] One of the major aims of education, according to the Committee, 'was the development of a sense of Sudanese unity among its citizens',[3] the inculcation 'in each child [of] a sense of nationhood and patriotism',[4] 'to teach him methods of peaceful and co-operative group work aimed at both individual and social welfare, and to imbue him with the spirit of international understanding and co-operation'.[5] The aims were finally summarized as follows:

Education in the Sudan should aim at producing a loyal citizen, strong in body and mind, sound in character, deep in his religious convictions, willing to defend the unity of his country, knowing his right and duties as a citizen, able to earn his living and to participate in the economic development of his country, able to express himself well, objective in outlook, independent in thought, courageous in action and willing to assume responsibility.[6]

The *Ten-Year Plan of Economic and Social Development* published in 1962 included among its targets the training of manpower at all levels, both technical and professional, and the improvement of the educational services 'with the object of creating a cultural and social environment capable of coping with the requirements of the new

[1] Ministry of Education, *a Report of the Sudan Educational Planning Committee*, Khartoum (June, 1959), p. 1.   [2] Ibid., p. 20.
[3] Ibid., p. 18.   [4] Ibid., p. 14.
[5] Ibid.   [6] Ibid., pp. 28–9.

economic life'.[1] Education is viewed for the first time as an investment. Out of the plan's public investment, amounting to £E285
millions, £E36·6 millions was allocated to Education.[2]

The *Report of the Unesco Educational Investment Programming
Mission to the Sudan*, submitted in 1963, emphasized the economic
role of education in the national plan. According to this report,
'economic development depends ultimately on people: no amount
of education or financing will secure it unless people are available in
adequate numbers at the right time and with the diverse knowledge
and skills required. If the educational system is not such as to produce the quantities and levels required when wanted, the economic
development envisaged will be retarded.'[3] The report concluded that
'the educational provision in the Sudan is inadequate to meet the
needs of an expanding economy'.[4]

The development of an educational system capable of fulfilling
these objectives depends, however, on a knowledge of the present
system and its background. The two published works by A. A.
Abdul Magid,[5] and V. L. Griffiths,[6] and the two unpublished studies
by L. Sanderson[7] and M. K. Osman[8] are directly concerned with
certain aspects of the history of education in the Sudan. Other books
and articles which include information on education shed valuable
light upon educational policies and changes. Little study has, however, been done on the relation between educational changes on the
one hand, and economic, political, and administrative changes on
the other. The study of these aspects of education, and how economic,
political, and administrative factors have influenced its development,
is a key to the understanding of the present system, and hence
valuable to the makers and planners of new policies, aims, and
systems. It is with these aspects of education under the Condominium
administration (1889–1956) that this book is concerned.

[1] The Republic of the Sudan, *The Ten-Year Plan of Economic and Social
Development, 1961/62–1970/71* (Khartoum, 1962), p. 6.
[2] Ibid., p. 2.
[3] United Nations Educational Scientific and Cultural Organisation, *Educational Investment Programming Mission—Sudan*, Unesco (Paris, 1963).
[4] Ibid., p. 29.
[5] Abdul Magid, A. A., *El Tarbia fi al Sudan fi al Qarn Al Tasia Azhar*, 3 vols.,
Cairo, 1949 (Arabic text).
[6] Griffiths V. L., *An Experiment in Education* (London, 1953).
[7] Sanderson, L. M., 'A History of Education in the Sudan, with special reference
to Girls Schools', M.A. thesis, University of London, 1962.
[8] Osman, M. K., 'Education and Social Change in the Sudan, 1900–1958',
M.A. thesis, University of London, 1965.

Education is viewed in the narrow sense of schools and institutions where formal instruction and training are carried out. All types and levels of education, whether government or non-government, modern or traditional, for boys or for girls, are dealt with. The word 'educated' is used to refer to those who have attended the modern schools. The word 'class' is used and preferred to the words 'élite' and 'group' when reference is made to educated persons. The word 'élite' implies a position of pre-eminence, and the word 'group' implies a closely knit collection of individuals. On the other hand, the term 'educated class' has been the most used and accepted term in the Sudan to describe those who have attended the modern schools. This is not to suggest that those who have attended the traditional institutions are not educated, nor to imply that these traditional institutions were not imparting useful knowledge.

The material largely derives from primarily unpublished sources. The Sudan Government Central Archives at Khartoum are the main source of information. These contain information on the Condominium administration in great detail. Material on educational development in the north and the south is available in both the departmental and provincial files. The Ministry of Education Archives, which, unlike the Central Archives, have not yet been classified, are another source for information on education in the Sudan. There are about 1,000 files containing detailed information on all aspects of education during the Condominium administration. It was not, however, possible to make full use of these files because of the disorganized state they are in at present. The Ministry of Interior Archives have not yet been classified. They contain information on administrative policy, especially in relation to the Southern Sudan, and on Christian missionary societies, which is not yet available in the Central Archives.

The Sudan Archives at Durham University contain the most comprehensive material outside the Sudan on the Condominium administration. The collection includes the papers of Sir Reginald Wingate, Slatin Pasha, H. C. Jackson, and other ex-officials of the Sudan. The papers and official reports include detailed information on the Sudan administration in all its aspects, Christian missions, economic development, education, etc. It was with the kind permission of the Sudan Government Archivist, the Director of Education, the Permanent Secretary to the Ministry of the Interior, and Mr. R. Hill, the keeper of the Sudan Archives at Durham

University, that it was possible to make use of the material referred to in this book.

Mr. G. C. Scott has been most helpful not only in providing me with his note on 'Education in the Northern Sudan' and letters to his mother but also in supplying me with first-hand information on educational policy during 1930–46. V. L. Griffiths and L. C. Wilcher were helpful in giving information on Bahkt or Ruda and higher education in the Sudan respectively. Mirghani Hamza has also been of immense help in providing material and information on the voluntary movement in education and the educational activities of the Graduates' Congress.

Of the published sources, the official reports and publications of the Sudan Government, the Gordon Memorial College, and the Education Department constitute the main source of information on education during the Condominium administration. A detailed survey of books and articles on Sudan education since 1900 has recently been compiled and published by Mrs L. Sanderson.[1] A great deal of research on Sudan education, however, remains to be done by economists, educationalists, political scientists, and others if some of the answers to the problem of economic growth and political development in the Sudan are to be found.

I would like to express my thanks to Mr. John Vaizey for his guidance during the preparation of my B.Litt. thesis at Oxford, of which this book is a revised version. I am indebted to the Rockefeller Foundation for providing me with financial assistance and thus enabling me to undertake this line of research. To my Sudanese friends and colleagues in Oxford during the period October 1963–June 1966 I am most grateful: their help, encouragement, and above all stimulating companionship were invaluable.

MOHAMED OMER BESHIR

Khartoum
March 1968

[1] Sanderson, L., 'A Survey of Material Available for the Study of Educational Development in the Modern Sudan, 1900–63', *Sudan Notes and Records*, xliv (1963), 69–81.

PART ONE
1898-1919

CHAPTER I

The Educational Background

MODERN education in the Sudan did not begin with the Condominium administration in 1898 when a number of schools of a 'Western' type were established by the Christian missionary societies in the main towns of the northern Sudan and a few in the south. Neither did the Sudan's cultural relations with the outside world nor the infiltration of 'Western' ideas start at the beginning of this century. The Sudan had been exposed to cultural influences from outside since ancient times. A traditional system of education had followed the spread of Islam in the country. The beginnings of a 'Western' type of education were laid during the Turco-Egyptian régime by both the government and the Christian missionary societies.

Although little is known about the history and development of education before the seventeenth century, Egypt's connections with the regions south of the present borders indicate that in most cases Egypt was the Sudan's most important link with the outside world. The regions to the south of Egypt and to the north of Khartoum, which were given different names at different times, Kush, Nubia, or Ethiopia, were in close contact with Egypt. The present southern provinces were, on the other hand, isolated and had little or no contact with the regions to the north.

Egyptian immigrants came to live in old Nubia (about 2000 B.C.) and a civilization developed similar in both character and spirituality to that of ancient Egypt. The independent kingdoms of Napata (750–300 B.C.) and Meroe (300 B.C.–A.D. 350) continued cultural relations with Egypt, and even regarded themselves as the true champions of Egyptian culture and civilization. The extent of cultural Egyptianization can best be indicated by the fact that today there are more pyramids in the Sudan than in Egypt.[1]

Christianity entered Nubia from Egypt in the sixth century as a missionary effort. The priests of Nubia were Egyptians and their language was that of the Coptic Church of Egypt. The fact that the Nubian Church was monopolized by a foreign element which did

[1] Arkell, A. J., *A History of the Sudan from the Earliest Times to 1821* (London, 1955), p. 109; Henderson, K. D. D., *The Making of the Modern Sudan* (London, 1953), p. 481.

not encourage the growth of an independent culture, nor create the incentive for learning and education, meant that Nubia had to continue being dependent on Egyptian learning and culture for a very long period. The Christian Church in Nubia, unlike that in Egypt, failed to develop an indigenous culture or centres of learning, because of its lack of vitality. Christianity was torn by the differences and hostilities between its Byzantine and Egyptian Churches, and between Jacobite and Orthodox sects. The clergy, who had lost touch with the Church beyond their borders, were corrupt and did not inspire any reform movement.[1] Christianity was therefore incapable of reforming the life of the people, or of inspiring a cultural and educational movement in the north.

With the spread of Islam in the ninth century a new culture was introduced and established in the north. Although the contact of the Arabs with Kush, Nubia, or Ethiopia had begun long before Islam, the dominance of their culture in these regions had begun after the spread of Islam. They had founded ports on the Red Sea and carried on trade in gold, ivory, spices, and slaves. Some settled on the coast, others penetrated into the interior. Some of these settlers intermarried with the local people and imparted their own pre-Islamic culture and ideas.[2] By the fourteenth century the immigrants and their culture became dominant. Arabic was adopted by the local population as a language and Islam as a religion. Two regions, however, were not affected by this language conversion—Nubia and the Beja land.[3] Few Arab tribes had settled among the Beja because their land was less attractive in comparison with the central regions as grazing areas for their livestock. The same applied to the Nubians in the north. In addition, the Nubian language had already been rendered into writing during the Christian period, and this has enabled them to survive in the face of the new language invasion up to this day.[4]

The establishment of the kingdoms of Sennar, Darfur, and Kordufan in the seventeenth century marked yet another period of trade and cultural relations with Egypt and Hejaz.[5]

Islamic ideas and culture failed to influence the south. Climatic

[1] Trimingham, J. S., *Islam in the Sudan* (London, 1949), pp. 48–59; Arnold, T., *The Preaching of Islam* (London, 1935), pp. 111–12.
[2] Abdin, A. M., *Tarikh al-Thaqafa al-Arabia fi al-Sudan* (Cairo, 1953), p. 12 (Arabic text); Abdul Magid, A. A., *al Tarbia fi al-Sudan fi al Qarn al Tasia-Ashar* (Cairo, 1949), 3 vols., pp. 18–20 (Arabic text); Crowfoot, J. W., 'Some Red Sea Ports', *Geographical Journal*, 37 (1911), 523–58.
[3] Trimingham, J. S., op. cit., p. 25.   [4] Ibid., p. 49.   [5] Ibid., p. 83.

conditions were not suitable for either man or beast. The Sudd was a natural barrier and the new ideas, associated with the slave traders, were resisted. The same applied to the Nuba of Kordufan, who, being a target for slave raiders, withdrew to their mountains.

A demand for education arose because of the spread of Islam, the settlement of Arab tribes, and the rise of Moslem kingdoms. Religious education, being a basic requirement of all Moslem societies, demanded a knowledge of the *Koran* and consequently the ability to read and write in order to 'inculcate and strengthen the faith'.[1] Learning the *Koran* was a duty of all Moslems, and parents were required to create the facilities for their children for its learning. The Arab settlers wanted to educate their children so as to ensure cultural dominance, and hence political dominance, over the original people of the country.

The type of education developed was similar to that existing in Egypt, North Africa, and Hejaz. Since the fifteenth century Moslem culture and education had been declining. The rigorous culture, and education which had concerned itself with science and philosophy in the past, became concerned in the fifteenth century and afterwards with the study of religion to the exclusion of other subjects. Political stagnation which followed the Crusades and internal wars led the many who suffered from poverty and ignorance to seek their salvation in the teachings of the *Sufis*. Therefore education in the Moslem world during the seventeenth century was mainly concerned with the study of the *Koran* and the teachings of the *Sufis*.[2] Al Azhar, in Cairo, was passing through a period of decline. Thus the foundations of Moslem education in the Sudan were laid at a time of decline in the Moslem world.

The aim of education was the study of religion and *Sufism*. The extent of its spread was determined by the proximity of the regions to Egypt, North Africa, or Hejaz, the number of settled Arab tribes among the local population, the type of economic life and political organization, and the internal communications.

The tribes in the northern region led a settled life on the banks of the Nile. They were in contact with the sources of Moslem education to the north and east, and had a developed political system. They were relatively easier to reach than other regions. As a result of these

[1] Ibn Khuldoun, *Muqadima* (Beirut, 1961), p. 779 (Arabic text).
[2] Kinany, A. K., 'Islamic Schools and Universities', *The Year Book of Education* (London, 1957), pp. 333–43.

factors they were able to establish and develop an educational system suitable to their needs. The region immediately south of Khartoum and around Sennar, although the centre of political authority, was not able to develop a comparable system of education because of its continuous involvement in wars with its neighbours to the east and west.[1]

The main teaching institutions were mosques and *khalwas*. The mosque, in addition to its purely religious function, had always been a centre of teaching in the Moslem world. As Moslem education during the first decades of Islam consisted largely of religious instruction based on the *Koran*, it was only proper that the mosque should also be used for teaching. The mosques of Al Azhar, Amzru, and Ibu Tulun in Egypt were used for this purpose. As more and more people became educated, and more children were being taught, only schools were developed for the purpose of teaching, and mosques became obsolete for this purpose. The disturbance which could be caused by teaching in the mosque led to the establishment of schools near mosques or adjacent to them.[2] This development in other Moslem lands did not, however, completely reduce the mosques in the Sudan to purely religious centres to the exclusion of teaching. The mosques of Dongula, Nuri, Damer, Halfaya, and Tuti were used for both the purposes of prayer and teaching.

The *khalwa* was, however, the more important institution of the two. It was called *al madrasah* or *kuttab* in other parts of the Moslem world.[3] The word *khalwa* is significant in itself. It is derived from an Arabic root indicating seclusion. The idea was that the teacher of religion sought seclusion to pursue his mystical meditation. As education came to be associated with *Sufism* and meditation, the *khalwa* became the main institution where the *Koran* was taught.

The *khalwa* constituted a response to the traditional needs of a Moslem society which led a simple, economic, and political life, with little contact from the outside world. Nomadism or subsistence cultivation did not require more than a simple knowledge of reading and writing, which was all that religion asked for. When demand arose for educated personnel as a result of the economic and political contacts with the neighbouring countries, the supply was found in those few who were educated in Al Azhar or Mecca.

[1] Shoqair, N., *Tarikh al Sudan al Qadim wal Hadith wa Jughrafiatuh* (Cairo, 1903), vol. I, p. 99 (Arabic text).

[2] Shalaby, A., *A History of Moslem Education* (Beirut, 1954), pp. 50–1.

[3] Heyworth-Dunne, J., *An Introduction to the History of Education in Modern Egypt* (London, 1938), p. 2.

The *khalwa*, on the other hand, was a product of a certain view of society which held that society was stable, unchanging, and governed by fixed principles of law and morality. The main purpose of education, therefore, was to transmit these principles from one generation to another, and this was done through the memorization of the *Koran*. Reading and writing were taught as a means to this end. No manuscript copies were used, and the teacher dictated from memory. The method of study was to divide the *Koran* into a number of sections and learn it by heart. The texts were written down, lesson by lesson, on wooden tablets from which they could be washed off when they had been learnt.

Next to the *Koran* the most popular subject was the *Fiqh*, studied from *al Risala* and *Mukhtasar Khalil*. Next to this was the dogmatic theology of *al Tawhid*, *Alagid*, and *Ilm Al Kalam*. The books most used were *Muqadimat al Sanousia*. Those who wanted to study further could study Recitation of the Koran, Tradition, or *al Tafsir*. Arabic grammar and rhetoric do not appear to have formed part of the regular course of studies, though references are not lacking in the *Tabaqat* to individual scholars who were said to have excelled in them.[1]

The teaching was done by the *feki*, who either was locally trained or received his education in Al Azhar or Mecca. Some came from outside the Sudan, either on their own or invited by the rulers. Teachers of theology, the *Ulama*, formed a distinct class from those who taught the *Koran*. Both groups were accorded a high status in the community. This was in accordance with the tradition of Islam that 'learned men are the inheritors of the prophets' and 'whoever teaches me a word I become his slave'. Some of them became advisers to the rulers or mediators in the wars between kingdoms.[2] They did not receive fees but were given gifts by the pupils or their parents. They had their own lands to cultivate and their pupils helped them. Sometimes the *fekis* were exempted from taxes.[3]

A certain teacher would be chosen for a certain subject, and when this was mastered the pupil would move to another place under another teacher.[4] Each *howar* or pupil attended the *khalwa* for the period he required. Sometimes attendance was for a period of seven

---

[1] Hillelson, S., 'Tabaqat Waddayfalla', *Sudan Notes and Records*, vi, no. 2 (December 1923), 199–201.

[2] Abdul Magid, A. A., *al Tarbia*, vol. i, pp. 199–216.

[3] Abdul Magid, A. A., *al Tarbia*, vol. i, p. 107.

[4] Wad Daifalla, Mohammed Al Nur, *Kitab al Tabaqat*, ed. Ibrahim Sidiq Ahmed (Cairo, 1930), Arabic text, p. 73.

to fifteen years during which time the whole or part of the Koran
would be mastered.[1] This long period of attendance was made
possible through the existence of slaves who worked the land, and
thus enabled parents to dispense with the service of their children
for long periods. Hours of study began at dawn and ended at noon,
and sometimes there were evening sessions. There was no examination
and no time limit, and at the end of the studies the student would
receive a licence called the *ijazah* which permitted him to establish
his own school and follow the tradition of his teachers. The financially
able provided free lodging for the foreign student.[2]

Discipline in the *khalwa* not only required the rendering of every
kind of service to the *feki*, but imposed long hours of study. Corporal
punishment was recognized as a means of education.

As *Sufism* spread and became dominant, it was included as a
subject of instruction in the *khalwas*.[3] In this way the system of free
and voluntary education, with its free and voluntary boarding
facilities, not only catered for the needs of the community, but also
provided for the spiritual needs of the individual, moulding him in
the stream of life through its character training, and enabling him
to enter and participate in the social and cultural life of the
community.

According to Wad Daifalla, it was Mahmoud Al Araki, coming
from Egypt, who laid the foundation of the *khalwa* among the
people.[4] Other authorities suggested that it was Gullam Alla, coming
from Yemen, who established Islamic education even before the
Funj kingdom.[5] The descendants of Gullam Alla became renowned
for their learning and teaching.

The most famous *khalwas*, as suggested by Wad Daifalla, were
those in the Shaigia region, where the descendants of Gullam Alla
lived.[6] Katb al Shuna suggested that it became famous because
the first seven teachers sent by Haroun Al Rashid came to live there.[7]

An important factor, however, was that theirs was a relatively
prosperous region and their political organization was more advanced

[1] Abdul Magid, A. A., *al Tarbia*, vol. i, pp. 98–110.
[2] Burckhardt, J. L., *Travels in Nubia* (London, 1819), pp. 70–1
[3] Trimingham, J. S., *Islam in the Sudan*, p. 116.
[4] Wad Daifalla, *al Tabaqat*, p. 163.
[5] MacMichael, Sir H. A., *History of the Arabs in the Sudan*, 2 vols (Cambridge, 1922), vol. ii, p. 10.
[6] Wad Daifalla, *al Tabaqat*, p. 6.
[7] Katb al-Shuna, A. *Tarikh, Muluk Al Sudan*, p. 1.

than their neighbours'.[1] The economic and political advantages of the Shaigia region attracted teachers and students to their schools. These teachers were patronized and helped by the *meks* and local rulers. For example, Idris Ibn Gabir, one of the famous teachers, was married to one of the Shaigia queens.[2] The students who came from other parts of the country were welcomed and looked after by the people.

The first and most famous of all schools at that time was that established by Ibrahim Ibn Jabir. He was one of the first Sudanese who had travelled, in the seventeenth century, to study in Al Azhar.[3] His school at Turung, near modern Karima, attracted students from different parts of the country, and when their studies were completed many of them started schools in their own regions. The Gabir family followed the tradition and became dedicated to learning and teaching. A brother, Abdul Rahman, established two more schools at Korti and Dongula, where he spent four months in each, teaching the *Koran* and other related subjects. A sister, Fatima bint Gabir, was not only learned and pious but also a patron of a number of students.[4] Other famous schools in the region established by the Gabir family or by graduates of their Turung school were at Nuri, Zawarah, Dueim Wad Hag, Tangasi, and El Gorair.

When J. L. Burckhardt visited the Shaigia region in 1813 he found that many of the Shaigia had learnt to read and write Arabic. He noticed that the learned men were held in great respect and in their schools 'all the sciences are taught which form the course of Mohamedan study, mathematics, astronomy excepted'.[5] Waddington and Hanbury, however, found that, in addition to reading and writing, the pupils were taught addition, subtraction, division, and multiplication.[6] Burckhardt noticed that 'whenever young men are sent to them [the Shaigia], from the adjacent countries for instruction, the chief of the Ulama distributes them among his acquaintances in whose houses they are lodged and fed as many years as they choose to remain'.[7] He observed that 'many of the children of Sukot and

[1] Maqar, N., Ahwal al-Sudan al-Iqtisadiah Qubail al-Fath al-Misri. M.A. thesis submitted to Cairo University, 1956, pp. 34–81 (Arabic text).

[2] Wad Daifalla, *al Tabaqat*, p. 7.

[3] Ibid., p. 6.

[4] Ibid., pp. 111–12.

[5] Burckhardt, J. L., *Travels in Nubia*, pp. 70–1.

[6] Waddington, G. and Hanbury, B., *Journal of A Visit to Some Parts of Ethiopia* (London, 1822), p. 249.

[7] Burckhardt, pp. 70–1.

Mahas are sent to the schools of the Arab Shaigia, where they remain for ten years and upwards, and are fed and taught gratuitously by the Ulema of that tribe'.[1]

To the north of this region schools were established in the Dongula region, at Al Dabah, Dongula, and Goshabi. The three most popular teachers who attracted students to their schools were Wad Isa Swar al Dahab, Doleib Nasi, and Habib Nasi.[2]

Further north no centres of learning were established. The Nubians who kept to their own language did not demand education in Arabic. On the other hand, this was a region controlled by the *Kushaf* who came from Egypt and ruled over the Nubian independently of the Funj kingdom.[3] The few Nubians who knew how to read and write were educated in the Shaigia or Dongula schools, or by the *Ulama* who came to settle among them for short periods on their way to Al Azhar in Cairo.[4]

Another centre of learning was at Berber. This was a trade centre on the caravan routes between the Red Sea and central Sudan. The tradition was established by Mohamed Al Masri, who came from Egypt and established his own school. The school at Berber served applicants from the Rubatab and Manasir tribes. To the south of Berber there was the famous Magadhib school at Damer which, like the Shaigia schools, attracted students from different parts of the country.[5] J. L. Burckhardt, during his visit to Berber in 1813, found that many of the families had a son or relative dedicated to the study of the *Koran* and that many had been taught at Berber, Damer, or in the Shaigia region.[6] He founded several schools at Damer to which young men from Darfur, Kordufan, and Sennar came to learn the *Koran*. The teachers at Damer were educated at Al Azhar or Mecca, and had many books on religious and legal subjects. The *Koran*, *Tafsyr*, and *Tawhyd* were taught in these schools.[7]

On account of its commercial importance and the fact that a number of Shaigia teachers, or those who were educated in their schools, came to settle and teach in the Shendi region, this became another important educational area. Among those who contributed

[1] Ibid., p. 51.
[2] Wad Daifalla, *al Tabaqat*, pp. 165, 57, 90.
[3] Maqar, N., *Ahwal al-Sudan al-Iqtisadiah Qubail al-Fath al-Misri*, pp. 6, 18.
[4] Burckhardt, J. L., *Travels in Nubia*, p. 51.
[5] Ibid., pp. 4, 71, 122.
[6] Ibid., pp. 227, 267.
[7] Ibid., pp. 4, 71, 122.

to the reputation of the Shendi schools were Abu Sinaina, whose seminar consisted of about a thousand students, Al Mudawi Al Masri, Sighayroun Aloudi, and Abdul Rahman Abu Fag of the Shaigia tribe.[1]

The other important regions in which education and learning were established were:

1. The Halfaya region, near modern Khartoum North. Al Bandari came from Egypt and settled in Halfaya to teach. Hamad Wad Ummariom had a number of women among his students.[2] Abu Surur Al Fadhli started teaching in Halfaya but later moved to Darfur. At Tuti, Khogali Ibn Abdul Rahman, who was taught by Aisha bint Al-Gadal, a woman who was learned and pious,[3] was the most famous teacher.

2. The Gezira and Sennar regions. Many learned teachers travelled there and started their own schools. Among these were Ibrahim Ibn Naseer, who was known for his great collection of books, Hassan Wad Hassouna, who maintained more than ten schools, Dafalla Ibn Mohamed Abu Idris, for whom a rich man built a mosque and endowed it with twelve slaves for the maintenance of students, and Arbab Ibn Oun, whose school had many students who came from inside and outside the Sudan.[4]

3. The White Nile region, where the schools of Al Masalami, Ibrahim Ibn Abboudi, and Mahmoud Al Araqi were famous. The region seemed to have been a popular centre of learning before the raids of the Shilluk tribes, and famines, made it insecure for students and teachers.[5]

Kordufan, Darfur, and the Red Sea regions seemed to have had their own schools. They were not, however, as numerous or important as those of northern and central Sudan. The famous *khalwas* in Darfur were those of Kibi, Nazgang, Gana, Kabkabia, and Nunwashia.[6] Occasionally in *al-Tabaqat* scholars from Tokar were mentioned.[7] The Beja regions were, however, served by the learned teachers who established *khalwas* such as the Mogadheb of Dazer.[8]

[1] Wad Daifalla, *al Tabaqat*, pp. 26, 32, 131.
[2] Abdin, A. M., *Tarikh al-Thaqafa*, p. 81.
[3] Wad Daifalla, *al Tabaqat*, p. 145; Abdul Magid, A. A., *Al Tarbia*, vol. 1, p. 225.   [4] Wad Daifalla, *al Tabaqat*, pp. 26, 46, 85, 31.
[5] Ibid., pp. 21, 22, 163; Hillelson, S., *al Tabaqat*, p. 192.
[6] Ministry of Education, *al Talim Fi Darfur* (Khartoum, 1962), p. 70 (Arabic text).   [7] Hillelson, S., *al Tabaqat*, p. 192.
[8] Abdul Magid, A. A., *al Tarbia*, vol. 1, p. 210; Okeir, A. G., 'Education among the Beja', *Overseas Education*, xxiii, no. 1 (October 1951), 18.

Thus it was along the main Nile and along the Blue Nile between Khartoum and Sennar that scholarship and education developed during the sixteenth, seventeenth, and eighteenth centuries. Since great importance was attached to the continuity of tradition and the saying held that 'one who studied without a *shaikh* could never become a true *alim*', the region was abundant with a class of *Ulama* and saints, whose religious ideas and educational practices were similar to those of other Moslem countries. The current thoughts which at different times agitated the Islamic world found their way to the Sudan. The scholars and saints referred to in the *al-Tabaqat* reflected, in their different attitudes and types, a variety of the spiritual and intellectual doctrines which dominated Islam at the time. But 'the isolation of the country and backward state of learning'[1] resulted 'in the scholarship being scanty and feeble'.[2] In spite of this situation and the fact that this was a period of stagnation in the Moslem world and there were few libraries and books in the country, the achievements in education were significant.[3] The *fekis*, scholars, and saints of the Funj period gave the country a system of education suitable to the conditions of the times and undisturbed by the new Turco-Egyptian régime in 1820.

The occupation of the Sudan by the Turco-Egyptian forces provided the country for the first time with a central government. The Sudan became part of Egypt and its economic and cultural relations with the latter were cast into a new mould. The new régime did not find the gold it thought it would find in plenty. When the slave trade was abolished, Mohamed Ali could not recruit from among the blacks the numbers he wanted for his wars. But the Sudan could not be abandoned, and the best had to be made of what looked to many at the time a bad bargain. It was necessary to develop agriculture and communications, and establish a better system of administration.

In the field of education the policy was influenced by the attitude of Egyptian rulers in Egypt itself, and the attitude of their representatives in the Sudan. It was obvious that the new economic and administrative structure required more than the simple knowledge supplied by the *khalwa* education.

Mohamed Ali's educational policy in Egypt aimed at encouraging the *koranic* schools already in existence and establishing a few state schools which would produce the personnel needed for his modern

[1] Hillelson, S., *al Tabaqat*, p. 195.
[2] Ibid., p. 195.   [3] Ibid., p. 204.

reforms. He relied at the beginning on Egyptian personnel to implement the economic and administrative measures he introduced. The
need for local personnel to carry out the new measures did not,
therefore, arise at the beginning. His educational policy was aimed
at encouraging the *koranic* schools, and not interfering with their
work.[1] Grants were paid to the local teachers and *fekis* who applied
for support. His interest in the economic development of the Sudan,
however, led him to send a number of skilled workers from Egypt
to train Sudanese in agriculture. Following his visit to the Sudan in
1838–9, six Sudanese boys were sent to Egypt for agricultural education in the school founded by him in Cairo. While in Cairo they were
looked after and supported by government grants, and their course
of study lasted for three years. On completing their studies they were
attached to the department of agriculture for practical training, and
to the school of languages. They were afterwards employed by the
government in the Sudan.[2]

When Mohamed Ali began to send Egyptians on training courses
to Europe as part of his policy for modernizing Egypt, a few Sudanese
from among those already in Egypt were selected and sent abroad.[3]
They returned to work in Egypt instead of the Sudan. Mohamed Ali's
decision to train Egyptians in Europe was a new departure in educational policy in Egypt and the Sudan. Al Azhar continued to attract
Sudanese in greater numbers as a result of the new links between
Egypt and the Sudan; and a Sennar residence—*Riwaq*—was established in 1846 to provide board and lodging. The *Riwaq* was subsidized by the Egyptian government.[4]

Khedive Abbas (1848–54) was neither a reformer nor a supporter
of education for either Egypt or the Sudan. During his time the
Sudan suffered from the lack of a stable administration. In the course
of his seven years of rule, six governors were appointed to the Sudan,
none of them remaining more than a year. As his policy was to reduce
the expenditure on the Sudan he encouraged his governors to employ
Sudanese in government service and replace the Egyptian employees,
who were more expensive, with Sudanese. With this aim in mind,
and perhaps to get rid of Rufaa Rafia Al Tahtawi,[5] he established a

[1] Abdul Magid, A. A., *al Tarbia*, vol. ii, pp. 11–12.
[2] Ibid., pp. 17–18.
[3] Heyworth-Dunne, J., *An Introduction to the History of Education*, p. 172.
[4] Abdul Magid, A. A., *al Tarbia*, vol. i, p. 20.
[5] Rufaa Rafia Al Tahtawi (1801–73), Egyptian scholar, educated at Al Azhar
and Paris. He became principal of the school of foreign languages and trans-

primary school in Khartoum in 1853. Rufaa, who was appointed
headmaster, was not keen on the school because he held that his
appointment was a punishment rather than a reward. He believed
that it amounted to deportation from Egypt. The plan was to develop
the school on the Egyptian pattern and admit the sons of tribal
chiefs from Dongula, Khartoum, Sennar, and Kassala, and also the
sons of Turkish personnel resident in Khartoum. It was also planned
that the course would last for three years and all the students would
be resident. The age for admission was 7–12 years and subjects
studied were reading, writing, Arabic, and arithmetic. There were
eleven teachers in addition to Rufaa and a medical officer who looked
after the students' health. Seven of the school's eleven teachers were
army officers and two were from Al Azhar. The majority of the army
officers employed as teachers were persons who had committed
offences in Egypt and were appointed to the school in Khartoum as
a punishment, for Sudan service was at that time unpopular with
the Egyptians.[1] When Khedive Abbas died the school was closed.
Khedive Saeed, who followed Abbas, did not favour education. The
grumblings of Rufaa and his colleagues, and the indifference of
Khedive Saeed led to the closure of the first modern school in the
Sudan only one year after its establishment.

   Khedive Ismail (1863–79), like his father Mohamed Ali, set out to
make reforms in both Egypt and the Sudan. His enthusiasm for
reform was reflected in his educational policy in the Sudan. Sudanese
were encouraged to go and study in Al Azhar. The traditional
education in the Sudan was also encouraged through the payment
of grants to the teachers in the *Khalwas*, and new *Khalwas* were
established by the government. A plan to reform the *Khalwa* education in the Sudan was proposed and approved by Ismail. He planned
to appoint a Sudanese to each province in the Sudan with a view
to supervising the work of the *Khalwas* and initiate new courses of
instruction. He also proposed to appoint a Sudanese inspector of
education in Khartoum to supervise the provincial policies of education. The plan was not put into effect, and the traditional system of
education remained the same as before.

   Development in agriculture and local administration in the Sudan

lated many foreign works into Arabic. His Sudan experiences are recorded in
his book *Manahijal-adab-al-Misrya*. Al Shial, *J. Rufaa Rafia Al Tahawi* (Cairo,
1958) (Arabic text).
   [1] Abdul Magid, A. A., *al Tarbia*, vol. ii, pp. 28–37.

during this period led to a demand for trained clerks and technicians. As work in the Sudan was still unpopular with Egyptians, and those who agreed to work in the Sudan demanded high salaries, the need for trained Sudanese became urgent. The Sudan was costing Egypt an average of £E 50,000 a year because its revenue failed to meet the expenditure. In order to economize and reduce the cost of administration, it was decided to intensify the training of Sudanese for government service.[1]

A system of religious courts, to which religious men and teachers were appointed, was established.[2] Arabic replaced Turkish as the language of government correspondence. As the need for trained Sudanese grew, the need for schools where the training could be done became urgent.[3]

Five primary schools were established in 1863, at Khartoum, Berber, Dongula, Kordufan, and Kassala; and a few years later two at Suakin and Sennar. One hundred and twenty-four students were admitted to the Khartoum school and 75 to each of the other schools. The schools which followed the Egyptian system were supervised by the Egyptian department of education and became part of its system.[4] The development of a net of telegraphic lines between Khartoum and El Obeid, Fazoghli, Alkawa, Musawa, Berber, Kassalla, and Suakin[5] led to the establishment of two vocational training schools in Khartoum and Kassalla in 1870. Admission was from among boys who had completed their education in the primary schools.[6] The steamers' department started a training course for primary school leavers with a view to employing them as skilled workers and artisans.

With the extension of medical services to care for the health of the increasing number of government employees, both Egyptian and Sudanese, the need arose for locally trained staff in this field. A training course in medicine and pharmacy was organized for those who had completed the primary course.[7]

In addition to these courses and schools, a special school was established at Suakin for the education of children of freed slaves. Parents were opposed to sending their children to the same school

[1] Martin, P. F., *The Sudan in Evolution* (London, 1921), p. 108.
[2] Hill, R., *Egypt in the Sudan 1820–1881* (London, 1959), p. 23.
[3] Abdul Magid, A. A., *al Tarbia*, vol. ii, p. 72.
[4] Ibid., p. 74.
[5] Shoqair, N., *Tarikh al Sudan*, p. 176.
[6] Hill, R., *Egypt in the Sudan 1820–1881*, p. 23.
[7] Abdul Magid, A. A., *al Tarbia*, vol. ii, p. 74.

as the former slave children, and it was therefore necessary to provide special facilities for the latter.

As the Egyptian empire expanded to include Darfur, the Upper Nile, and Equatoria provinces, and demands for clerks and technicians increased, more students were admitted to the training courses and schools in the provinces. Special teachers were provided for the army battalions stationed in outer districts, where no schools were available.[1] Plans were drawn to establish a technical school in the southern Sudan to cater for the local population, and to teach technical subjects in addition to instruction in Arabic and Islamic religion.

Another plan was drawn up for agricultural education. The plan included the establishment of a community development centre at Adfo, near Cairo, with a view to bringing 1,200 Sudanese between the ages of 12 and 15 (200 each year), settling them on an agricultural project and providing them with elementary education and training in agriculture. The plan included a special course in home economics, domestic science, and child welfare for their wives. The aim of the project was to provide experienced and educated farmers for the Sudan.[2] The project was, however, never executed.

Khedive Ismail's progressive policy in education was continued during the time of Khedive Tawfik (1879–92). The most outstanding development during his reign, however, was the establishment of a school of medicine and pharmacy to replace the training courses which were already in existence. The plans for the school were drawn during the time of Ismail but the execution was delayed. In 1879, a teacher of chemistry and physics was appointed and left for the Sudan to take charge of the new project.[3]

In the southern Sudan, which had become part of Ismail's Empire, an elementary school was established in Equatoria province[4] to provide education for the children whose parents were in the army battalion stationed there, and for the children of the local population. Very few of the latter group did, however, make use of this facility.

Another contribution of the Turco-Egyptian administration, besides opening the Sudan to modern types of education, was its encouragement of missionary education. The establishment of a unified government, and the relative peace and order which had been established, attracted Christian missions to the Sudan.

[1] Abdul Magid, A. A., *al Tarbia*, vol. ii, p. 87.
[2] Ibid., p. 82.
[3] Ibid., p. 91.   [4] Ibid., p. 95.

The missionary educational activities during this period arose from their interest in spreading Christianity not only in the Sudan, but also through the latter to other parts of Africa. The Sudan was important from the missionary point of view because of its position on the routes which led to West, South, and East Africa. They had always considered it as a door through which they could reach the Christian kingdom of Ethiopia, where they wanted to carry their missionary work and capture its Coptic church. Catholic missionaries belonging to the Franciscan and Jesuit orders were not only the first to recognize this fact, but also the first European missionaries to try and introduce missionary work into Ethiopia through the Sudan.

Franciscan and Jesuit fathers came to Sennar in the seventeenth century on their way to Ethiopia. Father Charles Francis Xavier de Brevedent, a Jesuit missionary, arrived in Sennar in February 1699 with Charles-Jacques Poncet. The Franciscan missionaries Pasquale a Monteller, Antonio della Terza, and Bernadette d'Abripalder followed them soon and spent two years in Sennar. In 1701 four other Franciscan missionaries followed, among whom were Krump and Joseph of Jerusalem, and two Jesuit missionaries, Grenleer and Paulet.[1] However, none of them was concerned with the spread of Christianity among the people of Sennar or with the establishment of schools to teach the local population. A proposal made by the Franciscans to the *Sacra Congregazione de Propaganda Fide* in Rome for the foundation of a mission in the Funj kingdom was approved in 1697 and a grant made to the Franciscans who had a post at Akhmin in Egypt.[2] In 1718 this proposal was not pursued as a result of disagreements between the different groups of the sect.[3]

It was not until the Sudan was conquered in 1820 that European Christian missionary interests in the Sudan were revived. This time it was not for the purpose of reaching Ethiopia but in order to introduce Christianity in the Sudan itself. English and French missionaries who had established themselves in East Africa wanted to gain grounds in the Nile Valley from where they could work against the slave trade.[4] The Turco-Egyptian régime provided them with the opportunity to carry out this plan and Mohamed Ali's liberal attitude to the missionaries encouraged them to take positive steps in this

[1] Crawford, O. G. S., *The Fung Kingdom of Sennar* (Gloucester, 1951), pp. 196–207.
[2] Ibid., p. 204.   [3] Ibid., p. 212.
[4] Oliver, R. and Fage, J. D., *A Short History of Africa* (London, 1962), pp. 142–4.

direction.[1] He instructed his representative in Khartoum to help missionaries and exempt them from taxes.[2] The Sultan of Turkey agreed, on the request of Emperor Franz Joseph of Austria, to extend to the missions in the Sudan the privileges given to them in other parts of the Ottoman Empire.[3]

The Prefect Apostolic of Tripoli and the Canon of Malta Cathedral drew the attention of the *Sacra Congregazione de Propaganda Fide* in Rome to the new possibilities in the Sudan and warned them against the dangers of Islam spreading into the heart of Africa, and the possibility of Protestant missionaries sending representatives into the newly discovered lands.[4]

In the meantime a Catholic church and school were established in the Sudan by Father Luigi Monturi. Monturi, a priest from Naples, who was fleeing from the persecution of the Coptic Patriarch of Ethiopia, came to Khartoum in the company of the Belgian Consul in Egypt, B. van Cuelebroelk, and obtained permission from the Governor of Khartoum to establish a church and school. The school provided education for the children of Catholic residents and freed Sudanese slaves. In addition to instruction in reading and writing the children were taught the gospel.[5] Monturi wrote to the Prefect of the *Congregazione de Propaganda Fide* that he was planning to establish two schools—one for the Shilluk in the south and one for the Galla in the eastern Sudan near the Ethiopian border. He proposed to train and educate young men for service as catechists among their own people so as to help in the spreading of Christianity to Central Africa.[6] Monturi was not able to do this as he had to leave the Sudan soon afterwards. His mission and church were left in charge of another priest, G. Serracent. The latter abandoned both in 1855.

The information from Monturi and the proposal made by the Prefect Apostolic of Tripoli led Pope Gregory XVI to create in 1846 the Apostolic Vicariate of Central Africa. Khartoum became in accordance with this decree the centre of Catholic missionary work

[1] Hill, R., *Egypt in the Sudan*, p. 78.
[2] Abdul Magid, A. A., *al Tarbia*, vol. ii, p. 100.
[3] Gray, R., *A History of the Southern Sudan 1839–1889* (London, 1961), pp. 25–7.
[4] Ibid., p. 25.
[5] Hill, R., *Egypt in the Sudan*, p. 78; Toniolo, E. F., 'The First Centenary of the Roman Catholic Mission to Central Africa', *Sudan Notes and Records*, xxvii (1946), 98–126.
[6] Dempsey, J., *Mission on the Nile* (London, 1955), p. 99.

in the Sudan. The objects of the mission were defined as the conversion of the Negroes to Christianity, the bringing of assistance to the Christians who were in the Sudan as traders, and the suppression of the slave trade.[1]

A party of Catholic Jesuit missionaries, consisting of M. Ryello, M. di Maureaster, Angello Vinco, E. Pedemont, and I. Knoblecher arrived in Khartoum in February 1846. Three others soon joined and a church and school were founded. The Khartoum Catholic school admitted Coptic and European children, in addition to Sudanese children who were bought in the slave market at Khartoum. The boys were taught Arabic, French, Italian, arithmetic, music, and handwork. The school flourished and at one time there were forty boys in the school, the majority of whom were Sudanese.[2] It was supported by the authorities and the local population. The latter did not oppose it as long as it did not admit Moslem children. Two of the Sudanese pupils in the school went to Malta for further training. Those who completed their training in the school were employed in the government service.[3]

Missionary work was extended to the southern Sudan when two missionary stations were opened at Gondokro and Holy Cross in 1850 and at Kaka in 1862. No educational work was, however, carried out in these stations because of the attitude of the local administrators and tribes. The former, in spite of the central government's favourable attitude towards the missionaries, were hostile. The exception to this was General Gordon, who, as Governor of Equatoria, wrote in 1871 to the Church Missionary Society in England inviting them to undertake missionary activities in his province. The society was not, however, able to do this because of its commitments at the time in other parts of Africa.[4] The southerners were suspicious because they associated the missionaries with the administration, the merchants and the slave traders. Missionary work was further hampered by bad climatic conditions which led to the death of many, and the difficulties of replacing these with new missionaries from Europe. Italy was occupied with its own wars, and little financial

[1] Toniolo, E. F., "The First Centenary of the Roman Catholic Mission," p. 98; Trimingham, J. S., *Christian Approach to Islam in the Sudan* (Oxford University Press, 1948), p. 9.
[2] Toniolo, E. F., "The First Centenary of the Roman Catholic Mission," pp. 101, 106.
[3] Toniolo, E. F., *Dawr Al Irsaliat al Katholikia fi Harkat al Kashf al-Goghrafi wa ilm al Agnas al-Basharia bi al Sudan* (Khartoum, 1958), pp. 21–2 (Arabic text).
[4] Trimingham, J. S., *Christian Approach to Islam*, p. 11.

assistance was forthcoming to bring out new missionaries.[1] The three mission stations were finally closed by 1862.[2] One of the Dinka boys who attended the mission in Kaka was sent to England to help with the revision of a Dinka translation of St Luke's Gospel, published in 1886.[3]

The success of the Catholic school at Khartoum encouraged the Protestant missionaries to establish work in the north. Two German pastors, Eppere and Hausman, established a missionary station in 1862, at Abu-Haraz, south of Khartoum. Owing to the suspicion of the local population and opposition by the administration this was closed and another station was started at Gallabat, near the Ethiopian border.[4]

Missionary educational work did not recover from its first setbacks until Daniel Comboni began a new missionary drive in the Sudan. Comboni, who had published in 1864 a pamphlet entitled 'Plan for the Regeneration of Africa', based on his experiences in the Sudan during 1857–9, was convinced that the conversion of pagans in Africa to Christianity could only be done through an African-educated priesthood. He believed that education was the means to conversion. In 1867, he established two missionary institutes at Verona in Italy. The first, the Institute for Negroland, aimed at educating and training priests and laymen for missionary work in Africa. The second, the Institute of the Pious Mothers of Negroland, aimed at the education and training of women missionaries. Two other institutes with the same aim were established by Comboni in Cairo. In Italy the Association of the Good Shepherd was founded to provide funds for the institutes.[5]

By 1871 three Sudanese, whom Comboni had arranged to send from the Sudan to Verona—Lodovico, Giovanni, and Bonaventina —and eighteen Sudanese women, trained in Cairo, were ready to embark on missionary and educational work in the Sudan.

Kordufan was chosen by Comboni as the field of his new work because of the better climatic conditions compared to those of the south, and because communications with Khartoum and Cairo were much safer. The Western Sudan, on the other hand, provided the

[1] Gray, R., *A History of Southern Sudan*, pp. 25–7.
[2] Ibid., pp. 32–40; Dempsey, J., *Mission on the Nile*, p. 100.
[3] Cook, Sir Albert, *Uganda Memoirs* (Kampala, 1945), p. 221.
[4] Abdul Magid, A. A., *al Tarbia*, vol. ii, p. 105.
[5] Toniolo, E., *Dawr Al Irsaliat*, op. cit., p. 27, and Toniolo, E., "The First Centenary of the Roman Catholic Mission," pp. 117–18.

possibility of developing links with the Roman Catholic missionary work which had already been established on the Niger.

A school was established at El Obeid. In 1876 no less than 150 boys were receiving instruction in different trades at the school. In 1881 a farm was started to the south of El Obeid on which 300 families were settled to receive agricultural training. Two other schools were established at Berber and Suakin. In 1877 there were 200 girls and 300 boys in the school at Khartoum, the majority of whom were Sudanese.[1] Comboni's successes encouraged Gordon, Jessi, and Amin Pasha to invite him to re-establish missionary and educational work in the south.[2] The death of Comboni in 1881 and the outbreak of the Mahdist revolution, however, prevented this from being put into effect. The Mahdist régime in the Sudan (1885–98) put an end to missionary work and the schools established by the Turco-Egyptian régime.

The Mahdi's teachings advocated a return to pure Islam and the rejection of *Sufist* teachings in favour of the *Koran* and traditions. He was not sympathetic to the *Ulama* who supported the administration. His teachings were therefore against the educational practices and institutions developed by the Turco-Egyptian rule. Although he supported the education of his followers and encouraged his wives, daughters, and sons to learn the *Koran*, priority was given to the *Jihad* and not to education. *Khalwas* for the teaching of the *Koran* were permitted only on the understanding that the teachers would not remain behind when they were called to the *Jihad*.[3]

The Khalifa Abdullahi, although preoccupied with wars and internal conflicts, encouraged the teaching of the *Koran*. On one occasion he ordered that 4,500 tablets should be made for this purpose. He gave instructions that the adults should learn the minimum needed to say the prayers, while the young should learn the three R's in addition to the Koran. There were no less than 800 *Khalwas* in Omdurman alone during the Khalifa's rule. The teachers were paid by the state.[4]

Omdurman, which became the Mahdi's capital, attracted a number of *Ulamas* and teachers. These made use of the printing press captured in Khartoum, and produced a number of books and

[1] Toniolo, E., *Dawr al Israliat*, op. cit., pp. 38–46.
[2] Ibid., pp. 48–52.
[3] Letters from Al Mahdi to Ahmed Hamad al Maghdoub, Al Murshid ila Walhaig Al Mahdi, numbers 508 and 509, *SGA*.
[4] *Al Nil* (newspaper), Khartoum, 21 December 1964.

writings. Ismail Abdul Gadir Al Kurdufani wrote his two books on the Mahdi and Ethiopia while in Omdurman.[1] Tahir Tatai wrote a book on the Mahdi's sayings and teachings. Others who made contributions in this field were Awad al Karim al Masalam and Al Hussain al Zahra.

Another centre of learning and writing was in the Eastern Sudan where the Maghdoub family lived. The two known to have contributed to the intellectual side of the Mahdia through their writings were Al Maghdoub Abu Bakr Yusif and Mohamed Al Maghdoub al Tahir. The first was responsible for the collection and reproduction of the Mahdi's letters to Osman Digna, and the second for a manuscript describing events in the Eastern Sudan during that time.[2]

The third centre was in Dongula where there was a great concentration of the Mahdi's armies. There, a number of persons interested in the teachings of the Mahdi met together and set out to copy or reproduce these teachings for distribution among the Mahdi's followers.[3]

The attitude towards modern and missionary education did not prevent the Khalifa from making use of the graduates of the schools of the previous régime. The graduates formed the core of the bureaucracy and technical staff of his rule.[4] Cultural relations with Egypt and the outside world, however, suffered as a result of the conflicts between the Sudan and Egypt. The latter's educational system and institutions were no longer a source for the education and training of the Sudanese. Education suffered as a result of the régime's preoccupation with wars and no educational organization of any significance was developed.

Modern education, the foundations of which were laid during the Turco-Egyptian rule, was therefore replaced by a limited number of traditional religious schools which were the sole source of education when the Sudan was reconquered in 1898.

[1] Abu Salim, M. I., " Marakiz al Thaqafa, fi al-Mahdia " (Centres of culture during the Mahdia), *Al Khartoum* (January 1968), pp. 6–9.
[3] Ibid., p. 8.
[3] Ibid., p. 9.
[4] Holt, P. M., *The Mahdist State in the Sudan 1881–1898* (Oxford, 1958), pp. 233–4.

CHAPTER II

Educational Policy

THE RECONQUEST of the Sudan by the Egyptian and British forces in 1898 and the signing of the Condominium Agreement in Cairo on 19 January 1899 marked the beginning of a new régime in the Sudan. The reconquest was made in the name of the Khedive of Egypt because it was held to be a province of Egypt which had revolted and had then been brought back into the fold. A unique status was given to the Sudan because the country was vast and because it was necessary to keep out the French and what Cromer called 'the paraphernalia of internationalism'.[1] Sovereignty was laid in the hands of the two conquering powers but the actual military and civil administration was entrusted to a Governor-General. The Sudan was not to be governed from London or Cairo but from Khartoum. Except for financial control, which was in the hands of the Egyptian Government, and decisions on major and important matters for which he had to refer to His Majesty's Agent and Consul-General in Cairo, the Governor-General was to decide on all matters of detail. Cromer, the architect of the Condominium Agreement and the representative of Britain in Cairo, was the real authority in the making of Sudan policy, and all major decisions were referred to him. Until his retirement in 1908, and even after that, his interest in Sudan affairs never lapsed.

This unique administrative set-up created by an ingenious agreement made it possible for the new administration to make policies and regulations which would not have been possible had the Sudan been a British colony or part of Egypt. Nothing which could be directly opposed to British or Egyptian interest would be done. Yet Sudan's immediate interests as seen by the administration or dictated by the local conditions guided decisions of the Sudan Government. The Sudan administration was in many ways acting as if it was an administration of an independent country. Priority was given to the establishment of law and order, and the requirements for this took precedence over all other aspects. In northern Sudan the government was faced, during the period 1901–16, with no less than fourteen

[1] Cromer, Earl of, *Modern Egypt*, 2 vols. (London, 1908), vol. ii, p. 114.

incidents or disturbances caused by religious fanatics. In southern Sudan, no less than twenty rebellions by southern tribes, including the Nuer and Dinka, took place between 1900 and 1919. The inhabitants of the Nuba mountains continued to resist government administration until 1919 and thirty army expeditions were sent against them.[1] The problems of security and pacification were therefore very real; energy and much of the available resources had to be spent on military expenditure. The establishment of a good administration, guided by the principles of justice, constituted another way of overcoming the problems of law and order, and therefore a fair amount of revenue was allocated towards this end.

The resources of the country were limited. The population, estimated at $8\frac{1}{2}$ million before the Mahdist régime, decreased through famine, disease, and wars, and had become about 5 million in 1900. Another estimate put it at 1,870,000.[2] There was a lack of a modern system of communications, especially railways. After fifteen years of wars and revolutions there was chaos in the system of land ownership and land titles. Skilled labour was lacking and the local officials held that the people were not industrious and had no desire to improve their position. Agricultural expansion was limited by the lack of water for irrigation and this could not be increased because of the fear that Egypt's interests would be harmed.

As it was held that the Sudan was conquered mainly for the benefit of Egypt and to safeguard her interests in the Nile waters and her southern borders, the British Government argued that it was Egypt's duty to meet the demands of economic and social development which the Sudan could not provide.[3] Britain was therefore not prepared to give funds. Egypt's contributions, on the other hand, were necessarily limited by her own financial condition and responsibility to the European debtors. Egypt made an annual contribution to the Sudan to meet the annual deficits. These contributions amounted to nearly £E4,000,000 during the period 1899–1913. In addition to this, £E1,000,000 was paid to the Sudan Government[4] for the maintenance

---

[1] *The Anglo-Egyptian Sudan*, H.M.S.O., London, no. 98 (1920), pp. 42–52.

[2] Cromer, Earl of, *Modern Egypt*, p. 545; Abdu, O. M. Osman, 'The Development of Transport and Economic Growth in the Sudan, 1898–1958'. Ph.D. thesis submitted to the University of London, 1960, p. 59.

[3] Wingate, R., *Wingate of the Sudan* (London, 1955), pp. 130, 141.

[4] Stone, J., 'The Finance of Government Economic Development in the Sudan 1899 to 1913', monograph in the Library of the Institute of Commonwealth Studies, Oxford, p. 19.

of the army. The total of the loans for capital development made
by Egypt amounted to £E5,414,525.[1]

It was not part of the Sudan Government's policy to encourage
private enterprise because it was afraid that this might lead to a
situation similar to that in Egypt and undermine the policies it
planned. Official reports often quoted General Gordon's remark
that 'the Sudan is a useless possession, ever was and ever will
be', and this could not be considered as an encouragement to
private enterprise, even if the government had desired such an
attraction.

Obstacles to economic development were therefore formidable.
Resources for development and for expenditure on social services,
including education, were limited by what the government could
raise from local taxation, and contributions from Egypt. The government's task was to use the available funds in the best possible way
and create an educational system which would contribute to the
solution of economic problems and to the establishment of a good
administration.[2] It was essential to avoid unnecessary expenditure
on a system that had no connection with Sudan's economic needs
and to find one that was within the limits of a poor country living
on Egyptian dole. This was the government's predicament.

So far as British policy in other colonies was concerned, it was
something of a novelty.[3] The theory of *laissez-faire* in education
reigned supreme in Victorian England. Although state participation
in education had been accepted in England, education remained
mainly in the hands of voluntary and private bodies and there was
a general distrust of state intervention. Education in the colonies
was similarly left to the missionaries and private bodies. Concern and
active participation by the Sudan Government in education was
therefore a departure from the pattern in other colonies. It was
made possible by its unique status and would have been impossible
under Whitehall departmentalism as it existed at the time.[4] This
status had not, however, always been to the advantage of the Sudan
in so far as financial help was concerned. As a consequence of its
ambiguous status it remained for a long time deprived of financial

[1] Ibid., p. 37.
[2] Currie, J., 'The Educational Experiment in the Anglo-Egyptian Sudan,
1900–1933', *Journal of the Royal African Society*, vol. xxxiii, no. cxxxiii
(October 1934), 361–71, and vol. xxxiv, no. cxxxiv (January 1935), 41–60.
[3] Currie, J., lecture at Oxford on 3 May 1935, *SAD/243/1*.
[4] Idem, 'The Educational Experiment in the Anglo-Egyptian Sudan', p. 361.

help otherwise available from Whitehall to British colonies of more specific dependent status.

Another factor was to avoid the faults of the Indian and Egyptian educational systems. Indian educational policy and practice had received greater attention than before owing to the political unrest which took place. During Lord Curzon's viceroyalty attempts were made to reform Indian education. These reforms recognized the importance of vernacular languages as the proper medium of instruction in the lower grades of education. They sought to give education a more practical character by stressing teachers' training and developing industrial, commercial, and agricultural instruction. The importance of establishing a system of boarding-houses under proper supervision was emphasized. These reforms marked the turning point from a policy of *laissez-faire* to one of constructive effort and control.[1]

Cromer's experiences in India and Egypt led him to believe that education in Egypt was full of faults. He held that the most suitable education was that which aimed at raising the educational level of the illiterate masses by means of the village and mosque schools, and the creation of an efficient Egyptian civil service. He wanted to limit the numbers allowed to enter higher primary schools, and promote technical schools and female education.[2] He believed that 'the great mistake in the education of the poor has been largely too ambitiously literary. Primary education should teach the poor to write well and to count well, but for the rest it should be much more technical and industrial than literary and be more concerned with the observation of facts than with any form of speculative reasoning or opinion.'[3] The development of elementary education had in Cromer's view certain dangers. He feared that this type of education, 'being necessarily based to a great extent on the teaching of the *Koran*, must rather stimulate religious zeal and fanaticism',[4] and the teaching of the *Koran* should therefore be tempered with 'instruction in very elementary secular subjects such as arithmetic'.[5] He considered it dangerous 'to create too wide a gap between the state of education of the higher and of the lower classes in an oriental country

[1] Chirol, V., *Indian Unrest* (London, 1910), pp. 230–3; Furnivall, J. S., *Colonial Policy and Practice* (Cambridge, 1948), pp. 373–7.

[2] *Governor-General's Report, 1903*, pp. 52–8.

[3] Ibid.

[4] Letter from Lord Cromer to Sir E. Gorst, 12 November 1908, *PRO/FO/ 633/vol. 14.*   [5] Ibid.

governed under the inspiration of a Western democracy'.[1] He did
not consider it wise or just to leave the masses 'defenceless in the
presence of the hare-brained and empirical projects which the
political charlatan, himself but half-educated, will not fail to pour
into their credulous ears'.[2] He warned against an education which
would become what he called a 'process of manufacturing demagogues'. The only remedy against the demagogue was to educate
those 'who are his natural prey to such an extent that they may, at all
events, have some chance of discerning the imposture which but too
often lurks between his perfervid eloquence and political quackery'.[3]

His view of religious education was that as long as it was limited
to obtaining 'a knowledge of the religion of Mahommed and anything beyond that is considered superfluous and even dangerous',[4]
the religious schools could not be utilized to promote suitable education. Their graduates in Egypt were conservative and suspicious,[5] and
could not be relied on.

This relationship between education and employment on one
hand and education and political change on the other hand was a
fundamental part of Cromer's ideas on the role of education. Such
education was needed as would help the administration to function
and distract the educated from revolt by giving them employment.
His emphasis on technical and vocational education was not only
because of the need for skilled workers but also for its political role.
He wrote that 'every carpenter, bricklayer or mason that you turn
out will be one unit detached from the ranks of the dissatisfied class
who necessarily become patriots and demagogues'.[6] Thus by limiting
general education to a small class, he aimed at weakening the
nationalist movement. As the natural consequence of education in
his view was the production of a class wanting to get rid of foreign
rule,[7] he advised that it should be confined to those who were needed
for employment. His objection to teaching the English language to
schools lower than the intermediate or primary schools was based
on his conviction that 'its teaching could furnish the subject races
with a very powerful arm against their alien races'.[8]

[1] Cromer, Earl of, *Modern Egypt*, vol. ii, p. 534.
[2] Ibid.   [3] Ibid.
[4] Ibid., p. 532.   [5] Ibid., pp. 185–6.
[6] Letter from Cromer to Sir E. Gorst, 12 November 1908, *PRO/FO/633/
vol. 14*.   [7] Ibid.
[8] Cromer, Earl of, *Ancient and Modern Imperialism* (London, 1910), pp.
106–7.

Similar ideas and attitudes were held by Kitchener, Wingate, and Currie, who laid the foundations of the Sudan educational policy. They believed in the same principles which governed Cromer's educational policy in Egypt.

Kitchener, who believed that education in the Sudan should be primarily vocational,[1] warned against 'any attempt to force upon a semi-oriental and half-civilized people an elaborate system of education suited only to a highly civilized Western nation'.[2] It was therefore rational for Kitchener to decide from the beginning that what he needed in the Sudan was a supply of native clerks.[3]

Wingate, who became Governor-General in 1902, was more interested in education than Kitchener. His ideas were not, however, different from those of Cromer. He believed that co-operation between the rulers and ruled could only be obtained by laying a sound foundation of a 'carefully considered system of training and elemental foundation'.[4] Successful development, in Wingate's view, could be attained 'by devising some means of guiding the aspirations of native youth into channels best adapted for the evolution of individual character and racial progress and—most important of all —in encouraging moral and religious instruction which requires a sense of duty, unswerving integrity, and loyalty in the public and private relations of life'.[5] He believed that for the achievement of progress the government should provide a class of natives who would be able to take an ever-increasing share in administration, commerce, trade, and agriculture and diffuse a sound elementary education which would 'enable the masses to cope on more equal terms with the continually increasing claims of material progress and national advancement'.[6]

Currie was appointed Director of Education in 1900. He saw that it was his duty to proceed slowly and 'setting nothing on foot that has no real vital connection with the economic needs of the country'.[7] The educational aims he set out to achieve were:

[1] *Gordon Memorial College Annual Report, 1916*, p. 10.
[2] *G.G.R., 1911*.
[3] Magnus, Philip, *Kitchener, Portrait of an Imperialist* (London, 1958), p. 146.
[4] Wingate, F. R., 'The Story of the Gordon College and its Work', *The Story of the Cape to Cairo Railway and River Route*, 1887–1922, ed. Weinthal, L. (London, 1923), part I, pp. 563–611.
[5] Ibid., p. 567.
[6] Ibid.
[7] *G.M.C.R., 1901*, p. 6.

1. The creation of a competent artisan class, which is entirely lacking at present.

2. The diffusion among the masses of the people of education sufficient to enable them to understand the merest elements of the machinery of government, particularly with reference to the equable and impartial administration of justice.

3. The creation of a small native administrative class who will ultimately fill many minor government posts.[1]

These ideas guided Sudan educational policy for a long time and influenced its pattern and aims.

Another aim which the educational system set out to achieve was to train Sudanese to replace Egyptians in the army, and Egyptians and Syrians in the junior administrative positions. The majority of army officers in the Sudan were either British or Egyptians. A few Sudanese who held commissions in the army had been trained in Egypt. The Egyptian officer, by virtue of his knowledge of the language, was in closer contact than his British counterpart with the Sudanese officers and soldiers. A report by an investigating committee, held after a mutiny of the 14th Sudanese Battalion in January 1900, concluded that the mutiny was instigated by Egyptian officers who were in contact with nationalist groups in Egypt.[2] The Egyptian officers were, therefore, not a desirable element and Sudanese should be trained for the army instead.[3]

On the other hand the Condominium administration was to a great extent operated by former Mahdists,[4] Egyptians, and Syrians who were not infrequently Christians.[5] The survival of Mahdism was a source of continuous worry to the government. The Egyptian employees were discontented and often held to be corrupt and unjust.[6] The administration never hid its 'distaste for even the small residue of Egyptian influence'[7] and feared the impact in the Sudan of Egyptian nationalism.[8] It believed that only by direct contact with the Sudanese could a good administration be achieved. For this reason, neither the Syrians nor the Egyptians could be entrusted with

[1] G.M.C.R., 1901, p. 9.
[2] Report by Colonel Jackson on the Omdurman Incident, SP/A/112.
[3] Letter from Colonel Jackson to Sirdar, Khartoum, 4 March 1900. SP/A/112.
[4] Hill, R., Slatin Pasha (London, 1965), pp. 88–9.
[5] G.G.R., 1902, pp. 78–9.
[6] Letter from Cromer to Salisbury, Cairo, 12 June 1900. SP/A/112.
[7] Hill, R., Slatin Pasha, p. 111.
[8] Ibid.

the job,[1] and it was therefore necessary to educate the Sudanese to a level where it was possible to have direct contact with them.[2]

The other important issues which faced the government were traditional Moslem and Christian missionary education. Immediately after the reoccupation governors of different provinces reported the existence of hundreds of *khalwas* all over the country. In Dongula province, for example, nearly every village had its own well-attended *khalwa*. In Khartoum province, a great number of these were also functioning. In Halfa and Kassalla provinces, koranic schools were widespread.

In these *khalwas* scattered all over the country

village children were taught a little reading, less writing and the repetition of the *Koran* and the Mahdi's prayers by teachers who were ignorant of the very rudiments of the art of instruction, utterly incompetent, illiterate to a degree and consumed by a spirit of the wildest fanaticism . . . buildings mere hovels, children huddled together under the most insanitary conditions and instruction carried on in the midst of a deafening babel.[3]

This did not, however, prevent them from being recognized as an essential part of a Moslem society which considered that education was a duty.[4] A proposal to create a grant-in-aid system to all *khalwas* and improve their educational facilities was rejected by Currie.[5] He felt that such a step would be premature and might prove a financial burden and hamper the development of a modern system of education. A system of inspection and control, also proposed at the time, was rejected[6] on the ground that it might be difficult to implement and administer. Currie sought to reform *khalwa* education through the creation of model *kuttabs*[7] and the payment of a grant-in-aid to a few *khalwas*. The grant consisted of a monthly payment to the *feki* and its amount was decided on in consultation with the governors of the provinces. The *fekis* were encouraged to introduce elements of secular education, such as arithmetic, into the curriculum of the assisted *khalwas*.

This combination of secular and religious education whether in *kuttabs* or in reformed *khalwas* became the basis of Sudan elementary education. It was hoped that these reforms would reduce the dangers of a revival of Mahdism and the development of hostile religious

[1] *G.G.R., 1902*, pp. 78–9.   [2] Ibid.; Hill, R., *Slatin Pasha*, pp. 88–9.
[3] Wingate, F. R., *The Story of the Gordon College*, p. 572.
[4] *G.M.C.R., 1901*, p. 6.   [5] *G.G.R., 1900*, p. 76.
[6] Ibid.   [7] *G.M.C.R., 1901*, p. 6.

orders which both Wingate and Slatin feared very much.[1] It was also hoped that the tempering of religious education with secular education in the government schools would go a long way in eliminating the ignorance of a people who had great respect for the written document.[2]

Following the uprising of Abdul Gadir Wad Habouba in 1908, Currie wrote that the people in the Gezira believed 'in the potential capacity of any man who attained the status of an accredited religious leader to bring water to barren wells at a word, to produce silver from the earth or squadrons of horses from the clouds at his bidding or to render his followers bullet-proof by incantation'.[3] He was convinced that this could only be 'exorcised from the minds by the provision of very elementary education at once religious and secular'.[4]

The role of the new *kuttabs* in dispelling 'ignorance and superstition which renders them [the Sudanese] an easy prey to those who play upon their amazing credulity either for pseudo-religious or other ends',[5] and in providing an education which would 'avoid engendering in the pupils a distaste for the agricultural pursuits of their fathers'[6] was emphasized again and again by Currie.[7] The *kuttab* was planned as a gradual replacement of the *khalwa* in the educational system.

Christian missionary education presented problems of a different nature and with far-reaching implications. Immediately after the reconquest Cromer, in Cairo, and Kitchener, in Khartoum, were approached with requests from Christian missionary societies and from individuals in Britain and the United States of America to open the entire country to Christian missionary enterprise. The image of General Gordon as a Christian hero who gave his life fighting the slave trade, their attitude towards Islam as an evil power, and their desire to contribute to the eradication of slavery in Africa were factors behind this zeal.

In fact missionary interest in the Sudan did not diminish with the lapsing of the Turco-Egyptian régime in 1885. Plans for a missionary drive were drawn long before the reconquest. In 1885 a Gordon

---

[1] Hill, R., *Slatin Pasha*, p. 88.   [2] *G.G.R., 1902*, p. 79.
[3] Currie, J., cited in letter from Sir E. Gorst to Sir E. Grey, 1905, *PRO/FO/36*.
[4] Ibid.
[5] Currie, J., cited in *Report of a Committee appointed by H.E. the Governor-General*, 7 March 1933, p. 14, *SGA/File EH/17.A.1/1*.
[6] Ibid.   [7] Ibid.

Memorial Mission was established in London. Major-General
F. T. Haig visited Suakin, which never fell to the Mahdists, on behalf
of the Church Missionary Society in 1886-7 and 1890-1 to examine
sites for mission stations. In his report he recommended the extension
of missionary work and insisted that the language of the Sudan
Mission should be Arabic.[1] Dr. J. Harper was sent to Suakin by the
Christian Missionary Society in 1890, where he established an
orphanage which he thought would be useful for future contacts,
and become a nucleus of missionary work among the Hedendena.[2]
Major-General F. T. Haig recommended the establishment of a
mission at Suakin as 'a first step towards evangelizing the Nile
Valley'.[3]

The Roman Catholic Verona Fathers Mission, whose work was
interrupted by the Mahdist revolution, had similarly withdrawn to
Suakin and continued their missionary work from there. In addition
to this they maintained, in Egypt, a Sudan Mission in Exile under
the direction of the Apostolic Vicar, Bishop F. Sogaro.[4]

With the reconquest of the Sudan, missionary activities were
renewed. The Church Missionary Society decided to extend its work
in the Sudan. The Verona Fathers and the American Presbyterian
Mission also sent representatives to Khartoum.[5] This presented a
problem to the new administration. The question asked was whether
proselytism should be allowed or not. The main concern of the
administration was to establish law and order and to win the confidence of the population and was therefore against allowing the
missionaries a free hand. This attitude was not well received in
England.

A memorandum was signed by the Archbishop of Canterbury and
Sir John H. Kennaway, President of the Church Missionary Society,
criticizing Sudan Government policy and accusing it of acting contrary to the policies of the British Government regarding religious
liberty and neutrality.[6]

[1] Hill, R., 'Government and Christian Missions in the Anglo-Egyptian Sudan
1899–1914', *Middle Eastern Studies* (London School of Economics), i, no. 2
(January, 1965), 113–34.
[2] Harper, J., Report on Work at Suakin 16.10.1890, *The Anti-Slavery Society
Papers*, Rhodes House, Oxford, MSS. British Empire 522/A25.
[3] Hill, R., *Government and Christian Missions*, p. 117.   [4] Ibid., p. 115.
[5] For a more detailed study of this period see Beshir, M. O., *The Southern
Sudan, Background to Conflict* (Hurst, London, 1968), pp. 23–7.
[6] *Annual Report of the Church Missionary Society* (London, 1901–1902),
pp. 150–1. Church Missionary Society Archives, London.

The result of these pressures was a compromise. Missionaries were to act freely in the south but not in the north. In the latter they were allowed to start their activities with certain restrictions.

Both the government and the missionaries agreed that their main objective in the southern Sudan was to eliminate Islam and Islamic influence. Each of the missionary societies was given an area in which its work was to be conducted. This course was known as the 'sphere system'. In order to help the missionary societies, they were given certain privileges, for example reductions of fares on Sudan railways and steamers.

As for the northern Sudan, they were permitted in 1900 to establish schools in Khartoum, where they could be supervised, for the Christian children only.[1] In 1901 they were allowed to start schools outside Khartoum and also admit Moslem Sudanese children provided that the parents clearly understood the conditions under which education was given.[2] These arrangements seem to have temporarily silenced the critics outside the Sudan. The need to allay the fears of Sudanese who might be suspicious of this policy and ensure that missionary education was not used for conversion led the government to consider, in 1905, a proposal to institute a system of inspection of mission schools where Moslem children attended. Cromer's view was that inspection could only be justified if the government was paying a grant. He feared that inspection might invite applications for aid, raise the suspicions of the Moslem population, and be misrepresented by hostile elements wanting to associate government with missionaries.[3] A committee[4] was convened to discuss the proposals, and it advised the Governor-General that a policy of inspection was necessary not only to allay Sudanese fears but to ensure that such schools would not be 'centres of influence and intrigues of a kind calculated to raise extremely awkward questions of jurisdiction'.[4] As there was a possibility of Egyptian and French schools being established in the Sudan, the government, in the committee's views, 'ought to be armed with powers that would enable the government to exercise a close observation over what was going on, what was being taught and the text books that were being used'.[5]

[1] *G.G.R., 1904*, p. 140.
[2] Letter from Lord Cromer to Gwynne, Cairo, 13 March 1900, *PRO/FO/633/vol. 8.*
[3] Letter from Currie to Wingate, 23 June 1904, *SAD/103.*
[4] Letter from Currie to Wingate, Khartoum, 2 January 1907, *SAD/103.*
[5] Ibid.

Different missions had different attitudes towards the proposal. The Roman Catholic Mission, which cared mainly for Christian children and admitted a few Moslem children, did not oppose inspection. The Church Missionary Society and the American Mission, whose schools were attended by a majority of Sudanese children, did not welcome inspection.[1] It was finally decided to institute a system of inspection and the following regulations incorporating the rules on the teaching of Christianity in mission schools were approved:

1. Before Mohamedan children are permitted to attend a mission school the Duiker or Head of the School will satisfy himself that the parents or guardians understand that the school is a Christian school.

2. The full consent of parents or guardians must be obtained by the Director or Head of the School before any pupil is given religious instruction, no matter of what nationality or religion the pupil may be.

3. When religious instruction is being carried out no other children except those whose parents have given the necessary consent must be present.

4. The school shall be open at all times to the Inspection of the Governor-General or his representative.

5. The Director or Head of the School will be held responsible that the above regulations are strictly adhered to. It must be clearly understood that the permission in writing to carry on the school is dependent on that regulation being observed.[2]

The corollary of such an educational policy was the development in the north of a modern system of education controlled and administered by the government, and a traditional and Christian missionary education supervised by the government. In the south, unlike the north, education was wholly controlled and developed by missionary societies.

[1] Letter from Civil Secretary to Wingate, Khartoum, 2 February 1907, *SAD/ 103.*
[2] Letter from Currie to Wingate, Khartoum, 2 January 1907, *SAD/103.*

CHAPTER III

Laying the Foundations

THE IMPLEMENTATION of the educational policy and the development of a modern educational system during this period were determined by the attitude of the population towards the government's plans, the financial resources available, and the availability of teachers. The attitude of the population was necessarily determined by their attitude to the new administration and the latter's success in winning their confidence and support. Cromer tried to allay their fears when he promised not to interfere in their religious life. Their knowledge of modern education was limited to what a very small minority of them had experienced during the Turco-Egyptian period. The modern type of school was therefore a foreign imposition by a foreign ruler and was looked upon with suspicion. They feared that it would replace the *khalwa*—the symbol of religious education—and lead to the abandonment of their religion and traditions. The *fekis* and religious families were afraid that it might deprive them of their status in society, and their source of income. Parents feared that the attendance of boys in the school terms would deprive the family of their help and support in agriculture and trade, and that there would be less supervision of their sons' conduct and behaviour. The town was associated in the minds of the rural population with corrupt morals and practices. Parents also feared that school education would lead to the boys being enlisted into the army or the police force.[1]

Senior administrators toured the country so as to persuade the leading families that the new schools were for the benefit of their children and the advancement of their country.[2] They assured them that the aim of the schools was not Christian education.

Suspicions and fears were, however, slow to disappear. As the material benefits arising from employment in government service for school-leavers became clear and the suspicions were found to be untrue, the attitude towards the new schools changed. The appointment

[1] Ministry of Education: *Al Talim fi al Mudiria Al Shamalia* (Khartoum, 1962), p. 22 (Arabic text).
[2] Udal, N. R., 'Education in the Northern Sudan', *Espratto Dagliatti dell' VIII, Conegnotea l'Africa*, Rome, 4-11 October 1938, p. xvi.

as teachers in the government schools of sons and grandsons of what Currie called 'the learned prophets' of the past helped to allay the fears and bring about a new attitude towards education.[1]

Although fears and suspicions were disappearing fast among the town population, they persisted for a long time among the rural population. In 1918 the establishment of an elementary school in the village of Mugrat near Abu Hamad was resisted by the leading religious family and the *feki* of the local *khalwa*. The new elementary school established in the nearby village of Singarab came to be known among the villagers of Mugrat as the 'Church of Singarab'.[2]

This reluctance in the early years left many vacancies in the schools and made it possible to admit Egyptian children for whom no special facilities were provided by the government. In 1911, for example, one-tenth of the whole school population in government elementary schools were of Egyptian origin. In the same year one-quarter of all boys attending primary schools were Egyptians, and in the Khartoum primary school alone 108 out of 241 pupils were of Egyptian origin.[3] Currie was convinced that a policy which would exclude Egyptians from these schools would lead to an exaggeration of racial differences. The object of a good educational system, in his view, was 'the mitigation and not the exaggeration of these differences'.[4]

The financial resources on the other hand were a further limiting factor on educational development. In 1899 revenue stood at £E126,596 and expenditure at £E230,238. It was not until 1907 that the government's revenue exceeded its expenditure.[5] The deficit in the budget was met through a grant from Egypt, until 1913, when it was discontinued at the request of the Sudan Government. The establishment of law and order, being the major concern of the government, represented the major item in the government expenditure. Most of the capital expenditure between 1899 and 1918 was spent on the construction of railways, harbours, and river services.[6]

Expenditure by the department of education represented less than 1 per cent of total government expenditure until 1903 and reached its highest in 1912 when it rose to 4 per cent.[7] Within these limited

---

[1] Sudan Government, *Annual Reports of the Education Department* (henceforth cited as *E.D.R.*), 1907, pp. 9–10.

[2] Ministry of Education, *Al Talim fi al Mudiria al Shamalia*, p. 22.

[3] *E.D.R.*, *1911*, pp. 19–20.

[4] Letter from Cromer to Wingate, Cairo, 3 February 1904, *SAD/275/4*.

[5] Appendix I, Table I.

[6] Appendix I, Table II.   [7] Appendix I, Table I.

funds the department of education had to establish and develop a network of schools and institutions to produce the required personnel.

The third limiting factor, the availability of trained teachers, was solved through the training of Sudanese for teaching in the elementary and primary schools and the employment of Egyptian and British teachers for teaching in the primary and the higher primary schools. Egyptian teachers were, however, difficult to recruit for service in the Sudan. They demanded high salaries, and their recruitment was also contrary to the general policy of discouraging Egyptian employment in the Sudan. British teachers were not only more expensive, but less useful because of their ignorance of the language of instruction. Their supply was short because teaching was not attractive to British graduates. It lacked the prestige accorded in the colonial service to the administration, and provided less opportunity for promotion and less remuneration.[1]

From an economic and political point of view the Sudan had to rely on its own resources to produce its own teachers. A training college was established, and in order to attract the small number of British teachers needed a new policy was adopted. They were selected by the same board that appointed candidates for the political service, and received the same salary as those in the political service during the first ten years of service. Before coming out to the Sudan they were asked to undergo a preliminary training course in Arabic and archaeology and on arrival were given the opportunity of obtaining first-hand information and knowledge of the people by secondment to the political service for up to four years, at the end of which they could rejoin the department of education if they wished.[2]

These arrangements succeeded in establishing cooperation between the two services which had not happened in India,[3] and prevented the educational service, as far as the British teachers were concerned, from developing into a watertight compartment with no attractive future prospects. This policy, however, resulted in education being closely associated with administration and political service. British teachers came to be associated in the minds of the people and the students with the governors and district commissioners who ruled over them.

These factors, taken in conjunction with the educational policy, determined the extent and pattern of education provided by the

---

[1] Mayhew, A., *Education in the Colonial Empire* (London, 1938), pp. 60–1.
[2] *E.D.R., 1911*, p. 6.   [3] Chirol, V., *Indian Unrest*, pp. 233–4.

government. The Gordon Memorial College was the centre around which the educational system was built. Its importance not only lay in the fact that it remained the major educational institution during this period, and for a long time after that, but also in the fact that it was financed from outside sources. Funds donated from outside the Sudan for the establishment of the college released internal resources for the expansion of primary and elementary education. Its establishment therefore represented the most important event in the history of Sudan education.

The idea of a college in memory of General Gordon was conceived by Lord Kitchener after the battle of Omdurman in 1898. He realized that the Sudanese could neither develop nor participate in the government of their country without being educated and that they could not support an army of highly paid foreign administrators, even at junior levels. The British press attack on Kitchener's cruelty in dealing with the Mahdi's followers after their defeat at the battle of Omdurman, and on his plan to send the Mahdi's skull, dug from the grave, to the Royal College of Surgeons in Britain made him keen to establish a college which would not only prove his own personal goodness but also contribute to the progress of the people whom he had conquered.[1]

The idea of a college in memory of Gordon appealed to the British public. The name of Gordon was a household name in Britain, and his image was that of a crusader and a saint. Kitchener, in spite of the reports of cruelty, was after all a popular hero. His name and that of Gordon's were sufficient to draw public support for the scheme. He launched his appeal for the foundation of the college on his arrival in England one month after the battle of Omdurman. But before the appeal was launched, he prepared the ground by telling the commercial interests that the conquest of the Sudan and the triumph over the French at Fashoda would open the whole valley of the Nile to their commercial enterprise. During his visit to Edinburgh to receive the honorary degree conferred on him by its university, and the freedom of its city, he expressed his hope that the British as a race would step in and do what the British Government could not provide—education.[2]

Although the British Government was in agreement with his

[1] Wingate, R., *Wingate of the Sudan*, p. 141; Magnus, P., *Kitchener, Portrait of an Imperialist*, pp. 130–7.
[2] Ibid., pp. 141–4.

scheme and thought it the only policy by which the co-operation of the Sudanese people could be achieved, they were not prepared to give financial aid from their own sources, nor agree to financial aid for this particular scheme from Egyptian Government sources. If the scheme was to be successful, the whole support, in the British Government's view, should come from the public, especially the rich, in England.[1]

The appeal was finally launched in a letter addressed by Kitchener to the public Press on 30 November 1898.[2] The appeal, for £100,000, was to establish a college where elementary teaching, and later advanced courses, suitable to the requirements of the Sudanese, would be provided under the guidance of British teachers. The establishment of the college would, in Kitchener's view, give Britain 'the first place in Africa as a civilizing power'.[3]

In less than two months the sum of £100,000 appealed for was subscribed, and the total amount eventually reached £135,000. Contributions came from Britain, Canada, Australia, New Zealand, the Cape Colony, India, Egypt, and the U.S.A. There were contributions from individuals, firms, churches, and theatre groups. The Lord Mayors of London, Liverpool, Manchester, Edinburgh, and Glasgow raised special funds for the project. The firms of Glyn Mills, Currie and Co., K. Cassel, Rothschild and Sons, Bert and Co., W. W. Aston, Wernher and R. H. Beauchamp each contributed £5,000.[4]

An Act of Parliament was passed on 1 August 1899, enabling the executive committee to invest the funds in bonds or securities, including Egyptian Government Bonds, or for the purchase of lands or buildings in Egypt or the Sudan.

The plans for the building were drawn by Fabricus Pasha, the Khedive's architect, and the foundation stone was laid by Lord Cromer in the name of Queen Victoria, who had agreed to be the patron, on 5 January 1900. The college was officially opened by Lord Kitchener in 1902, but it was not until 1903 that the buildings were completed.

In the meantime part of the endowment fund was used to establish the first two primary schools, one in Omdurman in 1900 and the other

---

[1] Letter from Salisbury to Kitchener, 21 November 1898, *SP/A/113*.
[2] Appendix II.
[3] Appendix II.
[4] Gordon Memorial College Fund, List of Donations, Legacies etc. from November 28th 1898 to February 9th 1920, *U.K.A.*

in Khartoum in 1901, and a training college for teachers and *Sharia*
judges in Omdurman in 1900 and an industrial school in Omdurman
in 1901. Omdurman was until then the seat of government. Thus in
1901 the educational set-up consisted of these four schools in addition to two primary schools in Suakin and Halfa. The Suakin and
Halfa schools, where few Sudanese attended, had been established
during the Turco-Egyptian rule and were continued with the purpose of providing education for the children of Egyptian officials.
The two schools were financed by the Egyptian Government until
1902, when they were taken over by the Sudan administration.[1]

The course in the primary schools was for four years, and the
syllabus was similar to that provided by similar schools in Egypt.
The aim was to produce junior clerks, telegraphists, and land
measurers. Admission to these primary schools at the beginning was
from among those who had had advanced instruction in *khalwa*.
Later, only those who had attended the government elementary
schools were admitted. Many of the students in the Omdurman and
Khartoum primary schools were sons of tribal leaders or ex-Mahdists.
About one-fifth were sons of Egyptians employed by the Sudan
Government in the army or administration. No one was admitted
without the specific approval of the Governor-General,[2] and boys
so educated were not guaranteed a government job; they would only
be considered as possible candidates for government service if there
were vacancies and they were otherwise qualified.[3]

When the Sudan was occupied in 1898 there was no system of
civil or criminal justice, and no legal training. A legal system which
borrowed from India, Turkey, and England was developed. The
Sudan Mohammedan Law Courts Ordinance of 1902 set up a High
Court in Khartoum and provincial and district courts. As the legal
system was unlike that of Egypt, and no Sudanese had received legal
training, there was an urgent need for the supply of legal assistants.
A training college for the training of *Sharia* judges was therefore
established and attached to the Omdurman primary school. The
duration of the course was five years, in which instruction was given
in religious law, Arabic, and arithmetic. Admission at the beginning
was from among those who had attended *khalwas* and mainly from

[1] Sudan Government, *Memorandum on The Financial Relations between
Egypt and the Sudan* (Cairo, 1910), p. 56.
[2] *Sudan Government Gazette No. 8*, November 1902.
[3] Ibid., *No. 44*, February 1903.

among boys belonging to families with a tradition of learning and influence.[1] A teacher's training section was added to the college to provide teachers for elementary and primary schools.

The industrial school, which was attached to the Omdurman dockyard, gave both theoretical and practical training on a production basis in building, pottery, carpentry, fitting, smithwork, moulder's work, and cotton-ginning. The course was for three years, and admission to the school was from those who had had preliminary instruction in the *khalwas*. The majority of the students were Sudanese, but a few Egyptian boys were also admitted.

On the completion of the buildings in 1903, the training colleges and the Khartoum primary school were transferred to the college buildings. A new technical training centre was added, and an industrial workshop was established as part of the college. The last was a gift from Mr. William Mather, M.P. for the Rossendale Division of Lancashire. Mather had visited Khartoum in 1901 and discussed with Currie and Dunlop[2] the question of education in the Sudan. As a result of these discussions, he offered to present the college with the necessary equipment for the establishment of a workshop. The course extended over four years, during which the usual school subjects were taught in addition to practical subjects including carpentry, pottery, technical drawing, and elementary mechanical engineering.[3]

The publication in 1904 of Sir William Garstin's report on the irrigation of the Sudan, and its adoption by the government, made it necessary for Sudanese to be trained in surveying and construction. £E15,000 was allocated from the government's budget to the college for the purpose of extending its curriculum to include a post-primary course where general education and engineering courses would be given. This secondary course was started in 1905. It consisted of two sections: a four-year course which aimed at the training of assistant engineers and overseers of works, and a two-year course for the training of land surveyors. The curriculum of the first course was adopted from the Rookee Engineering College in India.

In 1906 a new secondary section was added—a four-year course for the training of primary school teachers. Admission to the three secondary courses was for those who completed the primary schools.

[1] *G.G.R., 1904*, p. 122.
[2] Dunlop was the Secretary-General of the Egyptian Ministry of Public Instruction.
[3] Diary of Sir William Mather (1839–1920), *SAD/404/8/1*.

The college thus became a centre for advanced training and the main supplier of the administrative, technical, and teaching personnel required.

No teaching of Islamic religion was made in the secondary section of the college because of the criticism from certain missionaries.[1] The latter did not approve of the absence of Christian teachings in the college. One of these wrote that the Gordon Memorial College

as a whole must be put down as thoroughly Mohamedan as far as religion is concerned . . surely the name of Gordon College is a misnomer and can only be calculated to deceive the Christian people of Great Britain. General Gordon is not honoured in this institution but the prophet Mohamed is. Mohamed's divinity school of the Upper Nile would be a much more appropriate name; for it certainly teaches more of the prophet's Sacred Book than any other subject.[2]

The writer went on to criticize the employment of Egyptian lecturers in the schools and the college because they were the product of Al Azhar which in his view was 'known the world over as not the largest, but the most bigoted school of Mohamedan learning in existence'.[3] The policy with regard to religious teaching was viewed as an encouragement to Islam and not helpful to the cause of Christianity.[4]

At the Edinburgh conference of missionary societies in 1910, Giffen of the American Presbyterian Society said that the influence of the college was Mohamedan throughout and no provision was made for the teaching of the Bible.[5] In fact it was not until 1932 that Islam was taught in the secondary section.

In the primary section of the college no Christian boys were allowed to attend Islamic courses although requests were received from parents that they should be permitted in order to improve their Arabic.[6] The college authorities did not object to the teaching of Christianity to the Christian boys attending the college except for 'the practical difficulties and the risks in opening controversies between different Christians'.[7] The introduction of a minister of any

[1] Wingate, F. R., "Notes on the Warden's Report," *1933*, *U.K.A.*

[2] 'General Gordon and Education in the Sudan', *Missionary Review of the World*, xxxi (1908), 360–4.   [3] Ibid.

[4] Watson, C. R., 'Missionary Conditions in the Egyptian Sudan', *Missionary Review of the World*, xxviii (1905), 85–93.

[5] *The Scotsman*, Edinburgh, 21 June 1910.

[6] Letter from Cromer to McInnes, Cairo, 16 May 1906, *PRO/FO/633, vol. 8.*

[7] Ibid.

one Christian cult to give religious instruction would not have been accepted by the others.[1]

A new function besides teaching and training was added in 1905 when Sir Henry Wellcome donated a completely equipped bacterio- logical and analytical laboratory to the Sudan Government for the purpose of developing scientific research. The gift, made after con- sultations with the Sudan Government, was a recognition by the administration of the fact that scientific research was a prerequisite to economic development. The association of the Wellcome Research Laboratories with the college laid the foundations for its development from the beginning as a centre of teaching, training, and research. An economic museum was established in the same year as part of the college. A small library was established and in 1915 the Gibb Trustees gave a complete series of oriental publications and the authorities of the Sultania library in Cairo offered a number of classical Arabic texts.[2]

Although it was not part of the department of education or the college, the military school established in 1905 was housed in the college buildings. The students of the military school attended relevant courses with the college students. The proposal to establish the military school was made in 1900 after the mutiny of the Sudanese battalions stationed in Omdurman. Colonel Jackson, who was the President of the Court of Inquiry into the incident, recommended the removal of all Sudanese cadets from the military school in Cairo and the formation of a military school in Khartoum. He held that Sudanese officers trained in Cairo were 'no better than a young Egyptian officer. In Cairo they get ideas into their heads which increase the veistures of their own importance and consequently they refuse to mix with their own races and keep aloof from Sudanese officers promoted from the ranks, who are the backbone of Sudanese battalions.'[3] Selection to the school was from among those who had completed their primary education. Preference was given to what the administration called 'Black Sudanese' over 'Arab Sudanese' on the grounds that the Sudanese battalions for whom the officers were being trained were 'black soldiers'. Of the first fifteen officers gradu- ating in 1908 only three belonged to the 'Arab Sudanese' group.[4] The course was for three years and the subjects taught were 'Military

[1] Ibid.   [2] *G.M.C.R., 1915*, p. 24.
[3] Letter from Jackson to Sirdar, Khartoum, 4 March 1900, *SP/A/112*.
[4] Report on the Military School, Khartoum, *SAD/106/4*.

Law, Khedival Regulations, Army Regulations, Musketry Regulations, Field Training, Pay Accounts, Interior Economy, and Arithmetic'.[1]

Outside the Gordon College and the military school a network of primary and elementary schools for boys was established in the main towns. Two primary schools were established in 1906 in Berber and Wad Medani, in addition to the four schools in Omdurman, Khartoum, Suakin, and Halfa. The total number of primary school pupils in 1906 was 762.[2] The number of boys admitted was carefully limited to those who were likely to be required for the Gordon College advanced courses or for minor government posts, so as to avoid the creation of an unemployed educated class. In 1914 the number attending the six primary schools did not exceed 783—all destined either for employment or for further training in the Gordon College. The teaching of English was restricted to the primary and post-primary schools while Arabic was to be the medium of instruction in the elementary schools.[3]

In spite of the fact that the demand for primary education was growing, the policy was to give priority to the expansion of elementary and technical education.[4] The development of elementary education was made possible through the imposition of an education tax. In 1904 Currie proposed that an education tax should be introduced in order to supplement the resources of the department and make it possible to meet an increasing demand for elementary schools.[5] As the Sudan Government's tax policy was based on the principle that as few taxes as possible should be charged, the proposal was rejected after reference to the governors of the northern provinces. All governors, except those of the Gezira and Sennar, reported that there was no enthusiasm for such a tax. This was more an opposition to additional taxes than to education. It was finally agreed to levy an education tax in Sennar and the Gezira provinces, and any other area which in the future showed willingness to pay the tax. Several of the provinces reported in 1907 that their inhabitants were willing to pay the education tax. The education tax varied from one-tenth to one-twentieth of the *ushur* and was collected in cash or kind. It was used exclusively for the establishment of elementary schools in the areas which paid the tax. Thus the regions which paid more

[1] Ibid.
[2] *G.G.R., 1906*, p. 137.   [3] Ibid., *1901*, p. 67.
[4] Ibid., *1912*, p. 66.   [5] Ibid., *1904*, p. 144.

by virtue of the number of their inhabitants and better economic resources came to enjoy more educational facilities. Kordufan and Kassalla provinces, for example, did not agree to the principle of the education tax until later and did not, therefore, receive the same facilties in elementary education as other provinces. The increase in the local education tax from £E350 in 1906 to £E5,293 in 1913 enabled the department of education to provide additional facilities which would not have been possible otherwise.[1] Education taxes continued to be paid until 1913 when they were stopped by the government. In order to cater for the additional expansion, two elementary teachers' training courses were started in Suakin and Rufaa in 1907.

The number of boys attending government elementary schools rose from 1,280 in 1907 to 6,086 in 1918 in seventy-three schools.

Technical education developed at a slow rate. The extension of the railway from Suakin to Berber in 1906 created a demand for artisans and skilled workers. Two technical schools were established in Kassalla and Dueim in 1906 but were closed during the First World War for lack of funds and suitable candidates.[2] There were 281 boys attending technical schools in 1914.

A policy of education geared to employment did not, naturally, cater for girls' education, and women's education therefore lagged behind men's education. In the past, few girls had attended the *khalwas* with boys. There was no evidence of a general demand for girls' education after the reconquest, and whatever demand there was arose from the Egyptian and Christian populations of the towns. Missionary schools, however, catered for this. The few Sudanese who demanded education for their girls sent them to the missionary schools. It was not until 1906 that the provision of education for girls was seriously considered. A petition signed by Egyptian and Sudanese parents was presented to the government demanding the establishment of a government school for girls. Currie's view was that the government should not undertake the task.[3] But this view was reconsidered when an Egyptian newspaper in Cairo published an article suggesting that mission schools in Khartoum were trying to advance the cause of Christianity among Moslem girls.[4] To allay the fears of the Sudanese the first two classes for girls were added

[1] Appendix I, Table III.   [2] *G.M.C.R.*, *1918*, p. 11.
[3] Letter from Wingate to Cromer, Khartoum, 29 December 1906, *SAD/103*.
[4] *Al Moayad* (newspaper), Cairo, no. 5043 of 17 December 1906.

to the Khartoum elementary school for boys. This decision was opposed by the Church Missionary Society in Khartoum on the grounds that the opening of a government school would make the Church Missionary School in Khartoum redundant and lead to the withdrawal of the Sudanese girls.[1] Wingate informed Cromer that the Church Missionary Society was much upset by the possibility of a government girls' school[2] in Khartoum. Gwynne suggested that the education of girls should be left to private enterprise.[3] He wrote to Wingate that 'it would be a test to Islam to attempt to do for herself what Christian bodies were doing without any government assistance'.[4] In the face of this strong opposition from the Church Missionary Society representative, a compromise was agreed upon. The two classes in Khartoum were closed. Babiker Bedri, who had been trying unsuccessfully for some time to obtain approval for the establishment of a girls' school, was allowed to do so. The girls' school at Rufaa would be in Currie's view a test of the real demand and would not constitute a danger to missionary efforts in this field. It was also decided that in future government schools would charge fees so as to discourage the movement of girls from missionary schools.[5]

The opposition to government schools for girls hindered the development of girls' education. During this period, only five elementary schools for girls were established, in Rufaa, Kamlin, Merowe, Dongula, and El Obeid. Neither Khartoum nor Omdurman, the largest towns, had any provision for government girls' education until 1921, when an elementary school was started in Omdurman as part of the training college.

Thus by 1908 the foundations of a government system of education embracing elementary, primary, secondary, technical, and military schools was established. No additional facilities were added until 1914, when a special school was established for the training of Sudanese for junior administrative jobs in the political service. The Sub-*Mamur* School, as it was called, represented another step in the policy of employing Sudanese and replacing the Egyptian personnel. A proposal to establish an agricultural school in Khartoum North was turned down and instead an experimental farm was established in 1912.[6]

[1] Letter from Gwynne to Wingate, Khartoum, 13 March 1907, *SAD/103*.
[2] Letter from Wingate to Cromer, Khartoum, 19 July 1907, *SAD/103*.
[3] Letter from Gwynne to Wingate, Khartoum, 13 March 1907, *SAD/103*.
[4] Ibid.
[5] Letter from Wingate to Finlay, Khartoum, 20 March 1907, *SAD/103*.
[6] *SGA/GENCO/1/1/File No. 5 and File No. 6.*

Educational development was slow after that and until the end
of the First World War. The financial depression of 1908, the withdrawal of the Egyptian grant in 1913, the depression in trade in
1913, the abandonment of the education tax in 1914, and the outbreak
of the First World War all contributed to this slow progress. The
number of boys in the secondary section was decreased from 80 in
1908 to 45 in 1915 and in the teachers' training section from 178 to
23 respectively.

The other source of education in northern Sudan during this
period was supplied by the *khalwas* and the missionary societies.
Koranic schools in the government's view were fulfilling a useful
function in meeting the growing demand for education. Grants-in-
aid were paid to a few selected *khalwas* on the recommendations of
the local authorities. These subsidies were paid from the local
educational rates and charged to the local provincial budgets.

The koranic schools fulfilled another useful function. Until the
number of schools had increased and produced candidates for the
college, boys trained in the *khalwas* were selected to the training
college for teachers and Sharia judges. Some were admitted to the
industrial school in Omdurman for training as artisans. The majority
of pupils completing their education in the *khalwas*, however, found
their way back into their own communities as teachers in the local
mosques.

Like the Gordon Memorial College, the Omdurman *Mahad Ilmi*
was the centre of religious learning and teaching.

In the Omdurman mosque students attended religious lessons
given by the Sudanese *Ulama*. A board consisting of a president and
ten *Ulama* was appointed in 1901 by the Governor-General to supervise the teaching in the Omdurman mosque and recommend persons
for appointment as teachers.[1] It was also the board's duty to advise
the government on all matters of interest in relation to the teaching
of Islamic religion.[2] Teaching was normally done in the mosque and
the private residences of the *Ulama*, who were all paid a monthly
salary. On the death of Sheikh Mohammed Al Bedawi, the first

[1] Members of the board were: Sheikh Mohamed Al Bedawi (chairman),
Sheikh Al Nazir Khalid, Sheikh Isa Doleib, Sheikh Ibrahim Sharif, Sheikh
Mohamed Abdul Magid, Sheikh Mohamed Wad Al Geraif, Sheikh Mohamed
Amin Al Darir, Sheikh Alsayed Ismail Alwali, Sheikh Mohamed Ahmed Nur,
Sheikh Ahmed Al Magdhoud, and Sheikh Algaili Al Tilib (members).
[2] Mudathir, Hassan, Madi al Mahad al Ilmi, *Magalat Mahad Omdurman*
(25 January 1963), pp. 31–8.

president, Sheikh Abu Al Gasim Ahmed Hashim was appointed as his successor in 1912.

In the meantime a recommendation to reorganize the teaching in the mosque was discussed by the *Ulama*. The development of a modern system of education had attracted boys to the new schools and very few Sudanese continued to go to Al Azhar in Cairo. The modern educational system presented a challenge to traditional education. The Governor-General informed Kitchener that 'there was a strong feeling amongst the higher Moslem dignitaries in the Sudan that the study of Moslem Theology was being neglected and that the only way to provide Moslem teachers for the Sudanese Ulama was to send a few young Sudanese Ulama to Al Azhar in Cairo where they would go through the regular curriculum of study and return to the Sudan as qualified teachers on completion of the course'.[1] Wingate was against this suggestion on the ground that such a course would expose the Sudanese *Ulama*, while in Cairo, to ideas prejudicial to the administration. But he preferred such a course to the idea of bringing out Egyptian *Ulama* to teach in the Sudan.[2] The alternative proposal of providing more higher Islamic studies in the Gordon College work was out of the question because it would make the Sudan administration 'fall foul of the non-conformist and ultra conscience in England'.[3] The compromise agreed to was to reorganize and develop the teaching of the Omdurman mosque. Sheikh Abul Gasim Ahmed Hashim encouraged the *Ulama* to teach in the mosque instead of their private residences. He issued, after the approval of the Governor-General, the first 'Regulations for teaching Islamic Religious knowledge in the *Maahad El Mashikha El Almia* in Omdurman and Khartoum and in the Mosques of Provinces or Districts'.[4] These regulations defined the constitution and duties of the board of *Ulama*, the duties of teachers and students, the curriculum, qualifications, and discipline. The studies in the new *Mahad* were divided into three stages, each leading to a certificate: *al Ibtidaiya* (primary), *al Ahlia* (national) and *al Alamia* (higher). Arithmetic and Arabic composition and dictation were added to the subjects studied. In 1917, ten assistant teachers were appointed and the number of regular students rose to 138, of whom 76 per cent

---

[1] Letter from Wingate to Kitchener, Khartoum, 26 October 1911, *SAD/301/4*.
[2] Ibid.   [3] Ibid.
[4] Sudan Government, *Note on the Omdurman Mahad Ilmi*, Legal Department, Khartoum, 16 September 1946.

came from Khartoum province. Gradually the *Mahad* came under government control. Its *Ulama* and teachers were paid from government funds. In view of the fact that the president was a *Sharia* judge and because of the close connection between the *Sharia* law and Islamic religion its control was vested in the legal department.

Unlike the Gordon College, the training in the *Mahad* was not related to the needs of the government service. The board of *Ulama* understood its role as providing a class of *Ulama* and preachers capable of imparting Islamic teaching to their community.[1] Few of these, however, were employed in junior posts in the *Sharia* courts. The graduates of the Gordon College *Sharia* section looked upon the *Mahad* graduates as representatives of an old society with ideas unsuited to the requirements of a new society. The major contribution of the *Mahad* in Omdurman was to produce teachers for the *khalwas* and preachers in mosques.

The development of a modern system of education did not therefore lead to a complete disappearance of traditional education. An Azhar in miniature developed and as a result the class of *Ulama*, which the Sudan had known for centuries, continued to carry on the traditional Moslem teaching in the traditional way. Those who sought higher Islamic studies no longer went to Cairo but came to Omdurman. The Mahad, like the Gordon College, became a national institution.

Many missionary schools, on the other hand, were providing an education of a different type. Missionary schools which were started for the education of non-Moslems in the Sudan soon developed into an important source for the education of Sudanese boys and girls.

The Roman Catholic Verona Fathers were the first to establish schools in the north. In 1900, two schools for girls, St. Ann and St. Joseph, were started, in Khartoum and Omdurman respectively. In 1906, another school for girls was started in Port Sudan.

The first Church Missionary Society school was established in Khartoum in 1902. Soon the school, which was originally meant to provide education for the Coptic Christians, attracted Moslem girls, both Sudanese and Egyptians. Three other schools were developed, in Omdurman in 1905, in Atbara in 1908 and in Wad Medani in 1912. With the exception of the school at Atbara, which was co-educational, all the others were for girls.

The American Presbyterian Mission began its first school in

[1] Mudathir, Hassan, Madi al Mahad, op. cit., pp. 31–8.

4   BED

Khartoum in 1905 for boys. A second school for girls was established in Khartoum North in 1909. In 1910 a boys' school was started in Halfa, but was soon closed for lack of support by the local population. In 1912 a girls' school was started in Atbara. The Khartoum North school developed into an intermediate and secondary school for girls—the first in the field of girls' secondary education.

The majority of pupils in the missionary schools were Sudanese Moslem girls. Unlike the government elementary schools, missionary schools provided instruction in domestic science and home economics and were thus able to attract support from the more socially advanced sections of the town's population. English, as a subject, was taught at the elementary and post-elementary levels. Although each of the missions followed different curricula and practices in its schools, they all provided an education with a Christian foundation and outlook.

Christian missionaries were tactful in their educational work. Their aim of advancing Christian teachings, values, and morals did not blind them to the fact that their work was being carried on in the midst of a Moslem community sensitive to the question of religion. Their objectives were therefore not pursued in a way which would antagonize the Moslem population. They came to be accepted by both the administration and the local population as useful contributors to education and pioneers of girls' education.

Three systems of education, each with a different objective, were therefore developing side by side in the northern provinces. While government schools laid more emphasis on vocational training and less on liberal education, both the traditional Moslems and the Christian missionary schools emphasized the religious aspects of education, each from their own point of view. The first provided education with a view to employment and the other with a view to preservation of religious values or the introduction of new ones. As the economic benefits of the first in the form of higher incomes became clear, suspicion and reluctance disappeared and there was a demand for further modern education.

In northern Sudan, Arab and Moslem culture and the existence of *khalwas* provided a suitable basis on which an educational programme could be developed, but the situation in the southern Sudan was different. There was no homogeneity of culture, no tradition of an older civilization and no predominant literary language in the south. It was not, however, a question of introducing education into the south, but a question of introducing a new type of education. Education, in the sense of being the systematic training imposed on an individual by an outside agency, was not new to the societies of the south. The purpose of tribal education in the south, like that of *khalwas* in the north, was the moulding of the individual into his own society. Unlike European education, it did not teach how to make a choice between different ideas, traditions or customs. There were predetermined aspects of life which tribal education aimed at making the individual master rather than change. Thus the individual learned about his tribe and his environment. In this sense also it is, unlike European education, less abstract and more utilitarian. Character training such as the teaching of courage or good behaviour to elders, which in the European education is implicit in games, school societies, and religious instruction, is done in primitive societies as part of tribal ritual and initiations.

The school as an institution whose essential task was to teach the pupils the art of reading and writing was an innovation brought about by the new administration and the Christian missionary societies. This was not an easy task to achieve. International boundaries were not clearly defined and tribes related to each other lived on both sides of the Sudan borders with Ethiopia, Kenya, Uganda, and the Congo. There was constant intertribal warfare and resistance to administrative control. Thus the government's main concern was the establishment of its authority. Pacification and normalization of conditions were given priority over the other requirements of administration.

Vast distances, economic backwardness, the large variety of languages, disease, migration of tribes, and the lack of knowledge about the people all created difficulties in the way of spreading education.[1] In spite of these difficulties and as a result of government support and encouragement, schools were established. The Italian Roman Catholics, the Anglican Missionary Society, and the American Presbyterian Mission all contributed to the development of schools in the south.

While the Roman Catholics emphasized technical and industrial training in their schools, the other two emphasized reading and writing. Their educational activities were not, however, always welcomed by the local population. The elders feared that a Christian type of education would alienate the children from their tribes and families.

[1] Beshir, M. O., *The Southern Sudan* (London, 1967), pp. 30–4.

Arabic was excluded from the schools and English was made the official language of education.[1] The curriculum and teaching methods varied from one missionary school to another but all of them emphasized the teaching of Christianity and the use of English as the medium of instruction.[2] Most of the schools were for boys but a few elementary schools were established for girls where hygiene and domestic science were taught.

Educational progress was, however, very slow because of the many difficulties faced by the missionary societies. In 1914 there was a grave set-back when the government decided to expel the Verona Fathers, who were of German and Austrian nationality, for fear of their being a focus of anti-British activities.[3] The government became more and more aware of these problems. Bimbashi E. Grove, Inspector of Opari District, in a report to the Director of Intelligence in Khartoum suggested that the government should play an active role and establish its own schools.[4] His proposal was rejected on the ground that the time was not ripe for such an action.

Education in the south remained, therefore, completely in the hands of the missionaries. Like the central government in the north, the missionaries were successful in laying the foundations of a system of education suited to their own objectives and needs. Unlike education in the north it was not geared to employment. Each missionary society had its own educational policy and this did not help to promote unity between the different tribes. The exclusion of Arabic and the emphasis on English promoted cultural segregation between the north and the south.

In spite of all problems and difficulties which hindered educational progress in both the north and the south, the foundations of a system of modern education were laid during the first twenty years of the Condominium rule.

[1] Ibid.
[2] Sanderson, L., Educational Development in the Southern Sudan, 1900–1948, *Sudan Notes and Records*, xliii (1962), pp. 105–17.
[3] Beshir, M. O., *The Southern Sudan* (London, 1967), pp. 34–5.
[4] Letter from Grove, E., to the Director of Intelligence, Khartoum, 17 September 1918, *SGA/CIVSEC/File 17.A.2/6*.

PART TWO
1920-1932

CHAPTER IV

Education and Administrative Policy

THE END of the First World War marked the beginning of a new educational policy in the Sudan. This new policy was an outcome of internal and external factors which, in their reaction to each other, produced new attitudes in the minds of both the rulers and the ruled. The Sudan was no longer isolated from the outside world and was apt to be influenced by what was happening outside its borders. It was no longer the country of 'hopeless depression where revival seemed well-nigh unthinkable'[1] in 1898. Law and order had been established in the north. The last of the rebels, Ali Dinar, had been defeated and Darfur brought within the fold. Revenue increased from £E126,596 in 1899 to £E4,425,340 in 1920. Suspicions and fears of education gave way to confidence.[2] The foundations of a secular system of education in the north geared to employment opportunities were firmly laid. In the sphere of skilled labour, the Mather work-shops had turned out nearly 500 carpenters, blacksmiths, fitters, turners, and painters, and the Omdurman technical school had turned out 101 bricklayers and stonemasons.[3]

Out of 4,178 classified posts in the Sudan Government service in 1920, Sudanese held 1,544 posts, compared to 535 held by the British, 1,824 by Egyptians, 167 by Syrians and 108 by nationals of other countries.[4] In the education department 282 Sudanese were employed as teachers compared to 31 British, 53 Egyptians, 4 Syrians and five others.[5]

Expenditure on education increased from £E1,075, or 0·3 per cent of the total budget, in 1901 to £E85,159, or 2·4 per cent in 1920.[6] There were 7,649 boys in 1920 attending elementary schools; 1,106, primary schools; and 210, technical schools. Five elementary schools for girls were established during the first twenty years, and a Teachers' Training College for Girls was established in 1920. Several of the sons of the 'old boys' of the Gordon College were already admitted to the college to study.

[1] Wingate, F. R., *The Story of the Gordon College and its Work*, p. 572.
[2] Appendix I, Table I.
[3] *G.M.C.R., 1922*, p. 2.
[4] Appendix I, Table IV.
[5] Ibid.
[6] Appendix I, Table I.

The research side of Gordon College, built around the Wellcome
Research Laboratories, had been further expanded by the addition
of a geological section and three museums—one for antiquities, one
for natural history, and the other for ethnological collections. The
objectives of education laid by Currie in 1901 were therefore to a great
extent fulfilled.

The administrative policy embarked upon after 1920 had, however,
given a new orientation to education, arresting developments in
certain parts of the educational system and furthering the developments in other parts. Until then the keynote of the administration
was direct rule. The higher ranks of the administration were dominated by army officers and the system of government could best be
described as 'a benevolent autocracy on military lines for civil
purposes'.[1] The benevolent autocrats who founded the system had,
however, disappeared from the scene. Cromer, who had taken a
keen interest in all matters relating to education, left Egypt in 1907.
Currie retired in 1914. He was followed by Crawford, an archae-
ologist. It was his first appointment in the political service. The three
directors of education who followed from 1926 to 1932—Corbyn,
Mathew, and Winter—were all administrators and not educationalists. Kitchener left his post in Egypt in 1914 to be Secretary of State
for War in Britain, and died in 1916. Wingate was recalled from
Egypt to Britain in 1919. Slatin Pasha, the Inspector-General and
adviser to the Governor-General, was released from his post at the
beginning of the war. With the exception of Sir Lee Stack, the two
other Governor-Generals during the period—Sir Geoffrey Archer
and Sir John Maffey—did not have direct experience of Sudan affairs.
New men were therefore dominating the scene and the civilian
political officer was gradually replacing the military administrator.

Indirect rule became the gospel of Sudan administration. Lugard's
Dual Mandate, which appeared in 1922, became 'the *vade mecum*
of a generation of colonial servants',[2] including the Sudan's. Sudan
administration looked to Nigeria, and not Egypt or India, for its
example. The Powers of Nomad Sheiks Ordinance was promulgated
in 1922. A member of the political service was sent to Nigeria in the
same year to study the system of native administration.

Over the years, indirect rule had meant many things to many
people. The idea was not new. It had been tried out in Baluchistan,

[1] MacMichael, Sir Harold, *The Sudan* (London, 1954), p. 67.
[2] Henderson, K. D. D., *The Sudan Republic* (London, 1965), p. 69.

Sarawak, and Uganda.[1] What was new about it was the fact that it 'coincided with a phase of considerable pessimism and doubt of the civilizing value of Western European ways'.[2] The basic principle of indirect rule, therefore, was that there was nothing about 'Western' institutions which made them universally right *de natura*.[3] The advocates of indirect rule argued that some of them might be suitable to the local societies and some might not. It was, therefore, wiser to rely in the first place on indigenous institutions where they existed, rejecting the inefficient or undesirable and adopting the others.

The primary aim of education under Lugard's indirect rule philosophy was 'to fit the ordinary individual to fill a useful part in his environment with happiness to himself and to ensure that the exceptional individual shall use his abilities for the advancement of the community and not to its detriment or to the subversion of constituted authority'.[4] According to him, education had failed to bring happiness to the communities of India and West Africa, and the ideal of a sound educational policy should therefore be 'to exchange this hostility for an attitude of friendly co-operation, and to raise a generation which shall be able to achieve ideals of its own without a slavish imitation of Europeans, and be proud of a nationality with its own definite sphere of public work and its own future'.[5] Instead of making the town and village population unsuited and discontented with their life,

education should enlarge their outlook, increase their efficiency and standard of comfort, and bring them into closer sympathy with government, and it should, in particular, produce a new generation of native chiefs of higher integrity, a truer sense of justice, and appreciation of responsibility for the welfare of the community. As regards that smaller section who desire to enter the service of government or of commercial firms, education should make them efficient, loyal, reliable, and contented—a race of self-respecting native gentlemen.[6]

These principles were to be given effect, according to Lugard, through the following means:

[1] Ibid., p. 69.
[2] Fabian Society, *The Sudan, The Road Ahead* (London, 1945), p. 12.
[3] Henderson, loc. cit.
[4] Lugard, Sir F. D., Revision of Instructions to Political Officers on subjects chiefly political and administrative, cited in *The Principles of Native Administration in Nigeria, Selected Documents 1900–1947*, ed. A. H. M. Kirk-Green (London, 1965), p. 106.
[5] Ibid., p. 107.   [6] Ibid.

(a) Schools whose primary object was 'the formation of character and certain habits of discipline, rather than the mere acquisition of a certain amount of book-keeping or technical skill'.[1]

(b) The development of literary schools to train boys for posts in which a knowledge of English is required; technical schools for the training of artisans; and elementary schools suitable to village life.[2] The teaching of agriculture in the latter 'should be limited to very simple facts combined with manual work, as for instance, the value of rotation of crops and of leguminous crops and manures as renovators of the soil'.[3]

(c) The development of residential provincial schools where 'the boys would be detached from their home surroundings and come continuously under the influence of the staff'.[4] These schools would be 'located a mile or two from the native city',[5] and their buildings made 'in the native style of architecture and usually in the form of a parallelogram'.[6] Their aim would be the training of clerks for native courts and teachers for rural schools.[7]

(d) Teaching methods adapted to the needs of the pupils whether intending to be clerks or artisans or farmers.

(e) The training of teachers and improvement of their status.

(f) The exercise by government of 'some measure of control over all schools, even though not assisted by grants, and endeavour to bring them into line with the general policy'.[8]

(g) The recognition and utilization of religion 'as an agent for this purpose, together with secular moral instruction'.[9]

Lugard's *The Dual Mandate* warned against the discontent and indiscipline which might arise from the impact of a Western education undermining the respect for both traditional and European authority. Education should, therefore, emphasize the value of traditional society and employ traditional methods, including religious and moral instruction, which would form a major part of the curriculum. In the social sciences the students would be taught the geography and history of their own localities in detail, and the history and geography of their country and of the Empire in general terms. The teaching of the history of Britain and the evolution of its governmental system and democratic institutions would, according to Lugard, do more harm than good because it would induce the pupils to deplore the woes of their own countries and desire their regeneration, instead of attending to their lessons.[10]

---

[1] Lugard, op. cit., p. 107.

[2] Ibid., p. 108.   [3] Ibid., p. 112.   [4] Ibid., p. 109.

[5] Ibid.   [6] Ibid., p. 110.   [7] Ibid., p. 111.

[8] Ibid., p. 108.   [9] Ibid.

[10] Lugard, Sir F. D., *The Dual Mandate* (London, 1922), pp. 426–55.

The adoption of indirect rule and native administration in the Sudan began in 1921 with the publication of Milner's *Report of the Special Mission to Egypt*.[1] The report argued that decentralization and employment of native agencies was the best policy to achieve economy and efficiency, and the administration of the different parts of the country should therefore be left as far as possible in the hands of native authorities under the supervision of the British administrators. On the question of education Milner's report was critical of the educational policy in Egypt, because of the discontent which had been created as a result of the production of 'an increasingly large and ever-increasing number of candidates for official posts, provided with Examination Certificates but destitute of any real educational culture'.[2]

In order to avoid the faults found in the educational policy in Egypt, Milner's report advocated the training of Sudanese for employment in occupations other than those provided by the government service, such as agriculture, commerce, and industry. It also argued in favour of enabling the Sudanese to replace the non-Sudanese junior officials—mainly the Egyptians, who outnumbered them and were reluctant to be employed in the Sudan.[3]

Those recommendations which did not conflict with the basic objectives of indirect rule as applied to education were soon adopted. The Governor-General stated in 1924: 'It is our object, while interfering as little as possible with all that is good in native traditions and encouraging their maintenance, to promote the advancement of the community as a whole, fitting the natives to earn their own livelihood in the various capacities open to them in their own country and providing the government and business houses in the Sudan with staff to meet their requirements in every sphere.'[4]

The *khalwa*, which was originally looked upon as a picturesque but useful part of the social system, came to be regarded as a necessary part of the educational system. It was recognized as a simple type of school directed towards serving the needs of the local villages and tribes, by supplying in the simplest possible manner the local educational needs, religion, reading, writing, and simple arithmetic.[5] As the only careers open to the great majority of the boys from villages and tribes were in agricultural and pastoral pursuits, the *khalwa*'s

---

[1] *Report of the Special Mission to Egypt* (Milner Report), Cmd. 113 (H.M.S.O. London, 1921).   [2] Ibid., pp. 9–10.   [3] Ibid.
[4] *G.M.C.R., 1924*, p. 10.   [5] *E.D.R., 1928*, p. 33.

major role was to supply the educational need for these careers.[1] It was no longer part of the *kuttab* but a distinct institution designed to meet different requirements,[2] and remaining 'as close as possible to the traditional circumstances and conditions of the village or tribe'.[3] The only changes allowed were 'to give greater efficiency to the teaching',[4] and teach some simple rules of health and cleanliness.

In order to give effect to these aims a local inspectorate for *khalwas*, responsible to both the education department and the local authorities, was established to assist provincial officials and 'give greater efficiency to the teaching'.[5] Consonant with the policy of native administration, local *nazirs* and *sheikhs* were brought into closer contact with the local *khalwas* and encouraged to take an interest in the working of the new policy.[6] *Fekis* were divided into five groups and paid monthly salaries ranging from £E2 to £E6 per month. Training centres for the *fekis* in provincial headquarters were organized.

In 1927 an extra task was added to the *khalwa*. It was used as a supplier to the elementary school and the first year of the latter was abolished. The experiment did not, however, succeed. It was found to be educationally unsound and was abandoned in 1930.

As a result of this new policy the number of assisted *khalwas* grew from 6 in 1918 to 400 in 1927, 489 in 1928, and 768 in 1930. The number of boys in attendance grew from 200 in 1918 to 889 in 1923, to 5,444 in 1925, to 13,077 in 1927, and to 28,669 in 1930.

The number of elementary schools had, however, remained unchanged. The *khalwa* had taken its place. In 1920 there were 80 elementary schools with 7,000 boys in attendance. The number in 1928 was the same, but with 7,827 in attendance. In 1932 the number of boys attending was 8,943. The increase in the number of *khalwas* had temporarily checked the growth of elementary education, on which the education system was based during the early years.

The aims of the elementary schools were redefined. Their original aim of dispelling ignorance and superstition was replaced with a new one, 'making the children who attend them more useful members of the society into which they have been born',[7] and to 'train the sons of the *Sheikh*, the cultivator and the artisan alike better to assist their parents'.[8] The director of education emphasized that the

[1] *E.D.R., 1928*, p. 33.   [2] Ibid.   [3] Ibid., p. 34.
[4] Ibid.   [5] Ibid.   [6] Ibid., p. 36.
[7] Ibid., p. 30.   [8] Ibid.

elementary schools were 'not trying to disturb the existing order of things, but rather to minimize the natural disturbance inevitable' in what he called progress.[1] The syllabus was revised to include lessons in the elements of hygiene, natural history, geography, agriculture, and veterinary knowledge, and local and tribal history based on notes prepared by provincial officials and the civil secretary's office.[2] A new series of reading books, prepared by Sudanese teachers supervised by a member of the British staff of the Gordon Memorial College, replaced the Egyptian books which had been in use since 1900.

The demand for elementary school teachers decreased as a result of this policy. The number of students in the teachers' training college decreased from 81 in 1920 to 16 in 1923. The training college was closed in 1923 and was not reopened until 1925, when a severe shortage was felt as a result of the departure of Egyptian teachers in 1924.

In line with the native administration policy, governors of provinces were directed to constitute a local authority which might be the district commissioner, a *mamur*, or a committee of officials or notables, or both, to supervise the work of the elementary schools.[3] The new issue of the *kuttab* regulations stated: 'Pupils shall wear the native dress of the district; those, however, who are not natives of the Sudan may obtain permission from the Headmaster to wear the dress of their own country. European shoes and socks shall not be worn by natives.'[4]

As the success of native administration depended on the creation of a class of educated chiefs, and heads of tribes, who would be able to carry out the simple administrative work and stand up to the rivalry of the educated class produced by the town schools, it was decided in 1925 to establish a school for this purpose. It was suggested that the school would provide 'a liberal education on native lines, above the standard of the present elementary schools, for men whose lives will be devoted mainly to the management of their own estates and such unpaid public functions as are performed nowadays by men of this class'.[5] The school would 'admit the sons of native notables of good birth and position'[6] and be sited in a rural area 'where political and rebellious agencies might not be rife'.[7] Leading

[1] *E.D.R., 1928*, p. 30.   [2] *E.D.R., 1930*, p. 51.   [3] *E.D.R., 1928*, p. 31.
[4] Ibid., p. 32.   [5] *SGA/Dakhlia/File 17. D.16. vol. I.*
[6] Ibid.   [7] Ibid.

nazirs and *sheikhs* were invited to a meeting to discuss the project.[1]
Although the proposal was met with enthusiasm, doubts were
expressed whether there would, in actual practice, be any demand for
such a school and whether the potential applicants would be forthcoming. Some *nazirs* did not want training for their sons which would
not lead to government employment.[2]

The question was again discussed in 1929. It was suggested that
'native chiefs without education would not be able to stand up to
the *effendi* class'.[3] The governors, meeting in 1929, suggested the
establishment of elementary schools in tribal areas,[4] and accordingly
schools were started in Neyala, Fasher, Darmasalit, Abu Rikba,
Naima, and Jala al Nahal—all centres of important tribal authorities.[5]

The education of the nomads received attention for the first time.
It was decided in 1921 to begin a school in one of the Beja villages
as an experiment. As the Beja were reluctant to send their sons away
from their own village, it was decided to move the schools to another
village after a period of time.[6] A teacher was appointed to the
Kabolish tribe. He lived and travelled with the tribe as it moved
from one place to another.

The retarding effect of the development of native administration
and the handing of judiciary powers to native authorities was reflected
in the closing of the school of administration and the slowing down
of the training courses in *Sharia* law. The school of administration,
which was started in 1919 to train Sudanese junior administrators,
and in which short courses in law and other subjects were given to
those selected from among the clerks and schoolteachers, was closed
in 1926. The number of *Sharia* students in the Gordon College
decreased from 26 in 1921 to 19 in 1923 and the intake was made
once every four years.[7]

The early period of native administration coincided with a world
depression and a fall in the prices of cotton, gum, and sesame.

---

[1] The meeting was attended by the civil secretary; the director of education;
Sheikh Awad el Karim Abu Sin, *nazir* of the Shukria tribe in Blue Nile province;
Sheikh Mohamed Dafalla, *nazir* of the Mersairia tribe in Kordufan; Abdul Azim
Bey Khalifa of the Abadda tribe in Berber; Sheikh Hamid Abu Sin of the Shukria
tribe in Kassalla; Sheikh Adam Hassan of the Juamaa tribe in Kordufan; Sheikh
Bokkari Ali of the Juamaa tribe in Kordufan; and Sheikh Taib Mohamed Badr
of Massamalia in Blue Nile province.
[2] *SGA/Dakhlia/File 17.D.16, vol. I.*
[3] Ibid.   [4] Ibid.
[5] *E.D.R., 1929*, p. 3.   [6] *G.G.R., 1932*, p. 421.
[7] *G.G.R., 1923*, p. 40.

Revenue decreased from £E4,425,340 in 1920 to £E3,766,133 in 1923. It was not until 1925 that revenue started to increase again.[1] The reduction of educational facilities, therefore, was not only consonant with the basic principles of indirect rule, but also demanded by the economic conditions. One aspect of education which was affected by the policy of economy was primary education. The number of boys attending primary schools decreased from 1,196 in 1922 to 1,101 in 1924.[2]

Southern educational policy and development were similarly affected by the concept of indirect rule, but in a different way. Indirect rule confirmed and later led to the acceleration of the policy which had already been started through its emphasis on the removal of Islamic influence from pagan tribes.[3] The south had been treated since 1902 differently from the north. The removal of northern and Moslem influence was hastened when the Equatorial Battalion was formed in 1917, and the last of the northern Sudanese troops left the south. The recognition of Sunday throughout the south as the official day of worship in 1918, the adoption of English as the official language of the south in 1918, and the Passport and Permits Ordinance promulgated in 1922 which allowed the Governor-General and his authorized representatives to declare any part of the Sudan a 'closed district' aimed at removing northern influence. The last of these measures aimed at excluding northern Sudanese from the south and reducing the number of southerners who tended to look northward for employment. The significance of the concept of indirect rule lay, therefore, in justifying a policy which had already been started rather than in initiating it. Practice became an accepted policy justified by the principles of indirect rule.

The impact of indirect rule as an administrative policy on southern educational policy and practice resulted in the institution of a grants-in-aid system, and the development of vernacular languages. The policy of indirect rule advocated control of all education and schools, even though not assisted by grants, and co-operation between the missions and administration.[4]

This policy coincided with three developments in missionary and colonial policy. The First World War had shattered the faith of many

[1] Appendix I, Table I.
[2] *G.G.R.*, *1923*, p. 40. Appendix I, Table v.
[3] Kirk-Green, A. H. M. (ed.), *The Principles of Native Administration in Nigeria*, p. 14.   [4] Ibid., p. 108.

Europeans in the moral values which Europe had inherited from the nineteenth century and also their faith in the Church, which seemed to many of them closely connected with these values. Missions fell in the esteem of public opinion and this unpopularity was inevitably reflected in the lack of the public's financial support of them.[1] Government support for missionary societies to enable them to carry on their educational activities was, therefore, necessary. The war had, on the other hand, left behind it a new attitude towards the colonial peoples. The negative attitude which had prevailed since the beginning of the century gave way to a new concept of trusteeship. The ruling power was held to be responsible for the development and, ultimately, the bringing of the colonies to self-government.

The second other major development during this period was the concern which missionary societies showed about education in Africa, and their becoming alive to the needs of co-operation with the governments in Africa. As a result of the missionary conference held in Edinburgh in 1910 a Council for Missionary Education was formed. The council provided the machinery and platform for different missionary societies to discuss the educational problems and policies in Africa. The Phelps–Stokes Commission, which visited Africa in 1920 and 1921, and published two reports on education in Africa, was critical of the educational policy and practice of both governments and missions. Educational facilities were found to be inadequate and unreal as far as the vital needs of Africans were concerned. A system of grants-in-aid and supervision and inspection of schools was recommended.[2] A conference of missionary societies, held in 1924, agreed to a memorandum on 'An Educational Policy for African Colonies' submitted by Dr. Jesse Jones, chairman of the Phelps–Stokes Commission, in which the needs of adapting education to the needs of the African communities through the teaching of agriculture, industrial education, hygiene and health, and home economics were emphasized. The report urged the use of tribal languages in addition to the language of the European nation in control.[3]

The Phelps–Stokes Commission's recommendations were 'the educational analogue of indirect rule. In the same manner as the

[1] Oliver, R., *The Missionary Factor in East Africa*, pp. 232–3.

[2] Lewis, L. J., *The Phelps-Stokes Reports on Education in Africa* (London, 1962), pp. 8–10.

[3] *Christian Education in Africa, Conference at High Leigh, 8–13 September* (London, 1924), pp. 3–5.

colonial élite had believed it possible to utilize traditional political institutions in development, educators considered that it was feasible to adapt the schools more closely to traditional values by using some indigenous educational content as the basis of school curriculums'.[1] This is not to suggest that all missionaries accepted the doctrine. Many missionaries were hostile to indirect rule because it represented a policy of preservation against which Christianity was hostile.[2]

Nonetheless the reports had 'an abiding and continuous influence at the centre of responsibility in Britain, and upon the thinking of far-sighted individuals, and groups in African and British territories',[3] including the Sudan.[4] It 'found immediate favour with Colonial Governments in Africa who were becoming increasingly aware of the futility and even of the positive dangers of a literary education of the Western type in societies which were primitive'.[5]

The third factor in educational development was the setting up of the Advisory Committee on Native Education. A conference held at the Colonial Office in 1923, and attended by missionary society representatives and government representatives, discussed a memorandum submitted to the Secretary of State for the Colonies by the Education Committee of the Conference of Missionary Societies in Great Britain and Ireland. The principal outcome of this was the creation of the Advisory Committee on Native Education in British Tropical Africa 'to advise the Secretary of State on any matters of native education in the British Colonies and Protectorates in Tropical Africa, which he may from time to time report to them, and to assist him in advancing the progress of education in these colonies and protectorates'.[6] The committee's first report laid the guiding principles for a colonial educational policy. These included:

(i) The recognition of the responsibility of Britain as a Trustee for the welfare and moral advancement of native people and their education.

[1] Foster, J. P., *Education and Social Change in Ghana* (London, 1965), p. 164.
[2] Murray, A. V., 'Education under Indirect Rule', *Journal of the Royal African Society*, xxiv, no. cxxxvi (July, 1935), 227–88. Oliver, R., *The Missionary Factor*, p. 288.
[3] Wilson, J., *Education and Changing West African Culture* (New York, 1963), p. 64.
[4] *The Southern Sudan, Now and Then*, Church Missionary Society (London, 1950), p. 12.   [5] Oliver, R., op. cit., p. 265.
[6] Advisory Committee on Native Education in British Tropical African Dependencies, *Memorandum on Educational Policy in British Tropical Africa*. Cmd. 2374, H.M.S.O. (London, 1925), pp. 3–5.

(ii) The need to adapt education to the needs of the communities, whether economic, social or administrative.

(iii) The need to recognize religion and moral education as the basis of character training and good education.

(iv) The need for co-operation between governments and missions in the field of education.[1]

Currie, the first director of education, was a member of the advisory committee, and it was through him that the Sudan kept in close touch with these developments. The last of these recommendations had already been accepted by the Sudan Government. In 1921 declared that its policy was 'not to substitute a government system of education for the missionary schools, but rather to attempt the regulation of some of the missionary activities along lines likely to be of more immediate benefit to the government'.[2] This would be achieved according to this policy declaration through:

(a) Grants-in-aid to certain missionary societies 'to be expended on the training, in approved boarding establishments, of the sons of local chiefs recommended by local government authorities'.[3]

(b) The establishment of a two-year course in English for some of those who had completed their education in missionary schools so as to enable them to replace the northerners working in the south.[4]

A report in 1922 by S. Hillelson stated that the educational facilities in the south were not satisfactory. The educational side of the missionary societies, according to him, was 'hardly developed—they work in a haphazard way without a definite syllabus of teaching, without means of enforcing regular attendance, and with a poor quality of native staff. The Buganda and Uganda trained Acholi teachers cannot be regarded as a success. They are foreigners in the country. They lack personality and authority and therefore are not likely to exercise a healthy influence on character and the discipline of conduct.'[5] The provision of a widely diffused system of schools in the south, like those in the north, was not, however, the report's answer to the problem for three reasons:

Firstly: Economic and administrative development did not reach a stage whereby such a diffusion would have been justified.

Secondly: An elementary school similar to that in the north would not

---

[1] Ibid.   [2] *G.G.R., 1921*, p. 7.
[3] Ibid., p. 7.   [4] Ibid.
[5] Hillelson, S., Report on Education in Mongalla Province, 22 April 1922, *SGA/CIVSEC/17/1*.

have fulfilled a useful purpose among very primitive people like the Dinka or Latuka.[1]

Thirdly: Unlimited education 'would result in the breakdown of tribal standards and the loss of the primitive virtues'.[2]

The aims of education according to this report should be limited to:

(*a*) The provision of a better class of Chief or Chief Assistant.

(*b*) The improvement of the standard of native labour 'by the general training of mind and body'.[3]

(*c*) The provision of a class suitable for employment in the Police as messengers, and

(*d*) The influencing 'of native standards and ideals by moral and religious training'.[4]

The following means were suggested to achieve the above aims:

(*a*) The classification of missionary schools into two groups of recognized and unrecognized schools. Recognition of a school depended on the maintenance of a satisfactory standard. The recognized schools were given a grant-in-aid and received as a matter of right facilities for transport of their teachers and for the purchase of stores and local supplies, and assistance in enforcing regulations of attendance of their registered pupils.

(*b*) Recognized schools were asked to follow a definite programme agreed on through consultation between the education department and the owners of the school, who were required to agree to visits from a representative of the education department.

(*c*) The government had the right to second teachers to the recognized schools, limit the number of pupils admitted to any particular school, and oppose the foundation of schools in districts not ripe for education.

(*d*) The employment of Christian Coptic teachers from the north, and the appointment of a Resident Inspector of Education in the south.

(*e*) The establishment of another high school for the Roman Catholic students similar to that of the Church Missionary Society established in 1920 in Juba. The latter school would aim at the training of boys to be 'chiefs, schoolmasters, teachers, clerks, carpenters, etc'.[5]

It was not until 1925 that the first steps towards implementing these aims were taken. The Governor-General declared that it was being 'recognized that increasing economic and administrative development in the Southern Sudan demands additional educational facilities'.[6] A comprehensive scheme of education in the south was prepared by the government in co-operation with the missions[7]

[1] Ibid.   [2] Ibid.
[3] *G.G.R., 1921*, p. 7.   [4] Ibid.
[5] Ibid.   [6] *G.G.R., 1925*, p. 47.
[7] Ibid.

whereby the latter received 'considerable grants by way of subsidy for the execution of the scheme'.[1] An inspector of education for the south was appointed in 1926 and began his work with a visit to Uganda 'in order to study the methods adopted there among a population somewhat similar' to that of the south.[2]

At the beginning the amount of subsidies to be paid was left to agreement between the local authorities and the missionary societies concerned. In 1927, however, the grants-in-aid were regularized on the following lines:

1. For each elementary school a staff grant of £150 per annum to be paid to the missionary society headquarters in addition to £150 per annum to be paid locally.

2. A capital grant of £100 for each new school established.

3. An annual grant of £100 for each technical school. This was increased to £200 in 1930.

4. An annual motor transport grant of £150.

5. An annual grant of £150 for medical work.

6. Free occupation of land for school buildings.

7. Reduced fares on railways and steamers as practised in the past.

The grant-in-aid was made on the condition that the schools were supervised by Europeans and were maintained at an efficient standard. The reduced fares were to be made to European missionaries only. No missionary of African or Asian origin could qualify for assistance.[3]

The other condition was that the acceptance of grants by the missionary societies carried automatically with it the right of a Government representative from the department of education to inspect the schools. This condition was opposed by the Roman Catholic Missionary Society because the latter held that inspection would lead to interference in their educational work. It did not therefore receive assistance until 1927, when its attitude changed. Arthur Hinsley, the newly appointed Visitor Apostolic to Catholic Missions in British African Colonies, visited the Sudan in 1927 and appealed to the local missionary authorities to co-operate whole-heartedly with the government. He advised the Roman Catholic missionaries in Africa, including the Sudan, that educational work should be given priority over religious work.[4]

[1] Ibid., *1926*, p. 8.   [2] Ibid., p. 73.

[3] Letters from Director of Education to the Church Missionary Society, Khartoum, 17 March 1929 and 16 September 1930. *Précis Book, 1905-1934*, Church Missionary Society Archives, London.

[4] Groves, S. P., *Planting of Christianity in Africa*, 4 vols. (London, 1948-58), vol. iv, p. 119.

Grants-in-aid to missionary education in the south amounted to £E1,765 in 1927, increasing to £E3,900 in 1928, and £E7,450 in 1930.[1] The result was a rapid increase in educational facilities in the south. The number of schools at all levels increased as follows:

1926	1932
(a) 4 Elementary Boys' Schools with 630 pupils.	(a) 33 Elementary Boys' Schools with 3,103 pupils.
(b) 9 Elementary Schools for girls.	(b) 11 Elementary Schools for girls with 547 pupils.
(c) 1 Trade School with ten boys.	(c) 3 Trade Schools with 128 pupils.
(d) 1 Intermediate School with 35 boys.	(d) 3 Intermediate Schools with 280 boys.
(e) None.	(e) 2 Teachers' Training Schools with 82 boys.

The only government-controlled school at the time was the Sir Lee Stack Memorial School at Wau, established in 1925 from the Stack Indemnity Fund. The school provided a two-year course in English and office work. The hope was that this school would develop into a Gordon College of the south, but this hope was not achieved. In 1927 the school was handed over to the Roman Catholic Mission in Wau.

The grants-in-aid system therefore enabled the missionary societies to increase the educational facilities in the south. Missionary control of education and the segregation of southern education were further strengthened by a new language policy. The development of the vernacular language had an adverse effect on the growth of education. Until then the most widely used language besides the vernacular in the Sudan was a debased form of Arabic. Its use as a means of communication had increased in spite of the restrictive policy agreed on earlier. English was learnt only by those who went to mission schools. The development of trade and administration required a language of communication between the trader and administrator on one hand, and the local population on the other. Arabic was the only possible medium for this and the Governor-General wrote in 1927 that:

wherever I penetrated, whether to the top of the Imatong or to the Belgian Congo border, I found Arabic in ready use by the local spokesmen of the

[1] *MIA/File SCC/46.A.1.*

people. In the face of this *fait accompli* we shall have to consider very carefully how far it is worth effort and money to aim at the complete suppression of Arabic. Indeed, we shall have to consider whether Arabic after all, in spite of its risks, must not be our instrument.[1]

This was the subject of the Rejaf Conference in 1928. The conference, under the chairmanship of the Director of Education, was attended by representatives of both missionary societies and governments from the Belgian Congo, Uganda, and the Sudan. D. Westermann, of the International Institute of African Languages and Cultures, also attended. The issues before the conference were: the value of the use of the vernacular as a medium of instruction, and the use of Arabic as a foreign language. The general opinion held by the missionary societies at the time was that, from an educational point of view, the use of the vernacular in elementary schools in Africa was the best instrument for acquiring knowledge and learning a foreign culture.[2] The difficulties in applying this to the south, because of the multiplicity of languages, the absence of a vernacular language spoken by the majority of the people, the lack of personnel able to teach in each or some of these languages, and the non-existence of textbooks in these vernacular languages, did not, however, lead the conference to disagree on this general principle.

It concluded that there were ten language groups in the south, and as it was impossible to patronize all the languages and dialects in the south, the principal members of six of these groups were chosen for purposes of development and for use as the medium of instruction in the village and elementary schools. These were the Dinka, Bari, Nuer, Lotuka, Shilluk, and Zande languages. Textbooks would be prepared in these languages. As regards Arabic the conference rejected its use on the grounds that 'it would open the door for the spread of Islam, Arabicize the south, and introduce the northern Sudanese outlook which differed from that of the southern people'.[3]

Arabic was held to be incapable of fulfilling the functions of a language of intercommunication, and it was accordingly decided not to encourage its use either in administration or in the schools.

[1] Note by the Governor-General on 12 June 1927, *SGA/CIVSEC/File 17.A.2.6.*

[2] Schmidt, P. W., 'The Use of the Vernacular in Education in Africa', *Africa*, iii, no. 2 (April 1930), 138–45.

[3] Note on the Case for the Vernacular, *SGA/Equatoria/File EP/17.* Tucker, A. N., 'The Linguistic Situation in the Southern Sudan', *Africa*, vii, no. 1 (January 1934), 28–38.

If it became necessary to use it in the communities where it was strongly entrenched, roman script and not arabic script should be used.[1]

One aspect of the language policy which was not settled by the conference and which had curious repercussions at a later stage was the question of a standard orthography. This became more serious when two or more missionary societies were involved in the writing of one language. The nationality of the missionaries made agreement in certain cases difficult to reach[2] and this led to delay in the production of textbooks, for 'nobody likes to put out a book only to find it banned in another mission because of the spelling'.[3]

Problems also arose out of the policy of adoption of certain languages and the realization at a later stage that some of these were not in fact spoken by the majority of the tribes for which they were selected.[4] The eradication of Arabic in certain parts of the south, such as Bahr al Ghazal province, was not easy to achieve. Contact with the Arabic-speaking tribes in the north, the existence of numerous northern traders, the teaching of Arabic in the missionary school at Wau, and the absence of a group language made it difficult for the authorities to achieve their aim immediately. The measures suggested to minimize the spread of Arabic in those areas were to eliminate the principal Arabic-speaking population at Wau by removing the Stack School to a place outside the town and the substitution of Arabic in the missionary schools through the use of English and a vernacular language.[5] All these suggestions were carried out and the result was a language confusion in the first years. Energy which could have been spent on extending education was directed towards solving these language problems.[6]

In spite of these difficulties, grammar books appeared by 1934 in Shilluk, Dinka, Nuer, Bari, Zande, and vocabularies in Shilluk, Annuak, Nuer, and Zande.[7] Learning English became the passport to the better-paid jobs in the government service in the south as well

[1] Sudan Government, *Report of the Rejaf Language Conference 1928* (London 1928), p. 26.
[2] Tucker, A. N., 'The Linguistic Situation in the Southern Sudan', *Africa*, vii, no. 1 (January, 1934), 31–4.
[3] Ibid., p. 31.
[4] Ibid.
[5] Letter from Governor Bahr al Ghazal province to Civil Secretary, 22 March 1932, *SGA/File N.B.G.P./SCR/1/C.6.*
[6] Tucker, A. N., loc. cit., p. 33.
[7] Ibid., p. 34.

as the north. English-language classes, especially for the army, police, and other southern employees, were started. In 1935, for example, there were thirty-five classes teaching English outside the schools in Bahr al Ghazal province. Southern employees were further advised that a knowledge of English would be a qualification for further promotion.[1] Non-English-speaking missionaries were encouraged to learn English and special courses were arranged for them in the University of London. It was suggested that English-speaking missionaries should be encouraged as a substitute to the Italian, Austrian, and German Roman Catholics.

Meanwhile the same educational policy was being applied in another part of the Sudan which lay virtually within the boundaries of the southern provinces. The population in the Nuba mountains in Kordufan province, like the southern population, was pagan. Unlike the southerners, the Nuba lived in the midst of an Arab Moslem population and were therefore in constant contact with them and influenced by their culture. When the pacification of the Nuba was completed in 1920, missionary societies showed the same willingness and enthusiasm they showed for the south. The spread of Christianity among them was important for two reasons. First, the region was adjacent to southern Sudan and the spread of Christianity and the conversion of the Nuba would discourage the spread of Islam and Islamic ideas to the south. The Nuba, from the missionary societies' point of view, held a key position in the struggle between Christianity and Islam in Africa.[2]

Second, from the government's point of view the preservation of the traditional Nuba life necessitated the introduction of measures which would protect the 'Nuba culture against a bastard type of Arabization'.[3] As the introduction of a modern type of education similar to that of the Moslem north would have destroyed their culture and become contrary to the concepts of indirect rule, the educational policy aimed to teach the Nuba boys their own traditions, and promote their education under Christian influence.[4]

[1] Letter from Governor of Bahr al Ghazal to Civil Secretary, 20 January 1932, SGA/File BGP/SCR/1.C.14.

[2] Cash, W. W., The Nuba Mountains, Church Missionary Society (London, 1930), pp. 21–31.

[3] Sanderson, L., 'Educational Development and Administrative Control in the Nuba Mountains region of the Sudan', Journal of African History, iv, 2 (1963), 233–47.

[4] Gillan, J. A., Some Aspects of Nuba Administration, Sudan No. 1 (1931) SGA, pp. 11–20.

The Sudan United Mission Society, which was invited to work in the Nuba area and provide educational facilities assisted by government subsidies, founded two schools, at Heiban in 1920 and Alliri in 1922. Both places were chosen because the inhabitants were backward and difficult to administer—education would facilitate the task of the administration. Village schools similar to those in the south were established and English became the medium of instruction in the majority of elementary schools. Arabic was, however, used in areas where the influence of Arabic and Islamic culture was greater.

Work among the Nuba proved as difficult as it was in the south. First there was the problem of the vernacular languages which had to be studied before any valuable communication with the Nuba could be made. Many of their vernacular languages did not extend more than ten miles from the mission's doorstep. Students, therefore, had to be taught Arabic at the beginning. Second, the existence of government elementary schools where Arabic was taught and school leavers had the opportunity of service in the government offices attracted the Nuba to government schools. Missionary schools were therefore in less demand. The process of Arabization and Islamization was continuing at a greater rate than in the south, in spite of the official policy. In order to discourage this process it was decided not to admit Nuba boys to government schools without prior permission from the district commissioners. Instruction about Islam without the consent of the parents was made illegal and the use of any language besides the vernacular in all missionary schools was prevented.[1]

By 1930, however, this policy failed to achieve its purposes. The Secretary of Education and Health confessed that 'Arabic is the only possible language of inter-communication',[2] and recommended that 'Arabic in roman script should be taught as a subject in the elementary schools'.[3] The use of roman instead of arabic script was recommended for two reasons. In the first place the children would learn roman script when being taught to read and write their own language, and no difficulty of teaching two scripts would therefore arise. In the second place, the use of roman script would prevent the pupils from reading Arabic literature which would 'introduce influences tending to disintegrate their social life'.[4]

[1] Ibid. [2] Ibid.
[3] Ibid. [4] Ibid., p. 34.

The teaching of Arabic in roman script created a number of technical problems. Although these problems were recognized from the beginning it was better from the administration's point of view to try and get over the difficulties rather than to give up.[1] What mattered primarily was to conform to the ideals of indirect rule and protect the traditional society from outside influences.

It would be wrong to assume that this policy in the Nuba Mountains or in the south, which led to a complete control of education by the missionary societies, was always accepted with no reservations or objections. Some administrators feared that by allowing religious bodies to be in complete control of education, the products of the schools would be so under the influence of the missionaries that they would be too easily recruited to their support in the event of a disagreement between the missionary societies and the government.[2] The Resident Inspector of Education, for example, warned against entrusting the Roman Catholic mission 'with the education of boys destined for government service', because they were 'nationals of a foreign country',[3] and because they were unable to 'provide a sufficiently good education'.[4] The governor of the Upper Nile province reported that the Italian Roman Catholic missionaries were 'disruptive of tribal life and discipline; their medical work and elementary education poor and merely a poor means of conversion';[5] and the American Presbyterian mission 'squalid and of low standard, with some good elements, but too impregnated with the atmosphere of Middle West',[6] and the Sudan United mission 'a failure in all respects'.[7]

Others feared that 'boys educated in the schools would not be content to go back to their homes and live the normal life of the tribe'.[8] Missionaries, in the view of one district commissioner, 'were out to break the indigenous customs, traditional usage and beliefs of the natives, and anyone passing through their hands became de-tribalized—they became either converts apeing Europeans, or types of the *effendi* class despising their own people'.[9]

[1] Gillan, J. A., *Some Aspects of Nuba Administration*, p. 34, 35.

[2] Letter from N. B. Hunter to Director of Education, 12 November 1925, *SGA/CIVSEC/File 17/D/48*.   [3] Ibid., 29 January 1929.

[4] Letter from N. B. Hunter to Director of Education, 12 November 1925, *SGA/CIVSEC/File 17/D/48*.

[5] Report by Governor Upper Nile province, June 1929, *MIA/File/SCO/14/A.1*.   [6] Ibid.   [7] Ibid.

[8] Minutes of the 6th Educational Conference of Mongalla Province, Juba, 16 April 1932, *SGA/CIVSEC/17/1/File 17.A.2.6*.   [9] *File SGA/ND/SCR/1.C.1*.

The Governor-General, after a tour in the south, wrote that he was far from satisfied with the work of missionaries there. According to him the missions 'made no adequate effort to seize their opportunities. They lack vision and are hedged in by pettiness of outlook and by their bias against the social and matrimonial customs of the people.'[1] He advocated direct activity by the government in the educational field, hoping this might stimulate the missions 'to justify their existence and to act more broadmindedly'.[2] He suggested the establishment at Juba of a good government technical school. The British High Commissioner in Cairo questioned the wisdom of entrusting the missionaries with educating the boys destined for government service because 'experience elsewhere showed mission education to be faulty',[3] and suggested that government schools should be started to train the boys needed.

Fears, doubts, and criticisms of the competence of missionaries or the wisdom of Sudan Government policy did not, however, lead to any changes. A memorandum by the Governor-General in 1929 re-affirmed the educational policy.[4] An Educational Conference held in Juba in 1932 under the chairmanship of the Director of Education confirmed that the government would not provide its own schools, but co-operate with the missions in providing an education which would not only aim at guarding against 'the destruction of native social institutions and the diversion of the African from his natural background',[5] but also at 'teaching him to adapt himself and his institutions to changing ideas and conditions'.[6]

Education in both the south and north had, therefore, conformed to the new administrative policy. The application of indirect rule in the north, and the policy in the south, had different impacts on education in each of the two regions. Differences between the north and the south were getting larger and larger and each region was developing along different paths as far as education was concerned.

[1] Note by the Governor-General, 12 June 1927, *SGA/CIVSEC/File 17.A.2.6.*
[2] Ibid.
[3] Letters from High Commissioner, Cairo, to Governor-General, 20 March 1929 and 13 April 1929 and letter from Lord Lloyd to the Foreign Office, 19 June 1929, *MIA/File SCO/46 A.I.*
[4] Memorandum by the Governor-General, 17 December 1929, *MIA/File SCO/46 A.I.*
[5] Minutes of the 6th Educational Conference of Mongalla Province, Juba, 16 April 1932, *SCA/CIVSEC/17/1 File 17.A.2.5.*   [6] Ibid.

CHAPTER V

Educational Development

THE DOMINANCE of the concepts of native administration over educational policy coincided with a period of growing tension in Anglo-Egyptian relations, the growth of Egyptian and Sudanese nationalism, an economic development represented by the establishment of the Gezira Cotton Scheme, and the extension of railways. Educational policy did not only reflect these economic and political developments, but was used to implement policies arising out of these. The final outcome was stagnation in education.[1] The policy of 'admitting the native to share in the management of affairs'[2] through the selection and appointment of educated Sudanese to government posts 'carrying direct administrative duties'[3] was abandoned after 1924 in favour of a policy which aimed at the gradual reduction of the number of educated Sudanese in the administration.[4] Educational policy, which aimed in 1918 at producing 'in greater number, not merely clerks and artisans, but officers and administrators', so as 'to meet the increasing demand for students of a higher standard for the more liberal professions and employments of the country',[5] was replaced by one in which 'the opportunities of employment in the Departments have been curtailed'.[6] Although the Governor of Berber province had warned his colleagues in 1920 against the mistake of creating an educated class and the need 'to strengthen the solid elements in the country—sheikhs, merchants, etc.—before the irresponsible body of half-educated officials, students and town riff-raff takes control of the public mind',[7] the appointment of 'executive officials selected for the public service from the ranks of the native population'[8] continued. The development of education was seen by the Milner report in 1921, and a memorandum by the Governor-General in 1924, as an essential part of the policy of indirect rule.[9] Enthusiasm for education, however,

[1] Letter from Lord De La Warr to Governor-General, 16 October 1937, *SGA/CIVSEC/17/3/File 17.B.1.*   [2] *G.G.R., 1921*, p. 5.
[3] Ibid.   [4] *G.G.R., 1926*, p. 6.
[5] *G.M.C.R., 1918*, p. 7.   [6] Currie, J., *The Educational Experiment*, p. 56.
[7] *SGA/CIVSEC/1/9 File L.F, vol. I.*
[8] Note by the Governor-General, 12 June 1927, *SGA/CIVSEC/File 17.A.2.6*
[9] Ibid.

evaporated after 1924 and instead there was no desire to employ educated Sudanese.[1]

The reason behind this change of attitude towards education and the educated class lay in the political events of 1924. These events were in themselves a product of the development of education. The gradual expansion of the latter, though geared to employment and administrative purposes, had produced an educated class imbued with new ideas, conceptions, and interests. The schools and modern education had weakened tribal differences and encouraged the growth of a sense of nationalism. The similarity in background of the educated class, their way of living, and studying in the Gordon Memorial College, and being all employed by one agency, created new loyalties in place of the old and traditional ones. The First World War, the outbreak of the Arab Revolt in 1916, the Fourteen Points of President Wilson, and the rise of Egyptian nationalism not only stimulated their interest but contributed to the growth of a sense of nationalism. The Egyptian Press was widely read by the educated Sudanese, and the Egyptian nationalist propaganda was directed at them. Efforts, too, were made by Egyptian officers and officials stationed in the Sudan to enlist the support of these Sudanese for the furtherance of their nationalist aspirations. Circulars which called for revolution in the Sudan, signed by 'Sons of the Nile', 'The Society for the Defence of the Faith in the Sudan', and 'The Society for the Deliverance of the Country', were secretly distributed in the Sudan in 1921.[2] The growth of Sudanese nationalism was not discouraged by the British administration, hoping that, by having an identity of its own, the Sudan would ultimately be separated from Egypt. The Sudan Government's efforts, however, were not directed towards the educated class, but towards the traditional leaders.[3] The educated class organized itself into clubs and societies. The School Graduates' Club was founded in Omdurman in 1918. The first Sudanese newspaper—*Hadarat al Sudan*—appeared in 1919. The 'League of Sudanese Union' was formed in the same year. 'The Sudan United Tribes Society' was formed in 1921, and the White Flag Society in 1924.

In the meantime a rift between the educated class and the

[1] Currie, J., op. cit., pp. 48 and 54.
[2] Memorandum on the Future Status of the Sudan by Sir Lee Stack, 25 May 1924. *Milner Papers*, Bodleian Library, Oxford.
[3] Memorandum on the Sudan 1920. *Milner Papers*, Bodleian Library, Oxford.

administration was growing. The former suspected the policy of indirect
rule and native administration as calculated to preserve tribal society
by promoting allegiance to the tribes and tribal leaders, and as such
contrary to modernism, nationalism, and their own interests. They
found that the basic conceptions of indirect rule were contrary to
the modern ideas which were taught to them in the schools, and
aimed at reviving a tribalism which had been almost completely
destroyed by the *Mahdiya* and the previous twenty years of direct
rule. They did not agree to the hereditary principle which recognized
accident of birth and not merit and service. They objected to a policy
in which their role was being reduced and sacrificed to an alliance
between an alien government and a national aristocracy.

Suspicion was further accelerated by the decision in 1921 to raise
the fees in the Gordon College and the other schools,[1] and in 1923
to reduce the number of free places in the primary section of the
Gordon College. An article by Ali Abdul Latif criticized the government's educational policy as one providing too few and poor facilities.[2]
The dismissal of seventy-one Sudanese in government service for
purposes of economy added to an already growing discontent.[3]

Demonstrations organized in Khartoum in June and August 1924
by the White Flag Society broke into revolt in 1924. Sir Lee Stack,
the Governor-General of the Sudan, was assassinated in Egypt on
19 November 1924. The Egyptian troops stationed in the Sudan were
asked to leave. Sudanese troops, led by Sudanese cadets of the
military school and officers, revolted in support of the Egyptian
troops but their revolt was suppressed.

The 1924 revolt was organized, led, and supported by the educated
class who had been brought up in the Gordon Memorial College,
the military school, and the other schools. Many of them had taken
part in the revolt, either directly or indirectly. Their sympathies were
not with the Sudan Government but with the nationalists. The
government's confidence in the educated class was shaken and its
apprehensions about the educational system were increased. Any
confidence which it might have had in the urbanized educated
Sudanese as suitable repositories of future political responsibility[4]

[1] *Hadarat al Sudan* (newspaper), Khartoum, 24 April 1921.
[2] Ali Abdul Latif cited in *Magalt Hamiyat al Khartoum* (Khartoum Garrison
magazine), no. 3, November 1960.
[3] Letter from Director of Intelligence to Governor Khartoum Province, 23
February 1924, *SGA/File DI/LB/257*.
[4] Hill, R., *Slatin Pasha*, p. 141.

was diminished. Strong personal antipathies existed between the British officials and the educated Sudanese.[1] When Currie visited the Sudan in 1926 he 'noted a change of attitude towards education among many of the higher grade English officials'[2] and 'the utter want of sympathy shown to young Sudanese by technical officials'.[3]

A British administrator wrote that when he arrived in the Sudan in 1929 he found 'strong disapproval of education, especially of the Gordon College, amongst most of the British officials, and an equally strong suspicion amongst the educated Sudanese that the government was determined to relegate them to technical posts and debar them from any real power in the country'.[4] Many of the British administrators held that education for the Sudanese was either wrong or unimportant.[5] The average of these were not in favour of too much education or an education which would 'put ideas of political power into their Sudanese heads';[6] the Civil Secretary held that the educated class had developed

an attitude of mind which in its lowest form is envy, and its worthier form a sense of thwarted aspiration and romanticism. The young modernist sees himself in a dream as a brilliant member and potential leader of a progressive and enlightened community, and the possessor of wealth enough to bring all the resources and pleasures of civilization within his reach. In reality he is a minor employee on modest pay, born into a primitive social group which he despises, bound in his domestic life by the fetters of unenlightened custom, and conceives in his hidden heart of hearts that his culture is a veneer and his daydreams things of fantasy.[7]

He held that the educated class did not assimilate the new ideas imparted by Western education, nor did they develop a critical faculty, with the result that an intellectual malaise had arisen among them.[8]

The government thus proceeded to act after 1924 'as if the Western-educated class as a whole was its inveterate enemy, to be checked and circumscribed in the interests of political stability'.[9] The appoint-

[1] Atiyah, E., *An Arab Tells his Story* (London, 1946), p. 163.
[2] Currie, J., *The Educational Experiment.*
[3] Ibid., p. 47.
[4] Ali, Nasr el Hag, *Education in the Northern Sudan, A Report to the Institute of Education,* University of London (October, 1951), p. 70.
[5] Scott, G. C., Appendix V.
[6] Griffiths, V. L., *An Experiment in Education* (London, 1953), p. 6.
[7] MacMichael, Sir Harold, *The Anglo-Egyptian Sudan* (London, 1934), p. 269.
[8] Ibid.
[9] Holt, P. M., *A Modern History of the Sudan* (London, 1961), p. 131.

ment of Sudanese to public service was no longer an essential part of the administrative policy, but a mere convenience.[1]

The second effect of the 1924 revolution was the closure of the military school, which since 1905 had supplied the core of Sudanese officers, and the discontinuance of the training courses for junior administrative officers. The third effect was the loss by the department of education of all its Egyptian teachers working in the Gordon Memorial College and many of those in the primary schools. The shortage of teachers created by the departure of Egyptian personnel hindered the development of education. In the Gordon Memorial College this problem was solved partly by the recruitment of Syrian teachers and partly by the promotion of a few Sudanese from the primary schools.

The dominance of the political outlook over education led to a new policy in recruitment of British teachers. Their training in administrative matters became an important factor in the preparation for their job. It was, therefore, decided to appoint teachers and tutors from among those who had worked in the political service. 'They were there in the dual capacity of masters and rulers, and the second capacity overshadowed the first.'[2] The atmosphere at the Gordon College at the time has been described as similar to the atmosphere of a barracks where military authority and discipline were dominant.[3]

This mistrust of education was felt mostly in primary education. No primary school was founded during the period 1920–32. The number of elementary schools in 1928 was the same as that in 1920. The scheme, started in 1922, through which nine Sudanese graduates of the Gordon College were sent to the American University of Beirut was discontinued.

Unlike the north, growth of education in the south was not interrupted by the political events or outlook. The intensification of efforts to replace the northern officials, and the inadequacy of agencies to which the authorities of native administration could be delegated, left no alternative for the government but to encourage educational development. The Governor-General's report of 1925 recognized that 'increasing economic and administrative development in the southern Sudan demands additional educational facilities'.[4]

---

[1] Minute by His Excellency the Governor-General, 1 January 1927, *MIA/File 33*.
[2] Atiyah, E., *An Arab Tells his Story*, p. 138.
[3] Ibid.   [4] *G.G.R., 1925*, p. 47.

The rise in the number of the pupils in the Gordon College from 118 in 1920 to 555 in 1930, and in the technical schools from 255 in 1922 to 387 in 1930, had been dictated by the need to replace the Egyptian personnel who had left the country, and for economic reasons. In 1925 a new economic era began with the completion of the Sennar Dam. Railways were extended from Kassala to Tirinkitat in 1921 and to Haya in 1924. They were further extended to Gedaref in 1928 and to Sennar in 1929. Economic progress created a demand for the employment of trained Sudanese but the supply fell far short of the demand. In 1925 the vacant posts in government service were 101, while only 50 graduates from the Gordon Memorial College were available for employment. In 1926, only 42 graduates were available for 103 vacancies; in 1927 it was 53 for 129 posts; and in 1928, 62 for 145 posts.[1]

The most significant development in education, however, was the foundation of the Kitchener School of Medicine. The original idea of the school lay outside this period. During his visit to the Sudan in 1911 Kitchener had proposed the foundation of a medical school to provide the doctors needed to carry out medical and health work essential for the future economic and agricultural development. When Kitchener died in 1916 the Governor-General appointed a committee to consider the best way to found a project in memory of Kitchener. The two proposals before the committee were the establishment of an agricultural school or a medical school. The latter proposal was adopted, but the appeal for an endowment fund, supported by Lord Cromer, was made in September 1916 by Wingate, in England and the Sudan. A subscription list was opened in December 1916. No work could, however, be started before the end of the First World War. The decision for the foundation of the school was therefore made before 1924, when the political outlook became dominant. Even then economic, administrative, and political considerations commended the establishment of the school. The planned economic development required sufficient manpower to sustain it. The prevalence of malaria and other diseases, however, threatened the steady increase in population needed to meet further development.[2] From the administrative point of view the doctors would be valuable as a means of civilization and pacification through the influence and power they would obtain on a backward society.[3] Political considerations

[1] *G.M.C.R.*, *1925*, p. 7; *1926*, p. 27; *1927*, p. 25; and *1929*, p. 23.
[2] Appendix III.   [3] Ibid.

6

also came into the project. It was held that there was 'no safer or more desirable channel into which the energies of the mentally active and intellectually restless can be directed than that of medical work and medical research, a sphere of work and line of thought that leads many from a narrow territorial and racial outlook, to a wide humanitarian view of life'.[1] Sending Sudanese for medical education in Cairo, Beirut or London was undesirable because 'it would have involved removing them from the influence of their homes, customs and traditions, and exposing them to intellectual and moral influences which they are not yet ready to meet'.[2]

Until 1924 the majority of doctors in the medical service were either Syrians or Egyptians, and Sudanese were needed to replace these two groups for both economic and political reasons.[3]

By 1924 a total of just over £E50,000 had been collected. The largest single contribution came from the British Red Cross Society, which paid £E12,000, this being the amount subscribed to the society in the Sudan during the war. The Rhodes Trust paid £E2,000; the British Cotton Growing Association £E500; the Sudan Plantation Syndicate £E2,500; the Greek community in the Sudan £E1,000; the Sudan Schools Club £E429; and Sayed Abdul Rahman El Mahdi £E500. The Lord Kitchener Memorial Fund, in addition to a contribution to the Endowment Fund, allotted £E2,000 towards the annual expenditure of the school. The Sudan Government contributed £E8,000 to the fund. The school was formally opened on 29 February 1924. Ahmed Hashim al Baghdadi, a Persian merchant resident in the Sudan, endowed the school with his entire fortune for the maintenance of the pupils.[4] The Kitchener School was the first medical school with a comprehensive syllabus to be established in northern tropical Africa.[5] From the beginning it was felt that the school should not follow too closely the British model. Its graduates were not intended to take higher qualifications or diplomas in the United Kingdom, but to be trained as general practitioners for work in the Sudan only. The provision of post-graduate training was left to the future when the need arose.

Although the original appeal stated the school would be an integral part of the Gordon College, this was abandoned in favour of an

[1] *Kitchener School of Medicine, Annual Reports*, 1924–5, p. 10.
[2] Ibid.
[3] Ibid., pp. 12–13.
[4] Squires, H. C., *The Sudan Medical Service* (London, 1958), p. 65.
[5] Ibid., p. 66.

independent institution in which both the medical and educational departments would co-operate.

The Trustees of the Gordon Memorial College were appointed Trustees of the Kitchener School of Medicine, assisted by a General Board consisting of the Director of Education, the Financial Secretary, the Director of the Medical Service, the Director of Intelligence as *ex-officio* members, and seven other members. The executive committee consisting of the *ex-officio* members managed the affairs of the school and approved the school budget on behalf of the General Board.

The academic and day-to-day administration of the school was entrusted to a School Council consisting of the Director of Medical Services (chairman), the Director of the Wellcome Tropical Research Laboratories, the Directors of the Khartoum and Omdurman Civil Hospitals, the Government Chemist, the Government Entomologist, and the Registrar. Training and teaching was carried out by the Sudan Government's medical staff and the scientific staff of the Wellcome Research Laboratories. This arrangement not only reduced the costs but also helped to associate medical research with teaching.

Like its predecessor, the Gordon Memorial College, the Kitchener School of Medicine marked the beginning of a new era in Sudan education. The primary section of the college was moved out in 1924 to give room for the increasing number of students and became a full vocational secondary school catering for post-primary education and consisting of six courses as follows:

1. A course for *Sharia* judges which extended over five years. Instruction was given in English, maths, geography, history, Arabic, and Islamic theology. Over 75 per cent of the teaching time was allocated to the last two subjects.

2. An engineering course which extended over four years. The first two years were allocated to general instruction in English, Arabic, history, geography, maths, science, natural history, and civil engineering. The last two years were devoted to Engineering in addition to English, maths and science.

3. A teachers' course which extended over four years. In the first two years instruction was given in languages and general subjects. The last two years were devoted mainly to instruction in the theory and practice of teaching English, Arabic, maths, history, and geography.

4. A clerical course which extended over four years. In the first two years instruction was given in languages and general subjects. The last two years were devoted to instruction in clerical work and languages.

6-2

5. An accountancy course, which was similar to the clerical course, except that students specialized in accountancy.

6. A science course which extended over four years. The first two years were the same as for teachers, clerks, and accountants. The last two years were devoted to instruction in maths, chemistry, physics, and biology.

The last course was introduced in 1924 with a view to preparing boys for entry to the Kitchener School of Medicine.

The Gordon College, in its new role as a secondary vocational school, was the subject of investigation by a commission invited in 1929 to inquire and report upon the curriculum and textbooks, the staff and organization, the physical training, and the standard attained.[1] This was the first inquiry into the affairs of the college since its foundation. The members of the commission were chosen from the Board of Education in England, the Colonial Office, and the Egyptian Ministry of Education.[2] The Commission recommended reforms in the contents of the courses and their general organization. It advised the exclusion of the clerical subjects from the general course, and the revision of the mathematics and science syllabuses with a view to making them more suitable for the future requirements of training teachers, engineers, and doctors. The chief defects observed by the commission were connected with the teaching of English and history.[3] The commission did not recommend new departures in the organization or aims of the Gordon Memorial College. Its importance lay in the fact that this was the first time since its formation that the College was subjected to an inquiry by an outside body.

The second major development was in the field of girls' education. The number of girls' elementary schools increased from five attended by 146 girls in 1919 to ten attended by 694 in 1927. In 1928 alone seven new elementary schools for girls were established. By 1931 there were 23 schools with 2,095 girls attending. This expansion in girls' education reflected the growing demand of parents for the education of their girls. The political outlook and the administrative

---

[1] Sudan Government, *Report of a Commission of Inspection on the Gordon Memorial College, February 1929* (Khartoum, 1929), p. 11.

[2] The members were: Mr. M. F. Simpson, Controller of Secondary Education, Egyptian Ministry of Education (chairman); W. Gannon, H.M. Principal Inspector, Board of Education, England; F. O. Mann, H.M. Inspector, Board of Education, England; and Mr. Hanns Vischer, Secretary and Member of the Advisory Committee on Education in the Colonies.

[3] Sudan Government, *Report of a Commission of Inspection on the Gordon Memorial College, February* 1929, p. 11.

policy seemed to have had little effect on the growth of elementary education for girls.

Until 1922 only men teachers from *al Mahad al Ilmi* and the Elementary Teachers' Training College were employed to teach the *Koran* and Islamic religion in the girls' elementary schools. Occasionally, and when available, women were employed to teach embroidery. With the expansion of girls' education the problem of training Sudanese women as teachers became urgent. J. D. Evans was appointed in 1920 to take charge of girls' education, and her first act was to establish in April 1921 a training college for women teachers, to which the first sixteen students were admitted. At first parents were reluctant to send their daughters to the training college. To them the idea of a girl employed in the government service and earning her own living was entirely new and strange. They were afraid that on the completion of the course the girls would find it difficult to marry. The early marriage age in the country was another difficulty. Parents preferred to see their daughters married rather than to continue their education. Even when they agreed the teaching life of a trained teacher tended to be a short one, they were reluctant to leave their young daughters in the care of others who were 'of a different race and religion'.[1] These difficulties were partly overcome by the decision to allow the girls to be accompanied by their mothers or grandmothers, who lived with them during their course of study, and to pay a bonus equivalent to one month's salary for every year worked, provided that the trained teacher had worked for four consecutive years after graduation. The example of Babiker Bedri, who established the first girls' school in Rufaa in 1908 and who agreed to send his own daughter and two nieces for training, helped in persuading the reluctant parents and allaying their fears and prejudices.[2] The number of students in the Girls' Training College rose from 20 in 1922 to 28 in 1925, and 61 in 1930. Many of those trained, however, left the service. The shortage in the number of trained teachers did not allow the government to meet the growing demand for girls' education, but private efforts and missionary societies helped in meeting this demand. Two private elementary schools were established in Omdurman in 1924. Two similar schools were founded in Dueim and Getina through voluntary contributions. In 1927 the Church Missionary Society started an elementary school

[1] *E.D.R., 1928*, p. 41.
[2] Ibid.

for Sudanese girls in Omdurman. The Unity High School was established in 1928 by the Church Missionary Society to provide a Christian English type of secondary education for those who desired it.[1] In 1930 the Roman Catholic mission established two schools at Atbara and Port Sudan. The success of missionary societies in attracting an increasing number of Sudanese girls to their schools was not only owing to the fact that they were satisfying an urgent and immediate demand but also to the fact that the contents of their syllabus, although based on Christian morals and values, included subjects such as home economics, domestic science, and child welfare.

There was less expansion in the provision for boys' education by the missionary societies in northern Sudan during this period because their efforts were directed more towards the south. As their schools did not aim in the first place at providing an education with a view to employment, which was the main incentive until then, there was no general support for it. There was also suspicion of the education they provided. In 1925 the American Mission School in Omdurman asked its Muslim pupils to attend lessons on Christianity. When this was reported to the parents, the boys were withdrawn and representations were made to the administration protesting against the action of the American Missionary School. The latter did not deny that their policy was to give compulsory instruction in Christianity with the object of inculcating moral values common to both Christianity and Islam,[2] rather than conversion.

A meeting of the leading citizens of Omdurman sent a petition to the government asking its permission to establish a National Intermediate School. The *Mufti* of the Sudan, who was elected chairman of the board, stated that the aim was to meet the increasing need and demand for primary education, to provide the boys who had been taken out of the American Mission School[3] with primary education, and to found and maintain a national system of education to serve the intelligent and the poor. Permission was given on condition that the government would not hold itself responsible for the employment of the graduates of the school and that

[1] Jackson, H. C., *Pastor on the Nile*, pp. 203–4; *Sudan Diocesan Review*, Surrey, England, viii, no. 1 (15 January 1929), 30.
[2] Sudan Government, *Reports of Governors of Provinces* (Khartoum, 1925), p. 294.
[3] Letter from Ismail Al Azhari, Mufti of the Sudan to the Civil Secretary, 16 October 1926, *MIA/File 17/D/21/23*.

the school would be under government supervision and open to its inspection.[4]

The opening of the Omdurman *Ahlia* School in 1927 marked the beginning of the voluntary efforts in education which became a rallying call for the nationalistic activities of a disillusioned educated class. The educated found in the movement to establish the Omdurman School an opportunity to express their dissatisfaction with government educational policy. Some of them volunteered to help in its administration or teaching, and organized literacy and adult education classes in the buildings during the evening.

The success of the Omdurman *Ahlia* School encouraged private efforts in education. In 1929 Babiker Bedri, on retiring from the educational department, established an elementary school at Rufaa where he had previously started his first elementary school for girls. The school at Rufaa was transferred to Omdurman in 1931 and an intermediate section was added in 1933. The Ahfad Schools of Babiker Bedri and the Omdurman National School were the pioneers of a national voluntary system of education.

In order to control and supervise the increasing number of non-government schools, the Education (Non-Government) Schools Ordinance of 1927 and the Education (Non-Government Schools) Regulations 1927 were promulgated. The object of the ordinance was to regulate education in non-government schools in both the north and south. According to the ordinance no school would be established without prior approval of the Governor-General and no teacher would be registered or allowed to teach without the approval of the Director of Education. It conferred on the Director of Education the right to inspect all such schools. The Regulations of 1927 recognized for the first time the *de facto* division between the northern and southern educational systems, which had been existing since the beginning of the century, by requiring two separate registers to be kept for the north and south. The conditions laid down for religious teaching were now formalized and made into law. The regulations stated that

all parents desirous of the education of their children in Mission Schools shall, before their reception as pupils, be informed by the responsible school authorities that religious instruction will be given to the pupils unless objection is raised by its parents, in which case they shall be exempted from attendance at prayers and religious instruction.[2]

[1] Ibid. [2] *Laws of the Sudan*, vol. 3 (Khartoum, 1941), pp. 1554–62.

In spite of these clear terms and requirements the governors of the southern provinces were advised that they could disregard certain parts of the law when applying them to missionary schools.[1]

In the meantime economic conditions were having an adverse effect on educational development. The economy, which had been showing an upward trend since 1925, was beginning to show a downward trend in 1928. The expanding foreign trade had exposed the Sudan to the full force of the world's economic conditions. Its export trade, which was mainly cotton, received the biggest hit. Prices and the demand for cotton fell. Imports in 1930 decreased by 9·9 per cent and exports by about 24·1 per cent. Between 1929 and 1931 exports had fallen from about £E13½ million to less than £E6 million.[2] Government revenue dropped from about £E4·6 million in 1930 to £E3·6 million in 1933. The problem was thought to be how to balance the budget rather than how to provide capital for development. This was done by the following three measures: (a) retrenchment in the government service; (b) reduction of salaries; (c) reduction of expenditure on services, including education. In a statement published in 1930 the government declared that as a corollary of the depression, government service would be reduced and there would be less opportunity for everyone graduating from the Gordon College to get employment. The intake in both the Gordon Memorial College and primary schools was accordingly reduced and parents were asked to sign an undertaking to the effect that they would not hold the government responsible for not finding employment for their sons. In 1931 the posts of 1,000 classified officials—about 20 per cent of the total government staff—including 207 British officials, were retrenched. The number of posts in the budget was reduced from 5,888 in 1930 to 4,793 in 1932; and 4,753 in 1933.[3]

Salaries for all government officials were reduced in 1931 by 5–10 per cent. The starting rate for the Gordon College graduates was reduced from £E8 per month to £E5.500 milliems per month. The fees in the college for day boys, which had already been raised from £E10 to £E12 per year in 1928, were raised to £E15 in 1931. The fees for boarders were similarly raised from £E25 to £E28 per year. Fees in the primary schools were increased from £E8 to £E10 per

[1] Letter from Director of Education to Governor Bahr al Ghazal, 30 March 1929, SGA/File SCR/17.A.1.
[2] MacMichael, Sir H. A., The Anglo-Egyptian Sudan (London 1934), p. 229.
[3] G.G.R., 1931, p. 12; G.G.R., 1932, p. 9; G.G.R., 1933, p. 9.

year for day boys.[1] In addition to this the number of free places at
the different schools was reduced.

The total expenditure on education was reduced from £E179,609
in 1929 to £E112,393 in 1933.[2] The effect of these policies was to
reduce the number of boys and girls attending schools in the north.
During the period 1930–32 their total number was reduced from
43,022 to 38,809. The numbers at different levels were as follows:[3]

	1930	1932	1933
Elementary schools	9,342	9,323	?
Primary schools	1,315	1,059	970
Gordon College	555	436	338
Technical schools	387	213	?

In addition to this the number of subsidized *khalwas* was cut down
by 33 per cent and the number of girls admitted to the training
college was reduced.

These policies created a general discontent[4] and brought the
educated class, for the first time since 1924, to an open clash with
the government. A delegation of graduates met the Governor-
General in January 1931 and expressed their disagreement with these
decisions. A petition to the Governor-General in June 1931, signed
by ten leading graduates,[5] stated that the reduction in the salaries
and number of Sudanese in the government service was 'a terrible
shock' to the educated class.[6] As an immediate solution they suggested the dismissal of non-Sudanese and non-British. As a long-
term solution they proposed reforms in the system of education with
a view to qualifying the Sudanese for private pursuits outside the
government service through:

I. raising and adapting the present standard of instruction in the existing
sections of the Gordon College to such a degree as will qualify the educated
Sudanese to compete with foreigners who are now monopolising almost
all private occupations in the country on account of their higher standard
of education;[7]

[1] *SGA/CIVSEC/File 17.A.3.*
[2] Appendix I, Table 1.   [3] *G.G.R. 1932*, pp. 77–8.
[4] Letter from Governor Khartoum Province to Civil Secretary, 7 December
1935, *SGA/CIVSEC/File 17.A.3* and *SGA/CIVSEC/File 1*, p. 13, vol. I.
[5] The petition was signed by: Ahmed El Sid Elfil; Omar Ishak; Mohamed
Nur Khogali; Mirghani Hamza; Abdul Magid Ahmed; Mohamed Ali Shawki;
Mohamed El Hassan Diab; Osman Hassan Osman; Hassan Ali Hashem, and
Mohamed Salih Faried, *SGA/CIVSEC/File 1, P. 13*, vol. II.
[6] Ibid.   [7] Ibid.

and

2. extending the programme of education to include the various professions for which no institutions have yet been established, such as
Commerce, Law, Agriculture, Veterinary, etc.[1]

No agreement was reached and the students of the Gordon Memorial
College went on strike in November 1931. The college was closed
on 1 December 1931. A compromise was, however, reached and the
starting rates for government service were raised from the proposed
£E5.500 milliems to £E6.500 milliems per month.

The economic depression, therefore, not only led to a further
retarding of education but added to the rift between the educated
class and the administration. The retrenchment policy which followed
the economic depression was yet more evidence of the loss of confidence in the educated classes. The strike was, from the government's
point of view, due to the close connection between education and
government employment, which had been the object of its policy
since the foundation of the Gordon Memorial College. It was no
longer a satisfactory situation from either the educated Sudanese
point of view or the government's. The Warden of the Gordon
Memorial College appealed in his report of 1931 for a searching
examination of the system of education.[2] He proposed in his next
report to review the aims of education.[3] Currie, who visited the
Sudan in 1932, was critical of the educational policy and urged the
revival of the military school, the establishment of schools of law
and agriculture, and priority for Sudanese in employment.[4] He was
in agreement with those educated Sudanese he met during his visit.

The administration thus became conscious of the need to reform.
Action, however, had to await better economic conditions and men
with new ideas and policies. The period of stagnation which followed
the political events of 1924, and reached its climax during the
economic crisis, was coming to an end by 1933.

[1] Ibid.
[2] *G.M.C.R. 1931*, p. 11.   [3] *G.M.C.R. 1932*, p. 11.
[4] Currie, J., *The Educational Experiment*, pp. 26–8.

PART THREE
1933-1956

CHAPTER VI

Educational Reform in the Northern Sudan
1933–1934

THE PERIOD of stagnation, an outcome of economic, political, and administrative factors, was giving way at the end of 1932 to a period of reform and progress in education. Examination of the system of education which had been urged by the Simpson Commission in 1929 was not carried out because neither the climate of opinion nor the economic conditions made such an examination possible. Although the retrenchment policy had brought to the fore the problem of employment of the educated Sudanese and the need to examine the possibilities of employment in fields other than governmental, such as agriculture and commerce, and of adapting the educational system if necessary, the execution of this had to await better economic conditions.[1]

There were signs of relief from the harmful effects of the economic depression at the end of 1932. During 1932–3 a comparatively higher export of cotton, lint, and gold bullion, due to heavy liquidation of gold ornaments for cash, brought about favourable conditions in the economy, and early in 1933 the budget was balanced for the first time since 1929.[2]

Political and administrative developments since 1924 prevented the implementation of the government plan of 1924 to appoint more educated Sudanese in the government service. A successful policy of native administration, however, depended on a supply of educated native executive officials to work in co-operation with the tribal chiefs. A new outlook and attitude towards the educated and the educational system was needed, if only for the sake of the success of native administration.

British and Sudanese opinion was becoming more critical of the educational system. Certain members of the education department thought that the educational system, through its emphasis on education for native administration purposes, and the rift it created between

[1] *G.G.R. 1933*, p. 11.
[2] Rahim, A. W. A., 'An Economic History of the Sudan', 1899–1956, thesis submitted for M.A. degree, University of Manchester, 1963, pp. 115–20.

the educated and the British administration, and between the educated and the tribal leaders, was not serving the interests of any of the three groups. Liaison between the three groups had to be maintained so as to achieve progress. A new educational policy was needed for this purpose.

Others, especially in the technical departments, doubted the value of preserving the traditional outlook. This concept was incompatible with advance on European lines, and a hindrance to the progress of Sudanese in scientific and technical fields, if pressed too far.[1]

Sudanese opinion, although weak and unrepresentative, was becoming more vocal in its criticism of the policy. These criticisms were made at private meetings rather than in public, because of the fear of victimization by the administration.[2] When Currie visited the Sudan in 1932, his visit was exploited as an event to express dissatisfaction and resentment at the policy followed after his departure.[3] When Currie returned to England, he expressed disagreement with what was going on in the field of education in the Sudan.[4] Indirect rule was seen by Currie as a hindrance to educational progress through its siding with tribal chiefs and its alienation of the educated class. These views, voiced during the visit and later published, encouraged the seekers of reform to press their views. On his return to England, Currie resigned from the membership of the Board of Trustees of the Gordon Memorial College as a protest, and did not return to the board until 1937, when it was evident that the old attitude was giving way to a new policy.

From an educational point of view, the value of the major agencies of education available for the majority, the *khalwa* and the elementary school, was being doubted. An investigation carried out in 1930 into the *khalwa* in northern Sudan proved that it was an unsuccessful substitute for the first-year class of the elementary school. Its value as a suitable instrument for development as the future elementary school was queried. Opinion on the solution was divided. There were those who believed that the Sudan would remain the same for a long time and that therefore the *khalwa* should be allowed to remain and fulfil its traditional function as an institute for character training and religious teaching. Another group, while dissatisfied

[1] Sudan Government, *Technical Training of Sudanese*, Report of the Committee appointed by His Excellency the Governor-General, Khartoum, 15 July 1935. *EDA*.   [2] *SGA/CIVSEC/1/58/File 1, P. 13*, vol. 1.
[3] Personal information from Mirghani Hamza.
[4] Currie, J., *The Educational Experiment in Anglo-Egyptian Sudan*, pp. 47–59.

with the *khalwa*, believed that it could be improved and become the foundation of the educational system. They argued that such a reform was in keeping with the general policy of preserving native ideas and institutions. A third group advocated its abolition because of its failure to be a substitute for the first-year class of the elementary school, and its inadequacy in meeting the needs of the population at that time. The future needs of the country required a training better than that of the *khalwa*.[1]

On the other hand, the elementary school, which in most cases was in the town, failed to attract children from the rural area. It was still suspected by the ordinary farmer who reasoned that it would make his boy useless for agriculture and animal husbandry. Others suspected that it would undermine a boy's religion and morals. Tribal chiefs, with a few exceptions, were reluctant to send their sons to the elementary schools. The association of native administration with education, which began in 1919, with governors empowered to constitute a local authority over elementary schools, failed to produce positive results. Native authorities did not show much co-operation because, in the first place, they were uneducated and, secondly, they looked upon education as government business and not their own. Elementary schoolmasters feared the interference of the uneducated tribal chiefs and hindered the development of an association with them.

The elementary school was not providing that type of education which suited the needs of village and town boys whose lives would be spent in ordinary occupations. The education provided by the elementary schools was not of a sufficiently high standard to supply the intermediate schools with the right calibre of boy. The Education Department tried to remedy these shortcomings in the schools by giving a rural bias to the schools, and by abolishing rote-learning through circulars and notes sent to teachers, but these experiments failed to achieve positive results. Teachers, themselves the product of these backward schools and *Khalwas*, were insufficiently educated, ill paid and, unlike other government officials, had no pension and were dissatisfied with their conditions. The teachers 'knew no English, had practically no Arabic books or magazines, only notes for their lessons'.[2]

[1] Letter from Secretary of Education and Health to Northern Governors, Khartoum, 19 January 1934, *SGA/CIVSEC/17/1 File 17.A.1.6.*
[2] Griffiths, V. L., *An Experiment in Education*, p. 4.

A review and reform of the educational policy was therefore
necessary. But it was the Gordon College students' strike in 1932
which 'set going the train of events which eventually led to reform'.[1]
Soon after the strike was over, the Governor-General appointed a
committee to look into the system of education. At first its terms of
reference were to look into the problem of 'over production of
educated boys whose only prospects lay in government employment'.[2] This was later changed to include a survey of lower education.
The appointment of the committee with such terms of reference
was a triumph for the advocates of reform and the opportunity was
taken by G. C. Scott, the Chief Inspector of Education, and one of
the reform-minded members of the Education Department, to argue
the case for change.

A *Note on Education in the Northern Sudan* was submitted by
G. C. Scott to the Director of Education in May 1932.[3] The note
was a novel piece of thinking because the ideas expressed were
generally ahead of the current thinkings of the Sudan Government
at the time. Its liberal, frank, and forward-looking attitude influenced
the committee. Although the note did not claim originality for the
ideas expressed because they 'were taken from books and from other
members of the department of education and the Political Service',[4]
it proved to be a landmark in educational reform. For the first time
since 1899 an evaluation of the educational system was made. It
went against the accepted British ideas of the time and it brought
home the case for a radical reform in education.

Scott argued that the reform of Sudan education was overdue and
that war, disease, injustice, and sedition could not be prevented if
the system of education was false. Failure in India, according to
Scott, was 'in great part due to a system of education similar to that
of the Sudan'.[5]

He argued that it was necessary to educate the Sudanese and give
them more education, because the government was committed to
such a policy, and because education was necessary if the destruction,
instead of the adaptation, of the old ways was to be avoided. The
policy of native administration, to which the Sudan Government
was committed, could not find in the first place 'a permanent foundation in ignorance'.[6] On the other hand, if the policy of native

[1] Ibid., p. 9.   [2] Ibid.
[3] Personal communication from G. C. Scott, Appendix IV.
[4] Ibid.   [5] Ibid.   [6] Ibid.

administration was to be successful, there was need 'for native rulers whom a wise education has enabled to understand the new conditions and to adapt their aims and methods. The rulers need servants to whom education has supplied the means of service without robbing them of sympathy for their people or belief in their traditions.'[1] 'Native Administration without education is a broken cart without a horse.'[2] It was only through education, Scott argued, that the government could cure 'indifferent agriculture, fanatical Mahdism, disease-carrying dirt, female circumcision, and all the cruelty and barbarity of a backward people'.[3]

The note stated that the main fault with the educational system was the rote system: parrot education which was inherited from the *khalwa* and transferred to the intermediate school and the Gordon College. The second fault was the examination system which encouraged rote-learning and persuaded the Sudanese that the object of education was employment. Therefore, from the educational point of view the most urgent need was to reform the lower levels of education. This reform was also urged by political and economic considerations because it was the most diffused type of modern education. Reform of the elementary school should come first, and only when it was certain that the schools would not repeat the faults of the old system could expansion be effected. To achieve this, an Elementary Teachers' Training College in which, among other things, research would be done by an educationalist with adequate knowledge of Islam, and of Arab history, literature and traditions, should be established. In addition to this, the conditions of service for teachers should be improved. This, Scott argued, was the key to reform and progress. But there were other proposals. The method of recruiting British staff should be improved. They should be selected from England

for their previous educational training, including practical experience in teaching and for the likelihood—so far as it could be judged—that they would be able and willing to devote their lives to Sudan education. On their arrival in the Sudan they should be appointed for at least two years as assistants to selected District Commissioners so that they may get some of that general knowledge and experience essential to their doing any good in the Education Department.[4]

The establishment of an agricultural school, whose main aim would be to encourage Sudanese farmers to improve their methods of

[1] Appendix IV.   [2] Ibid.   [3] Ibid.   [4] Ibid.

7   BED

farming, was proposed. The school would, in addition, enable the educated unemployed (a product of the faulty system of education) to go back to the land through a land settlement scheme. The pupils would be drawn from among the sons of landowners who would return home on the completion of the course, and from the landless government officials. The note recommended the establishment of a post-elementary school for the education of boys who would later succeed to positions of responsibility in the native administration. As a temporary measure, the note suggested, the Teachers' Training College could do this job. Introduction of adult education in the form of travelling libraries, cinemas, and travelling magic lanterns was suggested. Finally, the note suggested the reorganization of the administration of education by dividing the north into four districts, each of which would be in the charge of an inspector who would look after research, experiments, and reforms.

Six months after Scott's note, the Governor-General's Council appointed a committee[1] with the following terms of reference:

A. To review the educational system of the schools of the Northern Sudan and to suggest what steps, if any, are necessary to ensure that the system and training are adapted to the practical needs of the country.
B. To consider what steps can and should be taken in the immediate future to provide training for Sudanese in the administrative and technical departments of the government in order to increase their usefulness and provide openings for their gradual advancement.[2]

The committee, which became known as the Winter Committee, agreed with Scott's central proposal: that reform should begin with elementary education and that teachers' training was the key to this reform. Unlike Scott's note which aimed at radical changes in the system and was thereby likely to be expensive, the committee recommended, in view of the financial conditions, those measures which could be implemented without great cost.

The elementary education curriculum, according to the Winter Committee, was not suited to the Sudan because of its literary bias and because it was more suited 'to aspirants to the Government Service than those returning to the land'.[3] In order to correct this,

[1] The members of the Committee were: R. K. Winter, Director of Education (chairman); Sir Harold MacMichael, Civil Secretary; H. E. Fass and R. M. MacGregor (members) and V. L. Griffiths, secretary.
[2] Secretariat for Education and Health, *Education Policy, Northern Sudan*, Report of a Committee appointed by His Excellency the Governor-General, 7 March 1933, *EDA/File EH/17.A.1.1.*   [3] Ibid.

the curriculum should be adapted to the practical needs of the country, taking into consideration the limited scope for employment in government, the requirements of native administration, and 'the desirability of maintaining a friendly liaison between the educated residents of the towns and the responsible tribal leaders of the provinces'.[1]

The *khalwa* was brushed aside as an educational agency of little value, and the role of the elementary school, as the agent of reform, was emphasized. Its role was to give an education suitable to both the town and village boys, and of a sufficiently high standard to supply clerks for native administration and students for the Teachers' Training College and the intermediate schools. In order to fulfil the first role, agriculture and handwork should be introduced. To achieve the second object, the methods and contents of subjects should be reformed. The latter aim could only be achieved, the committee stated, by the establishment of an Elementary Teachers' Training College, which would:

(*a*) provide post-elementary education of five years, the last year being devoted to vocational training;

(*b*) provide instruction in English;

(*c*) provide handwork and agricultural training and have land on which agricultural training could be carried on;

(*d*) be built in a rural area from native materials and with a design and layout which could serve as a model for native villages and houses;

(*e*) provide refresher courses for teachers;

(*f*) provide education suitable for the sons of tribal leaders and probably 'giving a preliminary training to young men desirous of reaching the rank of officers in the Sudan Defence Force through the ranks'.[2]

Thus within the proposed Teachers' Training College a number of courses and ideas were to be organized and tested. Certainly it was the financial considerations and not educational principles which made the Winter Committee recommend the training of elementary teachers, of clerks for native administration, and of future army officers in one institution. None the less, the central idea was that of training elementary school teachers. On the question of the status of teachers, which Scott emphasized in his note, it was recommended that they should be on pensionable service but no increase in rates of pay was agreed to.

Regarding other levels of education, it was suggested that it should

[1] Ibid., p. 17.   [2] Ibid., pp. 22-30

not outstrip employment. The intermediate school should change its function from preparing boys for the Gordon College to that of providing sufficiently qualified employees for minor provincial posts and the requirements of commerce and agriculture. For this purpose it should have both a rural bias and practical training. The intermediate school was to be, in effect, a local province town school producing local employees. In this way the danger of young employees not kept under the influence of their parents and tribes during their most impressionable years would be eliminated. They would not be exposed to the harmful influences of the town, and politics, and would continue to maintain the ties with their own community. Further training for the intermediate schoolboys would be done in the provinces through in-service training.

The importance of girls' education was recognized and a steady advance was recommended by the Winter Committee. But two other recommendations which it made regarding girls' education made this difficult to achieve. It recommended the reduction in the numbers admitted to the Teachers' Training College, and the abolition of the system of giving a bonus to every teacher who completed four years of training. The reasons given for making these recommendations were the difficulty of absorbing all trained teachers in the service and the financial problems. One explanation given for this contradiction was that the Sudan administration was a male administration which paid lip-service to girls' education, but forgot about it. They were looking for economies to be made and the axe fell on this aspect of education.[1]

The committee was critical of the Gordon Memorial College and its pupils who, in its view, lacked balance in character and perspective in outlook. It urged that the college should rectify this fault and work towards producing a type who would accept opportunities for service in the government and outside it. Neither an increase in the number of Gordon College pupils nor facilities for higher education were recommended. The intellectual development of the country, in the committee's view, did not warrant such an increase. The economic conditions at the time would, in any case, make a development of this nature out of place. On the administrative side it was recommended that in each province or group of provinces a specially selected district commissioner should be made responsible for the supervision of education. This was not the same as Scott's suggestion

[1] Personal information from V. L. Griffiths.

of having an educational staff for such a job. The committee held that their proposal was less expensive than Scott's and also practical. The prospects of advancement for such special staff should be limited in future.

It was finally recommended to institute special training courses in certain departments, such as a commercial course for the customs officials and a two-year training course for engineers in the public works department. As for other government departments, the committee found that either the available training facilities were adequate or there was no need for them because of the lack of future openings.

It was this last recommendation which made the educated Sudanese disappointed with the committee's report. While the committee's suggestion was based on a static non-expanding economy and opportunities, the educated Sudanese viewed the situation in a different light. To these there were still a number of non-Sudanese in the service who could be replaced only if post-secondary education was provided. The educated Sudanese held that higher education had been an urgent requirement for the last ten years. This desire for higher education had manifested itself since 1924, in a number of ways, such as travelling by Sudanese students to Egypt for study purposes and requests by them to be allowed to join the American University in Beirut at their own expense.[1] The petition to the Governor-General signed by leading graduates of the Gordon College in 1931 had requested that higher education facilities should be provided.[2] The same points were made in another petition after the Gordon College students' strike. The committee's recommendations in relation to higher education, therefore, fell short of their expectations. Another aspect of the committee's report which they objected to was the recommendation to reduce the number of full and assisted places in the Gordon Memorial College.[3]

The direct outcome of the committee's report, which was accepted soon after it had been submitted, was the birth of Bakht er Ruda— the Elementary Teachers' Training College—which came to carry the banner of reform in education.

The cost of establishing Bakht er Ruda during a time of financial difficulties was taken care of partly by economies which were being made throughout the government departments.[4]

[1] Note by Udal, N. R., Khartoum 1928, *SGA/DAKHLIA/17/2, File 17.A.23.*
[2] *SGA/CIVSEC/1/58 File 1. P. 13, vol. I.*
[3] Griffiths, V. L., *An Experiment in Education*, p. 14.   [4] Ibid., pp. 9–10.

In 1934 the Elementary Teachers' Training School was transferred from Khartoum to Bakht er Ruda, near Dueim, in the White Nile province. The transfer was in keeping with the committee's suggestion that it 'did not feel that the present elementary Teachers' Training School, situated as it is in Khartoum, far from the *Kuttab* teachers' normal surroundings, is entirely suitable'.[1]

The committee did not specifically recommend Dueim, and its choice could be accounted for by the following reasons:

(i) A scheme of agricultural apprenticeship for elementary school-boys was already in existence. It was the only scheme of its kind in the whole of the Sudan. The scheme was intended to improve agricultural proficiency on the pump schemes.

(ii) Agriculture was one of the subjects taught at the elementary school in Dueim and the boys were given a plot of land on the pump scheme which they cultivated under the supervision of the agricultural officer.[2]

(iii) There was a small boarding school in which a few sons of tribal chiefs attending the school were living.

(iv) The administration in Dueim showed interest and enthusiasm for the ruralization of elementary education.[3]

(v) The administration was prepared to contribute towards the cost of the buildings if it was decided to establish the school in Dueim.

(vi) Free labour was contributed by prisoners in Dueim.

The co-operative attitude of the local administration, its enthusiasm for ruralization, the availability of irrigated land, and the economies that could be obtained at a time of short resources were decisive factors in placing the new training college at Bakht er Ruda, in spite of the adverse health conditions, the inadequacy of transport, and the distance from Khartoum.[4]

V. L. Griffiths, who had come to the Sudan in 1929 as a teacher in the Gordon Memorial College and acted as Secretary of the Winter Committee, was appointed Principal of the new Teachers' Training College. Before that he had been in India, where he came in contact with the education philosophy of Gandhi with its strong rural emphasis. While in India he was involved in the Scout Movement. He was inspired 'by the wave of distrust of old methods and

[1] Secretariat for Education and Health, *Education Policy, Northern Sudan*, p. 22.
[2] *G.G.R., 1932*, p. 151.
[3] Education Department, Occasional Note No. 2, *EDA/File DES/9.1.4*.
[4] Griffiths, V. L., personal information.

the desire for new ways which was a feature of the period immediately after the 1914–1918 war'.[1] India, the Boy Scout Movement, and the London Day Training College influenced his thinking and ideas. These ideas, which inspired parts of G. C. Scott's *Note on Education in the Northern Sudan,* later inspired and guided the reform work in Bakht er Ruda—indeed, educational development in the Sudan after 1934.

The aims of Bakht er Ruda were to create and train a rural teaching service, contented in rural surroundings and with reasonable high academic and professional standards and, at the same time, to provide refresher courses for working teachers. The latter purpose was essential if reform in elementary education was to be carried out in a relatively short time. On the syllabus side the aim was to devise syllabuses and produce suitable textbooks for pupils, and handbooks for the teachers, to suit the aim of ruralization. Thus its prime duty was to direct the interest of trainee teachers from academic learning to the practical affairs of rural life, to give them some knowledge of and skill in rural pursuits, and to inspire them with a spirit of service to the village community. In order to achieve this, the curriculum of the school was formulated in such a way as to strike a reasonable balance between deskwork and out-of-school activities. Agricultural and environmental activities were introduced with a view to gradually spreading a general interest in rural studies.

The work of syllabus reform for the elementary school began with the traditional subjects, Arabic and arithmetic, because 'they were the easiest to start with as the subject matter was already known to teachers and because it was essential to carry the teachers'[2] with the reform idea. Scott took charge of the reform in Arabic teaching, while Jamison, another advocate of reform, became responsible for the reform in arithmetic teaching.

The next stage in reform was the introduction of new subjects: elementary nature study, geography, handwork, and projects. Griffiths looked after the reform of history and geography teaching. Bacon, the agricultural specialist seconded to Bakht er Ruda, became responsible for science and agricultural teaching.

Although the majority of students came from rural surroundings, it was not easy to successfully introduce or implement the aims of

[1] Griffiths, V. L., *An Experiment in Education,* pp. 11–12.
[2] Griffiths, V. L., 'A Teacher Training and Research Centre in the Sudan', *Overseas Education,* xvi, no. 1 (October 1944), 1–6.

ruralization. Most of the Sudanese staff were not really rural-minded. The climate of Sudanese opinion was unfavourable to such a re-direction of education. Fathers did not want to send their sons to learn agriculture. Teachers did not think that agriculture was a progressive or intellectual subject. Government service and town life were more attractive to fathers, teachers, and pupils. 'The choice of the site raised Sudanese suspicions. To them the capital repre-sented civilization and progress, whereas the country represented backwardness and the new, loathed policy of boosting the hereditary rulers'.[1] In spite of this it was thought of one year after its establish-ment as the only real school in the Sudan and in which 'a properly organized attempt was being made to bring life and efficiency into the pathetic muddle of Sudan education'.[2] But, Scott wrote, it had 'an enormous weight of parrot-learning and indifference in the country against which to fight'.[3]

By 1936 Bakht er Ruda had developed into a large institution with five schools:

(i) An elementary school which, in addition to educating the local town boys, was used for testing the new syllabuses and methods and for demonstration purposes. It also had a few boarders—the sons of tribal leaders from various parts of the country.

(ii) The Teachers' Training School, a boarding school for specially selected boys from all over the Sudan being trained as elementary school-teachers.

(iii) An intermediate school at Dueim with a rural bias and with pupils from various parts of the country and a number of sons of tribal leaders.

(iv) Courses for the training school and intermediate school staff trained by the British staff in science, geography, and history.

(v) Courses for existing elementary teachers, who were brought in small groups from all over the Sudan, and given instruction in the method of teaching Arabic and arithmetic.

The task which Bakhr er Ruda set itself to achieve, namely the reform of the elementary and intermediate syllabuses on a practical basis and with a rural bias, and the improvement of teaching methods so that not only the majority of boys who did not proceed beyond the intermediate school would find real benefit, but also those who

[1] Griffiths, V. L., *An Experiment in Education*, p. 14.
[2] Letters from G. C. Scott to his mother, 31 July 1935 and 14 August 1935.
[3] Ibid.

proceeded to secondary education, was not an easy one to achieve.[1]
Its approach was based on an attempt to adapt the best methods and
ideas used outside the Sudan to the needs of the Sudanese child and
the needs of Sudanese society as seen by the reformer; this was not
easily accepted by the parents, the old teachers, or those of the
educated class who were suspicious of its aims. It took some years
before the aims of Bakht er Ruda were accepted and supported. Its
significance lay in the fact that its establishment marked the first
steps taken towards reforming Sudan education.

[1] Education Department, Occasional Note No. 6, 28 October 1936, *EDA/
File DES/9.1.4.*

CHAPTER VII

Educational Reform in the Northern Sudan

1935–1938

THE ESTABLISHMENT of the Elementary Teachers' Training College in Bakht er Ruda and the reforms initiated inspired more reform in education. In 1933 a new Governor-General, Sir Stewart Symes, was appointed. Unlike Maffey he was sympathetic to the educated class. He looked upon them as healthy members of a generation with new ideas on political and social subjects which 'were neither subversive nor revolutionary'.[1] In the same year a new civil secretary, Sir Angus Gillan, replaced Sir Harold MacMichael, the architect of native administration. The Department of Education, which had been part of a Secretariat of Health and Education since 1928, reverted to its old status as an independent department. These changes in personnel and structure assisted the process of reform. A committee was appointed in 1934 to examine the salary scales for government employees in order 'to provide for the progress of Sudanese to more responsible administrative and departmental posts'.[2] For the first time since 1931 the number of Sudanese in government classified posts increased by 84 posts in 1934, and the number of non-Sudanese decreased. A competitive examination— the Civil Service Examination—was instituted in 1934. In accordance with the Winter Committee's Report, training courses in building and architectural engineering within the Department of Public Works were started in 1934. The Winter Committee's Report had drawn attention to the complicated problems of education but did not suggest measures acceptable to the Sudanese which would further their efficiency and enable them to take more responsible jobs. The government's commitment to a policy of substitution and its desire to appoint more Sudanese to the senior official categories[3] required the provision of training facilities, and attention was focused primarily on problems of secondary and post-secondary education. 'The need was becoming apparent', wrote the Governor-General in 1935, 'and will become progressively more so in the future of more

[1] Symes, Sir Stewart, *Tour of Duty* (London, 1946), p. 222.
[2] *G.G.R. 1934*, p. 11.   [3] Symes, Sir S., *Tour of Duty*, pp. 224–5.

advanced training, particularly for Sudanese entering certain branches of government service'[1].

A committee[2] was appointed with the following terms of reference:

A. To review generally the progress made in the past ten years in the employment of Sudanese in more responsible posts in the technical departments.

B. To advise and wherever possible make specific recommendations as to whether this process of Sudanese dilution could be accelerated economically and without undue risks to the public service with particular reference to:

(i) the provision of better facilities for technical training of Sudanese candidates for appointment and after appointment, and

(ii) possible modifications of existing systems and practice in technical departments that could facilitate employment of Sudanese in more responsible posts.[3]

Although the committee, in accordance with the terms of reference, should have been concerned with employment, dilution, and training, its findings and recommendations dealt with the system of education in the Gordon Memorial College, which was the main source of Sudanese recruitment in classified posts. After a review of the facilities available for technical education, the supply and demand since 1921, and a survey of the supervisory and technical posts held by Sudanese in various technical departments, the committee reached two general conclusions: first, that the original aims of education, as seen by Kitchener in 1899, were no longer relevant to the Sudan conditions, and, second, that the real problem facing the Sudan was to devise a new system of general and technical education which would produce qualified Sudanese for new responsibilities, as the facilities available were no longer adequate for these objectives.[4]

While the committee recognized the need to train Sudanese in the new techniques brought about by the changes in science and technology, it warned against haste and 'premature utilisation of Sudanese in posts they are unqualified to fill'[5] because this would lead to disaster for them and the country. It also warned against hastening

---

[1] *G.G.R. 1935*, p. 14.

[2] The members of the committee were G. N. Loggin, Director of Public Works Department (chairman) and H. B. Emley, Manager Sudan Railways, S. L. Milligan, Director of Surveys, A. Lowden, Director of Agriculture and Forests, Captain H. B. Williams, Director of Veterinary Service (members).

[3] Sudan Government, *Technical Training of Sudanese*.

[4] Ibid., pp. 13–15.   [5] Ibid., pp. 13–16.

the replacement of non-Sudanese by Sudanese because the former were instruments of training, and unless proper training courses could be instituted the latter should not be unduly pushed to replace them. The failure of technical departments to employ more Sudanese in higher posts was not, according to the committee, due to lack of opportunity, but to the difficulty in finding men with the suitable education and standards. It complained that the Education Department had failed to consult the technical departments about their needs and there was no proper liaison between them as future employers and the Gordon Memorial College authorities as producers of future employees.

The Loggin Committee, as it came to be known, held that the Gordon Memorial College had failed to produce suitable candidates for the technical departments.[1] It was especially critical of the training of engineers. The system by which engineers were trained and which allowed for early specialization was not found to be good because it was being made on inadequate foundations and had left little time for general education. This was being done, in the committe's view, in spite of the fact that 'the mental development of a Sudanese boy of twenty years of age was actually only comparable with that of an English boy of sixteen',[2] and the realization that the students of the Gordon College did not really absorb the tuition given to them. It was also critical of the standard of English, the science syllabus, and the lack of thoroughness in engineering education. The latter 'was too comprehensive and elaborate having regard to the age of the boys under instruction'.[3]

The committee therefore recommended that the first step to be taken was to remove the scientific, technical, and highly specialized training from the Gordon College. In other words, it proposed that the Gordon College should become an ordinary secondary school after which the specialized training, scientific and technical, would follow. Post-secondary training would be done either in a post-secondary institution or within the departments. Training within the departments had, from the committee's point of view, the advantage of ensuring that intensive training in accordance with the departmental requirements would be followed. It would also identify the departments from an early stage with training and create a lively interest within them in the future careers of their trainees. The disadvantages in such a course were also realized.

[1] Ibid., pp. 26–32.   [2] Ibid., p. 27.   [3] Ibid.

Departmental training would be influenced by the immediate needs and requirements, and would therefore be narrow and wasteful. The shortage of British staff would make it difficult to carry out systematic training. The Loggin Committee concluded that although departmental training had been useful in the past and was until then required as an interim measure in certain departments, it should not be regarded as an adequate alternative for training in post-Gordon College schools, especially if the appropriate departments were associated from the beginning with the management of these schools in the same way as the Kitchener School of Medicine was associated with the department of health. The establishment of a school of science and a school of engineering at the post-secondary-school level was urged as a necessary step in order to cater for the immediate requirements.

The findings and conclusions of the committee were not wholly supported by the Director of Education. He felt that the committee's low estimation of Sudanese capacity to undertake responsible work was not borne out by the findings of his department and that their recommendations regarding post-secondary schools fell short of its plans.

The report was, however, finally accepted and the department of education was instructed by the Governor-General's Council to consider the educational questions raised in the report, and to incorporate the proposals into the educational system. Its major recommendation for the establishment of higher schools paving the way to establishing a university was ruled out. The Governor-General wrote that 'the advance to the University stage is, in my judgement, wholly unrealistic in the present generation'.[1] Instead of that, ten students were selected from the Gordon College scientific section in 1935 and attached to the Kitchener School of Medicine laboratories, where they were instructed in zoology, chemistry and physics with a view to their subsequent selection as agricultural and veterinary students. In 1936 the establishment of schools of engineering, agriculture and veterinary science was approved by the Governor-General's Council. The technical subjects which had been part of the Gordon Memorial College since its foundation were thus removed. The college was made, in 1936, into a general secondary school providing general education. The clerical and accountants' courses continued to be part of the college courses.

[1] *G.M.C.R., 1934*, p. 10.

In the meantime, another important development in higher education was taking place. In May 1935 the Governor-General's Council passed the Khartoum School of Law Order, establishing a school of law in Khartoum. This provided an opening for Sudanese as advocates and judges in civil courts.

Originally, the proposal for the establishment of a school of law came from the Legal Secretary in 1928. In a note addressed to the Civil Secretary he wrote that 'it is wrong and inadvisable that natives wishing to become lawyers (and there are sure to be some in the future) should be compelled to go either to Egypt or England, and it might be well worth while to consider proper training courses in the Gordon College which would remain under British tuition and guidance and would enable us to reject Egyptian qualifications'.[1] The last thing the Sudan Government wanted was the establishment of a class of lawyers. Although the Legal Secretary did not think that there was a need for Sudanese either at the Bar or on the Bench, he feared that if legal education was not provided, some Sudanese, who had already shown manifestations of modernism, would go to Egypt, where their political outlook would be affected, and receive legal education. Two Egyptians domiciled in the Sudan[2] and who qualified in Egypt had already returned to Khartoum and were permitted to practise. It was feared that if some Sudanese followed suit it would be difficult to reject their Egyptian qualifications.[3] If training was available in the Sudan, the inducement to go abroad would be reduced. On the other hand, it was desirable, the Legal Secretary wrote, 'to offer a career other than government employment to intelligent Sudanese' and if there were to be openings for advocates 'the people of the country should be given a chance'.[4] Some Sudanese were filling posts of judges in the Civil Courts and if they were to continue to do so with success the Legal Secretary thought 'they must receive proper training'.[5]

When the proposal was received in 1934 it was approved in principle on 28 February 1935, and the School of Law Order and Regulations received the final approval of the Governor-General on 11 May 1935.[6]

[1] Note on Legal Education by Legal Secretary, Khartoum, 14 April 1928, *SGA/DAKHLIA/17/2, File 17.A.23.*
[2] They were Labib Surial and Younis Nagm.
[3] Note on Legal Education, 3 February 1929, op. cit.
[4] Ibid., 1 December 1934.   [5] Ibid.
[6] Minutes of the 419th meeting of the Governor-General's Council. *SGA.*

Political developments in 1936 gave a further impetus to the development of higher education. The conclusion of the Anglo-Egyptian treaty of 1936 ended the exclusion of Egyptians from the Sudan. Although the treaty stipulated that when 'making new appointments for which qualified Sudanese are not available', the Governor-General 'will select suitable candidates of British and Egyptian nationality',[1] the Sudan Government was not prepared to 'restore to the Egyptians the share in Government Service which they had held in 1924'.[2] Sudanization was the alternative to employing Egyptians in the service, and could only be increased if more trained Sudanese were available. The need for higher education became urgent.

On the other hand Article II (1) of the 1936 treaty stated that the primary aim of the administration in the Sudan was the welfare of the Sudanese. Although the educated Sudanese felt that the treaty did not go far in recognizing their rights, they interpreted the article as a direction to the Sudan Government to provide better social services, including education at higher levels. The Sudan Government found itself pressed by both Sudanese opinion and Egyptian interests to give more attention to higher education.[3]

A review of education, especially at the Gordon Memorial College, had already been urged by Lord Cromer, as Chairman of the Trustees. He wrote that 'it is now some considerable time since the College was inspected by a competent technical authority and in accordance with the policy determined after the last inspection, a fresh one would probably prove helpful in the near future'.[4]

This competent technical authority was to be found in the De La Warr Commission,[5] which was invited by the Sudan Government, on the suggestion of Sir James Currie, to visit the Sudan in 1937.[6]

Its terms of reference were 'to enquire and report on the curriculum, staff and organization of the Gordon Memorial College at Khartoum; and to review the method and organization of the Elementary

[1] Article II (II) of 1936 treaty.

[2] Holt, P. M., *A Modern History of the Sudan*, p. 140.

[3] Griffiths, V. L., Summary of views on Extension of Higher Education in the Northern Sudan, 17 and 15 February 1937. *EDA*.

[4] *G.M.C.R. 1934*, p. 9.

[5] Members of the De La Warr Commission were Earl De La Warr (chairman) and Robert Bernays (M.P.), Miss Philippa C. Esdaile, B. Mouat Jones, Alexander Kerr, W. H. McLean, Z. K. Mathews, John Murray, Harold Nicolson (M.P.) (members).

[6] Personal information from Sir Christopher Cox.

and Intermediate school systems in relation to the Elementary Teachers' Training College and one or two selected schools'.[1]

The commission set out to make recommendations which would 'direct into beneficial channels'[2] the outcome of the impact of Western ideas and education upon the life of northern Sudanese. As the function of education in the Sudan was to harmonize the best elements in European civilization with Sudanese society, it was necessary to see that the schools and College kept in close contact with a primarily rural society and trained leaders 'who must be both superior to the mass of their countrymen and in sympathy with them'.[3] The educational system should in the commission's view avoid the 'bifurcation of the Sudan at this early stage in its growth with a small group of "effendis" in the town and government departments on one hand and a large group of native administrators in the countryside consisting of chiefs, sub-chiefs and village heads'.[4] This bifurcation, in the commission's view, appeared to be the 'greatest danger in the developments of the last ten years'[5] in the Sudan. One way of avoiding this danger was by encouraging tribal leaders to send their sons to schools beyond the elementary level. The financial needs of education should, therefore, be considered with great sympathy so that both expansion and reform could be achieved.[6] The commission was critical of the educational system. There was little education to be found in the khalwas. The teaching of facts was irrelevant to the environment. Teaching was subordinated to examinations.

The great fault of the schools was memorization, a consequence of the mental background of the pupils who had been brought up in the koranic tradition 'and to whom western civilization and education necessarily appear as foreign products'.[7] Intermediate schools lacked manual training, teaching of elementary and natural sciences, and suitable library books. Girls' education, which was 'one of the main causes of backwardness in the Sudan', and which was causing 'an unbridgeable gap between the two halves of society and home life of the Sudanese'[8], was inadequate. The pressure of vocational and technical courses in the Gordon College had resulted in a confusion of aims, methods, and attitudes. It had also hampered the development of the college into a proper secondary school.

[1] Sudan Government, Report of Lord De La Warr's Educational Commission (Khartoum, 1937), p. 5.   [2] Ibid., p. 6.   [3] Ibid.   [4] Ibid.
[5] Ibid.   [6] Ibid.   [7] Ibid., p. 8.   [8] Ibid., pp. 5–17.

The only institution which received praise was the Elementary Teachers' Training College at Bakht er Ruda and its elementary school. The latter was, in the commission's view, a contrast to other elementary schools. The children there were not only bright and eager to learn, but also 'learning to think and reason for themselves'. The commission had, however, the following to say: 'The time for experiment is over and the moment has arrived for advance upon the knowledge gained. The aim should be the creation of a Bakht er Ruda in every province.'[1]

In making these criticisms the commission was influenced by the views of the people it had interviewed. Among these were V. L. Griffiths (Bakht er Ruda), G. C. Scott (Warden, G.M.C.) and Mirghani Hamza, a leading educated Sudanese. The similarity between Griffiths' views and the commission's report could be seen in the views expressed by him to the commission:

V. L. Griffiths' views

(a) Educated Sudanese have no qualities of 'initiative, foresight, and adaptation to circumstances'.[2]

(b) The causes of this weakness are 'the lack of home civilization, the foreignness of education and the Koranic tradition in learning'.[3]

(c) 'The backwardness of women is one of the main causes of male backwardness.'[4]

Lord De La Warr's report

(a) Educational system failed to produce 'qualities of initiative, foresight, judgement and adaptation to circumstance'.[5]

(b) 'The mental background of boys is the Koranic tradition. Western civilization and education appear as foreign products.'[6]

(c) 'The inadequacy of women's education is one of the main causes of backwardness in the Sudan.'[7]

G. C. Scott's views are not much different from those expressed by Griffiths. He expressed these views in a letter to the commission in which he said:

[1] Ibid., p. 11.
[2] Griffiths, V. L., Summary of Views on Extension of Higher Education, 15 and 17 February 1937, EDA.
[3] Ibid.   [4] Ibid.
[5] Sudan Government, Report of Lord De La Warr, p. 8.
[6] Ibid.   [7] Ibid., p. 14.

The obvious and generally admitted fault prevailing in all Sudanese education at present is the tendency to memorize without understanding, and to look upon education as the mastering of impractical theorems and of exercises unconnected with life. As a result, not only do we usually fail to produce qualities of initiative, foresight, judgement and adaptation to circumstances but we also fail to reach an adequate standard even in the knowledge of the subjects themselves.[1]

These were views which were accepted and reproduced in the report.[2]

But it was in regard to the Gordon College that the commission relied to a great extent on Scott's views. The failure in the teaching methods was attributed, by both Scott and the commission, to the shortage of British staff and to their lack of knowledge of the Sudanese, due to their ignorance and poor standard in the Arabic language. It was also attributed to the quality of Sudanese staff whose 'intellectual interests were weak and knowledge of their country very limited'.[3] Mirghani Hamza held strong views on girls' education, and it was in this respect that his views were welcomed.

The commission's recommendations for improvement embraced the whole system. It recommended that, while the government should not interfere with the religious functions of *khalwas*, these should be improved by the introduction of better methods of teaching. Elementary schools should be in close contact with agriculture and thereby have a rural bias. In order to rid the children of the habit of repetitive learning which they acquired by spending two to three years in the *khalwa* before they entered the elementary school at the age of eight, it was recommended that admission to the latter should be at the age of five or six. Although the committee did not reject the proposal which V. L. Griffiths emphasized in his note, to increase the intermediate school's course to six years, it thought that the implementation of the proposal should depend on the possibility of recruiting boys to the elementary schools two years earlier. It opposed a proposal to reduce the secondary course to two years. Four years of secondary education was, in the commission's view, 'the irreducible minimum for a true secondary school'.[4]

Girls' education was to be expanded and the course in the training college for girls was to be lengthened. Technical education did not

[1] Letter from G. C. Scott to Lord De La Warr, 5 April 1937. *EDA*.
[2] Sudan Government, *Report of Lord De La Warr*, p. 8.
[3] Letter from G. C. Scott to Lord De La Warr, cited, and Sudan Government *Report of Lord De La Warr*, pp. 19–20.
[4] Ibid., p. 12.

receive the same attention accorded by the commission to other levels of education. All that the commission recommended was the expansion of facilities.[1]

With regard to the Gordon Memorial College, which had already started to change into a proper secondary school, it was recommended that the syllabus in history and science should be reformed. The number of both British and Sudanese staff should be increased and the latter should be given the opportunity to visit England. In order to establish closer contact with Sudanese life and with commercial and non-official activities, the formation of an advisory council, made up of the Director of Education, the representative of the Civil Security Department, representatives of other departments, the Old Students' Association and the Chamber of Commerce, was recommended. The function of this council was to advise the authorities on those matters relating to the welfare of the school. Certain proposals made by V. L. Griffiths regarding adult education for women and a Publication and Translation Bureau, and proposals made by G. C. Scott regarding the appointment of British teachers on a permanent basis and not on a contract basis, were either not mentioned in the final recommendations or rejected. Its support for contract appointment was based on the actual belief that this 'would secure a continuous supply of fresh blood which is essential for maintaining life and drive in any teaching staff, and which can scarcely be obtained in an isolated school such as Gordon College if all the masters are on the permanent basis'.[2]

The last part of the report was concerned with Higher Education. Unlike the Report of the Committee on Technical Training, and in opposition to the views expressed by different government officials, the commission recommended that the aim should be to establish in the future a university granting degrees of recognized validity. In order to achieve this aim the first step to be taken was to raise the standard of the Gordon Memorial College by making the students pass a public leaving-certificate examination which would enable the Education Department to have a yardstick by which to compare its own standards with those accepted elsewhere, and avoid the danger of continuing to work according to standards depending on local conditions and limitations. On the other hand such an examination would enable those proceeding to the professional courses to secure a recognized certificate which would open the way for them to secure

[1] Ibid., p. 45.   [2] Ibid., p. 20.

British qualifications. With this in view and in order to secure the necessary adaptations needed for the Sudan examination, it was recommended that the Education Department should approach one of the British examination bodies in order that its examinations should be adapted to Sudan conditions and requirements. Adaptations were required in English, Arabic, mathematics, history, and geography. At a later date, a local school certificate could replace the outside examination.

The next step, which did not need to await completion of the arrangement for a School certificate, was to establish Schools of Science, Art, and Commerce, to form, together with the already existing Schools of Medicine, Engineering, Agriculture, and Veterinary Science, the future University College and, ultimately, the University of Khartoum. These schools would at first award their own diplomas, the standard of which should be ensured by external examiners. The professional schools should aim at an academic standard equivalent to that of a recognized British professional qualification.

When the suitable standard at both the secondary and post-secondary schools had been reached, the next step recommended by the commission was to enter selected students for external degrees, for example, those of London University.

J. Murray, a member of the commission, made three qualifications to the commission's recommendations.

The first, included in the final published version, was his proposal to establish a college for the training of intermediate school masters which would be similar to Bakht er Ruda 'or at least be organized in the closest touch with indigenous life'.[1]

The other two, which were political and therefore omitted from the final report, were concerned with external examinations and education in the south. He argued against the use of a British external examination in the Sudan secondary schools on the ground that the Egyptian Government might claim equal rights for an Egyptian examination and advocated the establishment of a local certificate as educationally and politically sound.[2]

He suggested that education in the south should involve a fuller and better use of missionary societies, so that a complete system of education could be established and 'the arrears be made up'.[3]

[1] Sudan Government, *Report of Lord De La Warr*, pp. 51–2.
[2] Note on Publication of De La Warr and Garem's Reports, Khartoum, 27 November 1937, *SGA/CIVSEC/File 17.3.1.*   [3] Ibid.

A similar comment on education in the north was made by Lord
De La Warr. He informed the Governor-General that

a general and impartial view of education in the Sudan leads to the conclusion that the schools are inadequate in number and unsatisfactory in
quality. This is clearest in the case of the elementary and intermediate
schools but it applies also to the Gordon Memorial College which appears
to have been pursuing for many years a comfortable rut at an easy amble.
. . . The Gordon College, which should have achieved a continuously
rising standard throughout the thirty years of its existence, has failed not
only to attain the complete University standard which its founders
envisaged, but even to reach the stage of University entrance. Education
in the Sudan has tried to make up the accumulated arrears of many years
stagnation. . . . It is most unfortunate that the schools in the south are so
largely under the control of Italian missionaries. There is every reason for
the granting of government subsidies to the Church Missionary Society
Schools. The educational activities of native administrations should be
encouraged as part of the policy of indirect rule, but if the native authorities
are insufficiently developed to start schools of their own, we venture to
suggest that a possible way of meeting the situation might be for the
government to set up schools which will be handed over later to the native
administrations.[1]

Thus the Lord De la Warr Commission's recommendations laid
the foundations for the development of higher education. They represented a renewal of interest in higher education not only because of
Sudan conditions but also because of the concern which the Advisory
Committee on Education in the Colonies showed in this respect.[2]
In 1934 the Advisory Committee had submitted a report of a sub-
committee under the chairmanship of Sir James Currie 'in which
was laid down a plan foreshadowing in many ways that later worked
out by the Asquith Commission'.[3] The De La Warr Commission had
visited East Africa before coming to the Sudan and made recommendations for the development of higher education there.

Another investigation into the educational system carried out at
the same time, and closely associated with the work of the De La
Warr Commission, was made by Ali Bey El Garem of the Egyptian
Ministry of Public Instruction. He was invited by the Sudan Government to report on the teaching of Arabic and the training of teachers
in the Sudan. The need for well-trained teachers in Arabic for

[1] Letter from Lord De La Warr to Governor-General, 16 October 1937, *SGA/
CIVSEC/17/3/File 17.B.1.*
[2] Carr-Saunders, A. M., *New Universities Overseas* (London, 1961), pp. 28-9.
[3] Ibid., p. 28.

intermediate schools and the Gordon College was urgent. Up till
then the teaching of Arabic in these schools was by Sudanese graduates
of Al Azhar in Cairo, the graduates of *al Mahad al Ilmi*, in Omdurman,
or the Gordon College Teachers' Training Section. Owing to the fact
that fewer Sudanese continued to go to Al Azhar and fewer remained
at *al Mahad al Ilmi* to qualify, there was a shortage of Arabic teachers
in the intermediate schools.

The Anglo-Egyptian treaty of 1936 had opened the door for the
re-employment of Egyptian teachers and it was in this field of teaching
—especially Arabic teaching—that Egypt might have put up candidates. In order to meet such a situation, the training of Sudanese
became an urgent necessity. On the other hand, it was felt that the
employment of the traditional type of Arabic teacher was not in line
with the trend of modernizing the system of education. If the main
fault of education, the parrot-like learning, had to be remedied—
and the traditionally trained teachers were certainly fortifying it—a
new type of Arabic teacher was needed.

Al Garem's report suggested the establishment of a Higher School
—providing a four years tuition beyond Gordon College and specializ-
ing in Arabic, but including such subjects as history, pedagogy, and
English. In addition to their employment in the intermediate schools,
its graduates could be employed as headmasters of selected elementary schools. The purpose of this last proposal was to create more
jobs for the graduates. As such a suggestion, if accepted, would run
contrary to the plans of Bakht er Ruda and would create a new class
of teachers in elementary schools, whose special status would lead to
technical and administrative difficulties, it was decided not to accept
this part of the report. The report also suggested that until qualified
Sudanese were available for teaching Arabic in the high school, the
Sudan Government should seek assistance from Egypt to appoint
Egyptian teachers. The Minister of Education in Cairo indicated his
willingness to render such help, but the Sudan Government was
reluctant to take the offer until a few years later.

The Winter Committee's report, the Loggin Committee's report,
and the De La Warr Commission's report paved the way for two of
the most important developments in education in the Sudan during
this period: the development of secondary and higher education. It
was on the basis of these reports, their main conclusions and recommendations, that educational development in northern Sudan was
planned in 1938.

CHAPTER VIII

Educational Reform in the Southern Sudan
1933–1938

ALTHOUGH the need for educational reform in the north was felt as far back as 1932, it was not until 1934 that a reassessment of the educational policy in the south was initiated. The application of southern policy in the field of education was worked out in a number of conferences, the main one being the Educational Conference held in Juba on 16 April 1932. At this conference, the Director of Education emphasized the need to satisfy the demand for local staff in a few years. He pointed out that measures should be taken 'to ensure that the educational policy was entirely in accord with the declared policy of the administration'.[1] The conference resolved that educational development should aim 'not at the destruction of native social institutions or at divorcing the Southerner from his national background, but at teaching him to adapt himself and his institutions to changing ideas and conditions'.[2] The aim in the south, as in the north, was not to detribalize, but to make each boy a better member of his tribe. In order to achieve this aim, the missionary teachers, like the British teachers in the north, were encouraged to learn the tribal languages, customs, and lore with a view to teaching tribal history in the schools. Native music, dancing, and handicrafts were introduced into the schools. 'The school curricula were to be more biased towards tribal agriculture and pastoral pursuits and less towards literary subjects. Boys and girls were to wear native dress in schools. The Bush Schools were to be developed and encouraged because their teaching was done in the natural environment of the boys and girls'.[3] Entry into the elementary schools was to be at a younger age so that boys could find it easy to return to their tribal life before acquiring the habit of imitating the European or the northerner, and older boys already in mission schools were to be returned to their tribes. Missions should admit boys who came from 'better classes' and 'not waifs and strays'.[4] These concepts were basically the same

---

[1] Minutes of the 6th Educational Conference of Mongalla Province, Juba, 16 April 1932, *SGA/CIVSEC/17/1 File 17.A.2.6.*   [2] Ibid.
[3] Bowers, J. B., A Note on Missions and Educational Policy in Upper Nile Province, 14 December 1942, *MIA/File SCO/46.A.I.*   [4] Ibid.

as those advocated in the north during the period of the triumph of native administration.

But policy was one thing, and effective application another. For the success of such a policy two things were needed. A genuine belief by the missionaries in the aims of the policy, and a full and continuous co-operation between them and the administration. The learning of tribal languages and lore was difficult and needed time. Some missionaries had their reservations about tribal dances and dress. Although most missions accepted the education of better classes as an ideal, few were achieving it, either because they could not get the better boys, or because some were against it. They 'would not deny education from a Christian point of view to the "waifs and strays"'.[1]

As the southern policy implied that northerners should be replaced by southerners there was need to develop post-elementary education to satisfy the employment needs of government and missions. Such a development was bound to lead to detribalization. Limitation of opportunities, on the other hand, would not lead to replacement of northerners by southerners in the shortest possible time. It was therefore resolved that intermediate education should be in the appropriate tribal surroundings. The use of English in these post-elementary schools, as a language of instruction necessary for the purpose of employment as minor clerks, was again bound to lead to detribalization. To minimize this danger, it was advocated that the vernacular should be used as a medium of instruction. This was, however, rejected on the grounds of practicality, needs of employment, and the repercussions it would have had on the policy of developing English as a *lingua franca* in the south, all of which would suffer as a result. On the technical side, the use of English was not making much progress because of the lack of textbooks and the inability of Italian missionaries, who were in the majority, to teach in English. Arabic was spreading in spite of the efforts to curtail it. Northern merchants and officials, who came into daily contact with the southerners, helped the spread of Arabic.[2] The application of the policy in Bahr al Ghazal province, and particularly Wau, proved especially difficult because of the existence of a large Moslem northern community.[3]

The use of the schools as Christian agencies was bound to raise

[1] Ibid.
[2] *EDA/File DE/SCR/I.I.17.*   [3] *MIA/File SCR/I.C.7.*

the question whether such a policy would not conflict with the declared policy of developing native institutions. The conversion of the children to Christianity would alienate them from their tribe and the beliefs of their fathers. This was especially true in such tribes as the Dinka where the indigenous spiritual beliefs were highly developed. But such an argument could hardly be expected to convince the missionaries, since conversion to Christianity was their only justification for educational activity.

The practice of giving schoolboys foreign Christian names was seen by some administrators as contrary to the ideal of making them useful members of their tribes. The assumption of a foreign name would be a symbol of the foreignness of their religion and education and might lead to antagonism between the tribe and the school, and the latter might be looked upon as an enemy of tribal culture.

The sphere system made the missionaries regard their 'own schools as virtually autonomous and self-contained. There was little inter-communication between different missionary groups.'[1] This separation, chiefly due to sectarian differences, geographical isolation, and language barriers, resulted in different national characteristics and educational ideas being reflected in the schools.[2] In 1934, the Governor-General wrote to the Foreign Office in London that the sphere system was 'impossible to maintain as a sacrosanct Chinese Wall'.[3]

The application of southern policy to education was faced with many problems and contradictions. The co-operation between the missionaries and the administration was not always forthcoming. The solution of these problems became a real concern of the government.[4]

But there were other reasons for this growing concern. In 1935 the growth of Fascism and Nazism in Europe was threatening the peace of the world. In Africa, the Italian armies defeated the Ethiopians and conquered their country by the middle of 1936. The annexation of Ethiopia by Italy was seen as a threat to British interests in Africa and Asia. In the Sudan there was fear of adverse repercussions in having a hostile power on its eastern frontiers and the encouragement of nationalist feelings by either external or internal propaganda. The place of Italian missionaries, especially those

---

[1] Symes, Sir S., *Tour of Duty*, pp. 240-1.
[2] Ibid.   [3] *MIA/File SCO/46.A.I.*
[4] Symes, Sir S., *Tour of Duty*, p. 241.

engaged in religious and educational work in the south, was a matter
of great concern to the government.[1] Their number was more than
five times the number of British and other Protestant missionaries,
and as numerous as all other European officials and missionaries
situated in the south. Criticism and suspicion of this large Italian
community grew and demanded action.

The Anglo-Egyptian treaty of 1936 invited Egyptian intervention.
Three weeks after the treaty was signed the Grand Kadi, who was
usually an Egyptian, met the Governor-General to discuss the
possibility of sending Islamic missions to the south.[2] A month later,
the editor of *Al Sudan* newspaper published an article on 'Religious
Freedom and the Necessity of Removing the Restrictions on Islam
in the Southern Sudan', in which government policy of subsidizing
the Christian missions in the southern provinces, while putting
restrictions on the propagation of Islam, was strongly criticized.[3]
These two incidents were by no means isolated. The Nationalists and
Pan-Islamists in both Egypt and the Sudan were determined to open
the south for Moslem missionary activities. A new challenge to
government policy, in the administrative and educational fields,
presented itself, and the Sudan Government set out to find for itself,
in the Governor-General's words, how 'to steer a course between
the Scylla of a possibly hostile European Nationalist penetration by
Italian personnel and the Charybdis of a pernicious and obscurantist
form of Islam which would present itself quickly in the region'.[4]

Thus the government, prompted by different considerations,
started a review of the educational policy and practice in the south.
This review was not, however, concerned with the major policy lines
already applied, but rather with their application. The first of these
reviews was contained in a report by C. W. Williams, Assistant
Director of Education, presented to the Governor-General. In his
report, he wrote that 'an impartial examination into the situation
could not with honesty pronounce that the state of education is by
any means satisfactory. In theory the system has been soundly constituted . . . but in practice the whole edifice has been undermined

[1] Cox, Christopher, Report on Education in the South, July 1937, *EDA/File
DE/SCR/9.9.9.15*; Henderson, K. D. D., *The Making of the Modern Sudan*, p. 363.

[2] *MIA/File SCO/46.A.I.*

[3] *Al Sudan* newspaper, Khartoum, 25 December 1936.

[4] Letter from Governor-General to His Britannic Majesty's Ambassador
Extraordinary and Plenipotentiary, Khartoum, 7 December 1937, Cairo, No.
145/46.A.A, *EDA/File DE/SCR/9.9.9.14.*

and rendered unsound by the fact that the foundations have not been well and surely laid.'[1]

The chief defects in the system were the absence of trained native teachers, emphasis on religion and literary subjects, the shortage of staff in the Church Missionary Society schools, and the alien character of the Roman Catholics to both the rulers and the ruled. He found that the European missionary teachers were 'neither interested nor have any understanding or appreciation of the need for technique in their teaching'.[2] While nearly all teaching in the Church Missionary Society schools was left in the hands of untrained teachers, in the Roman Catholic schools the teachers failed 'to draw the best out of their boys or to imbue them with the fire, personality, and practical aptitude that are required of a successful teacher'.[3]

These defects were attributed to the insistence by all missionaries on the pursuit of religion to the exclusion of all other things, the narrow religious outlook of the Church Missionary Society, the indifference, especially of the old missionaries, to the importance of method and organization, and the contemptuous attitude of the Roman Catholic missionaries towards the native. The majority of Roman Catholic missionaries, the report stated, 'come of North Italian peasant stock, so that it is not altogether surprising to find them unappreciative and ignorant of British ideals and British methods of dealing with native peoples',[4] and were unpopular with the chiefs and the people.

According to the report, religion was not enough to enable the southerners to understand the impact of modern civilization, and to enable them to adapt themselves to the changing ideas and conditions, which was the object of education. Missionary education was neither teaching the native to be contented with his tribe and environment, nor making him a better tribesman and villager, which was another object of educational policy. The way out was to insist that the missionaries should 'in return for the funds allocated to them . . . take steps to see that the education which they provide is the best possible in the circumstances and not regard it as little but an important adjunct to their real work of evangelism'.[5]

Other recommendations made by the report were to consolidate rather than to expand, to train native teachers, to examine mission

[1] Williams, C. W., Report on Education in the Southern Sudan, 9 February 1936, *SGA/Equatoria/File EP/SCR/17.A.3.*
[2] Ibid.   [3] Ibid.   [4] Ibid.   [5] Ibid.

accounts and, generally, to exercise more control over missionaries. The government should, the report recommended, participate in education by establishing Government Farm Schools, Government Post-Elementary Schools, and provide secondary education either locally or abroad.

The Williams report, like the Winter and the De la Warr reports on northern education, was a landmark in educational policy in the south. For the first time missionary education was criticized by a senior official of the central government. For the first time also, government participation in education was advocated and urged.

This major recommendation was, however, considered unpractical. At a meeting held in the Foreign Office in London in October 1936, and attended by the Governor-General and the Civil Secretary, to discuss education policy in the Sudan, the Governor-General declared that he 'considered it preferable to improve the existing mission schools rather than to supplement them by government schools'.[1] He agreed, however, that the greatest need was for the provision of schools for the training of teachers, and for the increase in supervisory staff. Although no changes arose from the Williams report, it was a valuable assessment of the contribution of missions to education and a warning against a free hand for missionaries in the educational field.

The place of the Italian missionaries in southern education, which was another concern of the government at the time, was dealt with in a report by C. W. M. Cox (who was appointed Director of Education in 1937).[2] Although the report dealt mainly with the possible dangers which would arise from the existence of Italian missionaries in the Sudan in the event of war against Italy, it also dealt with the educational work of the Italian missionaries. Cox found that there was no evidence of political propaganda on the part of the missionaries. Instead there were instances when they were 'drawing attention to things Italian rather than those of the British Empire'.[3] He found them fanatics rather than patriots, who owed their allegiance to the Vatican and not to Fascism. But this did not lead him to the conclusion that they would not find a change of régime which would ensure and accelerate the triumph of Catholicism in the southern Sudan unwelcome. Such a change, together with the sphere system,

---

[1] Record of the Meeting held on 13 October 1936 in Foreign Office to discuss Education Policy in the Sudan, *EDA/File DE/SCR/9.9.9.14.*
[2] Cox, Christopher, *Report on Education in the South*, op. cit.   [3] Ibid., p. 21.

would probably lead to the disappearance of a Protestant administration and church, prevent the intrusion of Islam from the north,
and end the policy of indirect rule—all of which were aspects of a
southern policy of which the Italian missionaries disapproved.
Unlike the Protestant missionaries, who promoted 'an undisciplined
individualism as a result of their belief in the principle of native
leadership',[1] he found the Italian Roman Catholic missionaries
unable to appreciate the principles and ideals of the administrative
policy by virtue of their nationality, social upbringing, and inability
to speak or understand English well. Their existence in the south
was therefore a potential danger to the development and application
of native administration. Their educational policy, according to Cox,
made the boy 'a submissive member of a comprehensive, highly
organized society',[2] and it was difficult to reconcile this with the
aim of creating an educated leadership.

Educational policies of both missions were faulty. The administrators preferred the more disciplined Catholic boy 'to the more
independent Protestant boy whose training, in its stress upon initiative, may lead to the emergence of qualities of conceit, facetiousness
and unreliability'.[3]

As regards the Roman Catholic village schools, they were dis-
appointing because most of them were 'only Catechist Centres'.[4]
The elementary schools were not likely to turn out leaders and the
intermediate and trades schools were training subordinates and not
responsible clerks or skilled workers.[5]

The report recommended that, since the monopoly of education
by any foreign nationality in the south was undesirable as a matter
of principle, and as a precaution against any dislocation and vacuum
in education which might follow a breaking-out of war, the priority
should be given to replacing the Italian Catholic missionaries by
British Catholic missionaries. Secondly, the Italian missionaries
working in the south should be sent to Britain on training courses.
Thirdly, the government should immediately step in and provide
educational facilities in the southern provinces.

The Governor-General was again reluctant to accept a proposal
which would create a major change in policy. He held that a purely
secular system of education under government management would

---

[1] Cox, Christopher, *Report on Education in the South*, p. 7.
[2] Ibid., p. 21.
[3] Ibid., p. 23.   [4] Ibid., pp. 22–3.   [5] Ibid.

not provide adequate guarantees against the dangers of Islam or Italian nationalism. It would cost much more than the country would be able to afford without achieving much good.[1]

The British Ambassador in Cairo disagreed with the Governor-General on this last point. He pointed out that the continued domination by Italian Roman Catholics of education in the south was unsound and dangerous from a political and administrative point of view, and state education was the only real solution to the problem.[2]

The proposal regarding the recruitment of British missionaries for immediate work in the south, and the sending of Italian missionaries to take the colonial course at the London Institute of Education, were, however, agreed to by the Foreign Office. The British Minister to the Holy See was asked to approach the Vatican to obtain its agreement on the two proposals. The Vatican was also asked to appoint two British Roman Catholics to two of the key positions in Roman Catholic religious work in the Sudan, and agree to the appointment by the Sudan Government of a British expert on education to supervise the Roman Catholic mission schools.[3] These proposals were accepted by the Vatican,[4] and the British Roman Catholic Society of St. Joseph at Mill Hill, London, was assigned to take up religious and educational work in southern Sudan in 1938.

Thus the years 1933–8 were years of examination and review of the role, place, and implications of missionary work in southern education, from the political and administrative points of view. Several meetings were held with a view to reorganizing their educational work, and making it suit the new policy. It was on the strength of these new policies and agreements with the missions that the first development plan for education in the south was formulated in 1938.

The period of reform coincided with a period of expansion in educational facilities. The number of schools during the period 1927–38 was as follows:[5]

[1] Letter from the Governor-General to His Britannic Majesty's Ambassador Extraordinary and Plenipotentiary, Khartoum, 7 December 1937, Cairo, No. 145/46.A.A, *EDA/File DE/SCR/9.9.9.14*.

[2] Letter from British Ambassador in Cairo to Rt. Hon. Anthony Eden, 11 January 1938, No. 30/84/3/83, *EDA/File DE/SCR/9.9.9.14*.

[3] Letter from Foreign Office to His Majesty's Mission to the Holy See, 21 March 1938, J835/220/16 No. 18, *EDA/File DE/SCR/9.9.9.14*.

[4] Letter from the British Embassy to the Holy See, to the Foreign Office, 4 August 1939, No. 127/76/22/38, *EDA/File DE/SCR/9.9.9.14*.

[5] Despatch from the Governor-General to His Britannic Majesty's Ambassador in Cairo, No. 31/*I.C.I.*, 10 March 1938, *EDA/File DE/SCR/1.1.17*.

Type of School	1927	1932	1934	1936	1938
No. of village schools	—	189	310	392	585
No. of elementary schools (boys)	27	29	31	34	34
No. of elementary schools (girls)	—	5	16	17	18
No. of intermediate schools (boys)	3	3	3	3	3
No. of trade schools (boys)	2	3	3	3	3
No. of normal schools (boys)	—	1	2	3	2

The greatest increase was in the number of boys and girls attending village schools. The number of boys and girls grew from 13,839 in 1936 to 15,073 in 1938.

While village schools had grown to more than three times (300 per cent) compared to 1932, the number of elementary schools grew about 18 per cent and the number of intermediate and trade schools was constant. This was a reflection of the policy followed since 1933 of improving the standards rather than increasing the number of these schools.

The majority of the schools at all levels belonged in 1938 to the Church Missionary Society and the Roman Catholic Mission. Their distribution among the different missions in 1938 was as follows:[1]

	Number of Schools, 1938				
	Village	Ele-mentary (boys)	Ele-mentary (girls)	Trade schools (boys)	Inter-mediate and normal schools (boys)
Roman Catholic Mission	306	20	12	2	2
Church Missionary Society	271	10	4	1	3
American Presbyterian Mission	4	2	2	—	—
Sudan United Mission	4	1	—	—	—
Bible Churchmen's Society	—	1	—	—	—

[1] *E.D.R., 1938*, pp. 39–42.

Since the government was committed to a policy of replacing the northern personnel by southerners, it would have been expected that educational expansion, especially at the intermediate and trade school levels, should have been greater than it was. But the missionaries were short of staff and funds, and were unable, therefore, to assist the policy of southernization by accelerating education at the post-elementary level. The development of southernization in the government service during 1932-8 was as follows:[1]

	1932	1934	1936	1938
I. *Clerical staff*				
(a) Total number of staff employed by government departments in southern Sudan	260	147	148	159
(b) Number of southerners employed by government departments	72	78	85	100
(c) (b) as percentage of (a)	45%	54%	57%	63%
II. *Technical staff*				
(a) Total employed by government departments in southern Sudan	245	175	226	228
(b) Number of southerners employed by government departments	118	77	94	106
(c) (b) as percentage of (a)	48%	44%	41%	46·5%

Development was thus slow in spite of the fact that government grants-in-aid to missionaries in southern Sudan increased from £E7,605 in 1933 to £E9,155 in 1937.[2]

The missions could not effectively carry out an educational policy and bring education to influence a backward society in a short time. Their inability to do this was recognized by the government and encouraged the adoption of a new policy.

Educational policy in the Nuba area, which was similar to that in the southern provinces, was also reviewed. It had been evident since 1932 that the Sudan United Mission, to which the Nuba area was allotted as an exclusive sphere for religious and educational work, was unable to meet the demand for education because of the

---

[1] Despatch from the Governor-General to His Britannic Majesty's Ambassador in Cairo, No. 31/I.C.I., 10 March 1938, *EDA/File DE/SCR/1.1.17*.
[2] Education Department, *Annual Budgets, 1933-1937.*

lack of qualified staff and funds. The Church Missionary Society was invited to co-operate in providing educational facilities for the training of clerks, the provision of social welfare, research on language problems, and anthropological studies, and, finally, in relating educational work to the practical needs of the people. The central government agreed to pay a subsidy if qualified teachers were appointed. A school in Salara and a teachers' training course in Katcha were established by the Church Missionary Society in 1933 with substantial government aid. These developments were not, however, considered adequate. Douglas Newbold, who replaced Gillan as Governor of Kordufan province in 1932, saw that economic development in the Nuba area was outstripping intellectual and educational development.[1] A special tax was levied on cotton to finance expansion in education and four government elementary schools staffed by Egyptian Christians were established during 1936-9.[2]

The other problem facing Nuba education, the language problem, was also reviewed in 1935. The policy of teaching colloquial Arabic and writing it in roman script failed as a practical and educational proposition. A meeting held in Khartoum on 7 December 1935, and attended by the representatives of the Civil Secretary and the Director of Education, to discuss the problem resolved that the previous policy should be abandoned. Instead, literary Arabic, in arabic script, should be taught. It was, however, emphasized that the Arabic taught should not be classical Arabic, but a simple literary form which would satisfy the practical needs of the majority of pupils, form an adequate foundation for the further educational progress of the minority, and lessen the difficulties for the missionaries supervising education.[3]

This change of policy was objected to by the missionaries on technical and religious grounds. In their view, Arabic was a poor medium for teaching Christianity and it would open the Nuba area to Islamic ideas and culture, a danger which, by following a policy of teaching colloquial Arabic and writing it in roman script, they were trying to avoid.[4]

In spite of the increase in the amounts of grants-in-aid to the two

[1] Sanderson, Lillian, 'Educational Development and Administrative Control in the Nuba Mountains region of the Sudan', *Journal of African History*, iv, no. 2 (1963).
[2] Henderson, K. D. D., *The Making of the Modern Sudan*, p. 69.
[3] *EDA/File 17.A.2.7.* [4] Ibid.

9

missionary societies between 1933 and 1937, the results were unsatisfactory. School attendance in the missionary schools was
decreasing. This could partly be explained by the fact that more
Nuba children were attracted to the government elementary schools.
But the major cause was found to be in the Nuba's dislike of attending
missionary schools where religious instruction was practised. Their
highly developed religions, like the Dinka's, were a barrier to
missionary influence. In spite of the increase in the grants-in-aid to
the Sudan United mission from £E810 in 1933 to £E2,300 in 1937,
the number of boys and girls attending the missionary schools
decreased from 148 in 1933 to 59 in 1937. Nuba educational development thus presented special problems to the administration. An
anthropological study initiated by Newbold and carried out by
Nadel provided part of the answer to the problem. Nadel concluded
that the influence of Arabic culture was bound to increase as a
result of its association with higher material and cultural standards,
and the association of the Moslems of the northern provinces with
government and administration. Therefore, the assimilation of the
Nuba into the culture of their neighbours was inevitable and any
attempt to segregate the Nuba educationally would fail.[1] Thus the
era of developing education in the Nuba region differently from the
north came to an end. Missionary educational work in the Nuba
region began to resemble and be associated with their work in the
north.

In north and south, an era of progress followed the investigations
and reports made during 1933–8.

[1] Nadel, S. F., *The Nuba* (Oxford, 1947), pp. 481–512.

CHAPTER IX

Educational Development, 1938–1946

THE ACCEPTANCE of the principal recommendations by different committees and the reports on education in the north and south ended the period of isolation and stagnation. The financial conditions after 1934 made it possible for an overall increase in the facilities for education in both parts of the country. It was not only possible to found Bakht er Ruda and the higher schools, which were the corner-stones for future development, but also to develop all other levels of education.

The government was able to start a policy in both the north and south which would, in the words of Lord De La Warr, 'make up the accumulated arrears of many years stagnation'.[1] In 1938, for the first time, an educational plan to cover the years 1938–46 for both the north and the south was approved by the Governor-General's Council. The idea of a plan for education was first suggested by V. L. Griffiths in 1937 so as to ensure a balance of education between towns and rural areas, and an education for native administrators.[2] The plan, which replaced proposals made in 1936 for expansion, emphasized the needs for reform in the north and south.

On the financial side, the plan estimated that capital cost would amount to £E500,000, of which £E154,000 was earmarked for the rebuilding of the secondary school, recommended by the De La Warr Commission, and £E42,000 for Bakht er Ruda. The recurrent expenditure was to increase from £E140,000 in 1936 to about £E300,000 in 1946. This represented an increase in the share of education in the north and south in relation to the whole budget from 3·3 per cent in 1936 to 5·9 per cent in 1938.

The basic general principle on which the plan was based was that while the expansion of higher and secondary education was urgent, its achievement would depend on the progress of lower levels of education. Expansion at the higher and secondary levels should not be at the expense of elementary education, which was the only facility for the majority of the population. Thus, of the capital

[1] Letter from Lord De La Warr to Governor-General, 16 October 1937, *SGA CIVSEC/17/3 File 17.B.1.*
[2] Griffiths, V. L., Views on Higher Education, *EDA.*

expenditure to be spent over the years 1938–46, about 50 per cent was allocated to secondary and higher education, and of the recurrent expenditure over the same period about 75 per cent was allocated to the improvement and expansion of lower levels of education.[1]

The second general principle was that while education in the south was not satisfactory, it would not be desirable, on grounds of economy and principles, to introduce a widespread system of state education. instead a gradual expansion and participation by the government was agreed to. The missions were to continue to be the main educational agents. The share of the south in educational expenditure, mainly grants-in-aid, increased from $7\frac{1}{2}$ per cent in 1938 to 9 per cent in 1946.

The execution of the plan faced a number of difficulties, the most important being the shortage of teachers. Because of the war teachers' training, which was the key to the expansion of elementary education, faced the problem of the recruitment of expatriate teachers for training the teachers. The difficulties of importing building materials during the war years caused the school building programme to lag behind. Rising costs of both materials and labour resulted in an increase of recurrent costs of the programme in 1946 from the estimated £E300,000 to £E450,000. The achievements in 1946, especially in elementary education, were therefore less than the plan had aimed for.

In northern Sudan, instead of the target number of 150 elementary schools for boys and 82 schools for girls, only 128 and 69 respectively were achieved. The plan's target of increasing the number of men teachers in 1946 to 545 and women teachers to 302 was not fulfilled; there were only 469 men teachers and 225 women teachers. Teachers' training for elementary education suffered particularly from the uncertainty of moving the training college to a new site, and the lengthening of the course in 1940 from four to five years. Shortage of women teachers was caused by the increased rate of marriages, and by the lengthening of the course from two to three years. The number of boys attending elementary schools in northern Sudan increased from 13,773 in 1938 to 22,015 in 1946. The number of girls attending elementary schools increased from 3,411 in 1938 to 7,747 in 1946. This was less than the plan had set out to achieve. Sub-grade education came to play an important role because of the unfulfilled demand.

[1] Educational Plan 1938–1946, *SGA/GENCO/3/42*, p. 7.

In 1934, and in accordance with the Winter Committee's recommendations, subsidies to inefficient *khalwas* were discontinued and a new two-year elementary school, a sub-grade school, emerged. At the beginning, the sub-grade school was held to be an interim measure, aimed at providing literacy facilities in areas which, because of limited finances, were unlikely to be able to support full elementary schools. In fact they were viewed as forerunners of permanent elementary schools in the areas where they were established. In the 1938–46 plan they were, however, adopted as an integral part of the system, and the Governor's Fund, from which they were financed, was increased from £E6,393 in 1938 to £E9,450 in 1943, and the establishment of a training centre for their teachers was recommended. The grants to *khalwas* were to be confined to those which were efficient. As a result, the number of children attending *khalwas* decreased from 221,000 in 1935 to 9,992 in 1946. This development created problems and dangers. There was the danger of creating, as a result of developing sub-grade schools, a classified sub-elementary cadre capable of almost limitless expansion, and a teacher with a lower status.[1] On the other hand, it had the advantage of absorbing, as teachers, an increasing number of unemployed ex-elementary and intermediate school boys. The sub-grade school came to be viewed as a new rival to the *khalwa*. In certain places the *feki* was employed as a teacher in the sub-grade school, and the *khalwa* was closed. In others, as financial assistance was stopped, and a sub-grade school was established, the local people tended to withdraw their support from the *khalwa*, and turn to the school. The *feki* lost his traditional status and position. The headmaster of the new school looked upon the *feki* as an embodiment of reaction and conservatism, while the latter saw the former as an instrument undermining his influence, and even his living.

As for the provision of special educational facilities for the sons of tribal chiefs, the plan recommended increased facilities at Bakht er Ruda Elementary School to serve, in addition to its main purpose of teaching practice, as a school for the sons of chiefs. The provincial governors' meeting of February 1939 discussed this particular problem and decided that 'no Sheikh should in future be appointed who has not had elementary education, no *Omda* who has not received intermediate education, and no *Nazir* who has not been to

[1] Letter from Director of Education Department, Khartoum, to all staff, 16 March 1939, *EDA*.

Secondary School'.[1] Sons of tribal leaders were thus given special treatment for entry to elementary, intermediate, and secondary schools. At every level, places were reserved for them and they were admitted even if they did not qualify for entry.[2]

To meet the growing demand for girls' education, and in order to bridge the gap between boys' and girls' education referred to in the De La Warr report, the plan provided for expansion in elementary education for girls and, for the first time, an intermediate school for girls was provided in Omdurman. By 1941 it was recognized that this fell short of the demand and a revision was recommended by a meeting held in the Department of Education in March 1941.

Expansion of intermediate education for boys did not receive the same encouragement as that received by elementary education for boys, because of the controversy over its advantages and its soundness. The argument which started in 1936, when E. N. Corbyn, then Director of Education, suggested the institution of a six-year intermediate school, was not resolved by either the Winter Committee or the De La Warr Commission. The latter proposal did not go beyond recommending an improvement of the system. Although the 1938-46 plan suggested the implementation of the Corbyn proposal of establishing, at selected centres, six-year intermediate schools, with a vocational bias in the last two years, this was never carried out, owing to the difficulties of recruiting British teachers who would act as advisers to Sudanese headmasters in the proposed schools. Opinion in the Department of Education was divided on this issue, and although the general feeling was that there was something wrong in the existing system, the critics were not confident that the answer lay in the Corbyn proposal. Intermediate education was therefore allowed to drift on. The number of schools grew from eleven with 937 pupils in 1934 to thirteen schools with 2,027 pupils in 1946.

This relative growth in elementary and intermediate education had enabled Bakht er Ruda to concentrate on the reform work already embarked upon in 1934. The 1938-46 plan rejected the proposal for the creation of Bakht er Rudas in other provinces, on the grounds that it would be expensive and that reform work was not completed. A dispersal of effort would hinder reform work rather than accelerate it. The question of transferring the Teachers' Training College to another site was, however, given serious consideration in 1938. A number of places such as Shendi in the northern province,

[1] Ibid.   [2] *SGA/DAKHLIA/17/6/File 17.D.6.4.*

Gala al-nahal in Kassala province, Kosti and Kawa in the White Nile province, Tendelti, Rahad, Bara, and Tegali in Kordufan province, and Rufaa, Kamlin, Wadelhadad, Masid, Nuba, and Karkoj in the Blue Nile province were suggested as possible sites. The Gezira region, in the Blue Nile province, was excluded on political grounds. It was objected to because the Gezira had always been looked upon as providing a sphere for the propagandist. The introduction of students and teachers of such an institute would introduce subversive ideas and disseminate discontent among the tenants. As most students at one time or another in their careers would tend to be very liberal-minded, they would use their ideas and qualifications to spread doctrines which would cause harm to the scheme. The bad points in the scheme would be exploited by the teachers, and spread among the students. The introduction of an intelligentsia in the Gezira would accelerate the throwing of the scheme more and more into the political limelight, create new political focal points in the area, and influence the future farmers.[1]

Movement to other places which did not present political dangers was rejected on the grounds of cost, and the Teachers' Training college, after a period of uncertainty, finally remained in Bakht er Ruda, while the reform work of the elementary school subjects continued, and two new tasks were added in 1939 to its original aims. Up to then nothing had been done on the intermediate school reforms. A conference was held to study the problem and in 1940 Bakht er Ruda started a refresher course for schoolmasters. In 1941 it took over the responsibility for training the graduates from the higher schools. But the achievements here were slow compared to those in elementary education.

The second task was community development through adult education and character training. What was new about adult education in Sudanese society was its methods and not its aims. The study of religious subjects by adults in the study circles was part of the traditional system represented by the *khalwa* and the mosque. Literacy classes for adults were often organized on a voluntary basis by schoolmasters. The educational policy did not, however, recognize adult education and community development as a legitimate area of

---

[1] Letter from Bredin, G. R. F., to Governor Blue Nile Province, 30 July 1938. Letter from Hillard, A. J., to Governor Blue Nile Province, 30 June 1938; Letter from Governor Blue Nile Province to Director of Education, 1 November 1938, *SGA/Blue Nile/1/15 File SCR/17.O.6.*

activity because of the doubts as to the feasibility and effectiveness
of community education. It was generally regarded 'with a certain
amount of suspicion as carrying the taint of impracticable idealism'.[1]
But under the influence of the Advisory Committee on Education in
the Colonies, and the recommendations of the De La Warr report,
this attitude began to change.

In 1935 the Advisory Committee published its second important
Memorandum on 'The Education of African Communities'.[2] This
was a landmark in colonial educational policy in the same way as
the 1925 Memorandum was. It drew attention to the growing diversification of needs between urban and rural communities. The paper
emphasized the principle that education was one of a number of
social institutions concerned with social, economic, and political
betterment, and should, therefore, be directed towards the whole
community. The whole community must therefore move forward
educationally, otherwise there would be the danger of any one section
of the community lagging behind another. Adult education was
therefore a legitimate activity for education departments working in
close co-operation with other departments. The De La Warr report
emphasized the need 'to direct into beneficial channels the movement
set up by the impact of western ideas upon the life of northern Moslem
Sudanese'.[3] It was realized that if education was to be an instrument
of change this could only be effective if 'it could be carried forward
into manhood. For this to happen some kind of educational influence
would have to be exerted on the ex-schoolboy through the period of
adolescence and the outlook of his parents might also have to be
made more flexible.'[4] Traditional values and standards were being
disturbed and there was a need for a much broader understanding by
the individual of his own position as a citizen.[5]

The 1938-46 plan proposed the development of adult education
and M. F. A. Keen was appointed Adult Education Officer.[6]
Experiments in adult education were launched by Bakht er Ruda in
1944. These included a boys' club, a publication bureau, a children's
magazine and the Um Gerr project.

[1] *SGA/DAKHLIA/17/5 File 17/B/8/*.
[2] Advisory Committee on Education in the Colonies, *Memorandum on the
Education of African Communities*, Colonial No. *103*, H.M.S.O., London 1935.
[3] De La Warr Report, p. 6.
[4] Griffiths, V. L., *An Experiment in Education*, p. 135.
[5] Abbas, M., Interim Report on Um Gerr Experiment. *EDA*.
[6] *SGA/GENCO/3/42*. Also *SGA/DAKHLIA/17/5/File 17.B.8.*

The development of community and adult education was not always welcomed by the educated Sudanese. They suspected that it was a policy calculated to slow down educational progress. Having had a scholastic education themselves, they believed that policy should give priority to expansion in school education, because it was through such an education that an élite, able to take over the functions of government, would be produced. The limited resources should be spent on the education of this élite, and not on adult or mass education. Even when resources were available, preference should be given to the education of children in schools, rather than to the education of adults.

Concern with character training began in 1938 in Bakht er Ruda. V. L. Griffiths held that the educational system in the Sudan had failed to contribute to the character training of the Sudanese. This failure manifested itself, according to him, in the large proportion of educated Sudanese who retained traits of character more suited to tribal life than to modern society, such as 'quickness to suspect infringement of their personal honour',[1] and lack of initiative and adaptability. The majority 'did not realize the importance of certain qualities for posts of responsibility or the greater need for tolerance and co-operation in modern life'.[2] Action was therefore needed both inside and outside the school to instil qualities of self-discipline, tolerance, initiative, reliability, habits of observation, care of property, objectivity, and self-criticism. Inside the schools, the British staff of the education department were urged to study Sudanese ideals of character training, by reading and finding out about Islam, Arab ideals, and way of life, and to beware of the objectives and difficulties of character training. Sudanese teachers were taught to realize the importance of these qualities for their work and social life. Games, handwork, gardening, project-type lessons, camps, and school societies were introduced as part of the school curriculum. Youth clubs and a Translation and Publication Bureau as forms of adult education were established outside the school, and encouraged the development of certain character qualities.

These developments, especially those concerned with school societies, training in citizenship, and self-government in schools,

[1] Griffiths, V. L., Note on the British Contribution to Character Training in Sudan Education, also Letter from Director of Education to all British Officials in the Education Department, 15 November 1941. *EDA*.
[2] Ibid.

resulted in the development among the student class of an active attitude of mind, critical of both administration and society. Such an attitude was not always welcomed by the British and Sudanese traditionalists. The first saw it as a destructive attitude breeding anti-government concepts.

The Um Gerr experiment, which aimed at stimulating the interest of the cultivator, made the latter more restless and unwilling to do what he used to do, and this made the adult educator and his work unpopular with the agricultural authorities.[1] The Sudanese traditionalists, seeing that the policy was encouraging an attitude of mind which questioned the basic beliefs and assumptions of society, held it to be anti-religious and 'anti' the accepted modes of behaviour.[2] These controversies were proof that the reform in methods and aims started in Bakht er Ruda was having its impact on society.

The 1938–46 plan did not envisage expansion in numbers admitted to secondary education on the grounds that it would be unwise to precipitately reverse the considered policy of the government in order to regulate admission to secondary education by means of the estimated absorption capacity of the country.

Instead, the plan proposed, in accordance with the De La Warr Commission's recommendations, to transfer the Gordon College to a new site where full secondary education with no vocational training would be followed. The transfer to another site, like that of the Elementary Teachers' Training College, was dictated by considerations other than that of utilizing the buildings for higher education. Khartoum was thought to be an un-Sudanese town, and there was need to bring up the secondary school boy in a Sudanese atmosphere. Khartoum was unsuitable for the development of agricultural education and out-of-class activities. The town life attracted the students to unhealthy practices. In 1937, 6 per cent of the total of college students suffered from gonorrhoea, and it was desirable to bring them up in an environment 'where prostitutes were not available and where it was practicable to sublimate their sexual instincts by healthy occupations'.[3] The transfer, it was argued, would help to bridge the gulf between the educated classes of the towns and the

[1] Personal information from V. L. Griffiths.

[2] Letter from Director of Education to Civil Secretary, 10 January 1942. *EDA/File DE/9.1.1.9.*

[3] Note by Gordon Memorial College Warden on moving the secondary school out of Khartoum, Appendix C to the 1938–46 Educational Plan, *SGA/GENCO/ 3/42.*

majority who lived in the countryside, and would help to educate the rural population and broaden the outlook of the educated townsmen. From a political point of view, the boys in Khartoum were continuously exposed 'to the harmful propaganda and agitation against the government by the educated class, which had urged them to strike in 1932 and might very well urge them again'.[1]

There were arguments against the proposed transfer. First, it was expensive. Secondly, teachers would lose the benefits of contact with other professions. Many Sudanese teachers were against the transfer because, by being away from Khartoum, they would lose their role in the social and political life of the country. Other Sudanese suspected that the aim was to keep them down by making them associate with the backward areas and not with the progressive towns.

But the decision was finally taken to transfer the school to a place outside Khartoum. The entry of Italy into the war in 1940, however, led to the postponement of the transfer. The Gordon College buildings and the new buildings, completed in 1939 at Wadi Siednna, where the secondary school was destined to go, were taken over by the army. The college was transferred during the war years to Omdurman. The efficiency and unity of the college were difficult to maintain during these years. Many boys lived with relatives, and attended the college as day boys, and books and equipment were difficult to obtain. British staff were depleted, owing to the release of some of them to wartime duty. Sudanese were provided to fill their places and by 1941 most tutors were Sudanese.

It was not until 1946 that conditions returned to normal. The secondary school was transferred to Wadi Siednna and a new one established at Hantoub.

The college began to shed its vocational courses in 1936, and in 1937 it was decided to link its courses with the Cambridge School Certificate courses, thus enabling its students to take an internationally recognized examination, and to prepare them for a higher standard of entry into the high schools.

The number of students grew from 384 in 1934 to 528 in 1946.[2] Fifty per cent in 1944 were sons of government officials and army officers.[3] The second generation of educated Sudanese was already in existence there.

In 1936 G. C. Scott was appointed Warden of the Gordon Memorial

[1] Ibid.
[2] Appendix I, Table vi.   [3] Ibid., Table vii.

College, and new ideas and policies were initiated. Scott held that the main fault of education in the college was its premature teaching of skills which were considered appropriate for the lower branches of government service.[1] This fault was due, in addition to the verbal and formal tendencies of traditional education, to the influences of uneducated homes, the lack of research in the content and method of education suitable to the Sudanese, and the failure to recognize and apply, after adaptation, those methods and contents of education which had proved successful in the schools of England and other countries.[2] The result of this was that the system had produced men who were only interested in the salaries to be received, but who were 'inadequately equipped with real knowledge, and weak in the power of creative imagination, accurate observation and sound thinking'.[3] He argued that some of them lost their old religious convictions but failed 'to find instead any sound ethical rule of life whether based on a religious or some other foundations'.[4] Scott's new policy was to develop the creative mental power of the students; to provide knowledge which could be used, when they left the college, as a basis for further learning and which would help them in earning their living; to make good citizens of them and to 'provide for them some substitute for the no longer acceptable beliefs and sanctions of a primitive community'.[5] Civic lessons were introduced in 1937 to train the students to become good citizens.[6]

It was in the area of discipline that a radical change was made. Discipline through fear of flogging was the accepted method until then. This was replaced by a discipline based on respect for the rights of others, for the welfare of the community, and for oneself.[7] These changes in the aims and methods of secondary education were not always applied with ease or success.

By 1942 the result of the changes, especially the aspect concerned with creating a critical mind and attitude, was so obvious and alarming to the traditionalists that Scott had to defend the policy in a public lecture in the Sudan Cultural Centre. The development of nationalism and the ideas disseminated by the Second World War

[1] Letter from G. C. Scott to Members of the Gordon College staff, 1937. Personal communication from G. C. Scott.
[2] Ibid.   [3] Ibid.   [4] Ibid.   [5] Ibid.
[7] G.M.C.R., 1938, p. 24.
[6] Letter from Scott to members of Gordon Memorial College, 3 August 1938. Also lecture to the Sudan Cultural Centre, October 1942. Personal communication from G. C. Scott.

aroused keen interest in politics. The new educational methods encouraged this interest further, to the alarm of many British administrators. In Scott's lecture at the Cultural Centre, in 1942, the students' right to discuss political problems was defended as a healthy sign, the prohibition of which would defeat the aims of the new educational policy in the secondary school.[1]

The development of higher education urged in the De La Warr report received the approval of the Governor-General's Council, and in 1939 the schools of agriculture and veterinary science admitted their first students. The schools of engineering and science were also started in 1939. The school of arts, with courses for Arabic teachers, general teachers, and administrators, was started in 1940. During 1938-41 130 students, not all with school certificates, were admitted to the higher school. The entry into these schools was regulated by the needs of the various government departments. The primary function of the schools was seen to be the training for careers in government because the demands of future employment were constantly studied and kept in mind.[2] The number of students in the higher schools grew from 148 in 1942 to 163 in 1944.

The higher schools granted diplomas, which were roughly equivalent to a pass degree in an English university, or to the corresponding English professional examination. A final certificate of a lower standard than the diploma was also granted by the schools of science and arts. The schools were staffed almost entirely by members of the Sudan Government Service, seconded for either whole-time or part-time lecturing. A few lecturers were seconded from the Egyptian Government Service or employed on contract.

Until 1943, the schools were under five different departments of the government. The schools of arts, science, and engineering were under the department of education. The school of agriculture under the department of agriculture, and the school of veterinary science under the veterinary department.

A degree of unification was, however, obtained by the appointment of the Higher Schools Advisory Committee. The committee consisted of the Director of Education, the Civil Secretary, the Financial Secretary, the Legal Secretary, the Director of the Sudan Medical

[1] Scott, G. C., ibid.
[2] Progress Report on Higher Schools submitted by the Director of Education to Governor-General's Council Meeting on 5 September 1942, *SGA/GENCO/3/49.*

Service, and the Director of Agriculture. Each school had a board
of studies to advise on academic matters. A Board of Principals of
Schools, under the chairmanship of the Director of Education,
correlated the work of the various boards of studies. In 1944, the
Council of the Gordon Memorial College was constituted, and the
new Gordon Memorial College, embracing all higher schools, except
the Kitchener School of Medicine, came into being on 1 January
1945. The new college was officially inaugurated in February 1945.
Dr. J. D. Tothill, Director of Agriculture, became the first principal
of the college, assisted by G. C. Scott, who had left the old Gordon
Memorial College in 1942 to assist in the development and creation
of the new Gordon Memorial College, the forerunner of the
University College.

At its first meeting on 15 November 1944, the Gordon College
Council defined the functions of the college as teaching and research.
On the teaching side, it was stated that 'the students should acquire
not only a high standard of academic and professional knowledge,
but also those qualities of mind and character which are necessary
for good citizenship and professional competence'.[1] Another function
of the college was to encourage the advancement of education outside
its walls, and the development of extra-mural work. The rapid
development in higher education in spite of the difficulties of the
war years, the shortage of staff and equipment, and the inadequate
academic standard of the only two secondary schools in the country,
was urged on by the internal developments in the Sudan, and the
new attitude in Britain towards developing university education in
Africa.

The Sudan Government was realizing the urgency of training,
fairly quickly, adequate numbers of students for senior government
posts. The pressure of Sudanese nationalism and their desire for
political freedom made it necessary that educational development
should be brought up to the level at which its product could 'be
expected to cope with the multitudinous problems of good citizenship
and good government'.[2] Delay and hesitation would have endangered
the plans for self-government and encouraged the Sudanese to seek
education in Egypt's schools and university.

Since 1943, the question of the development of higher education in

    [1] Minutes of the Gordon Memorial College Council Meeting on 15 November
1944, *UKA*.
    [2] Letter from Tothill, J. D., to Christopher Cox, 29 October 1945, *UKA*.

Britain's overseas territories had occupied the attention of the Advisory Committee on Education in the Colonies. Professor Channon, Professor of Biochemistry at Liverpool University and member of the committee, presented a memorandum on Higher Education in the Colonies. As a result of this memorandum, the Advisory Committee recommended that a body should be constituted to advise the Secretary of State on the means whereby the universities in Britain could best assist. A sub-committee of the Advisory Committee presented a report which dealt with the problems and needs of higher education in the colonies. This and the Channon report argued the case from political and economic points of view. The slow development of higher education in Africa was caused by the limited financial resources, the absence of education for the majority of children, the small opportunities for secondary education, and the lack of men in the Colonial Service with personal experience of higher education and its development. Colonial administrators were, according to the sub-committee, concerned with the possible political and economic dangers of producing university men who had received a liberal education. They were concerned lest a situation like that of India would arise, and the numbers receiving university education were therefore limited to the number of posts available. Vocational training and not liberal university education was emphasized by the colonial administrations in Africa.

During the Second World War new factors were introduced into the situation. The British Government emphasized that the guiding principle of its colonial policy was that the colonies should become self-governing. These public pronouncements, together with the expectation that they would be rewarded for their war contributions and sacrifices, led the colonial peoples to expect help from Britain in their development. Higher education was an obvious need and a necessary step if self-government was to be achieved. From the political point of view, it was argued, a new policy which encouraged higher education would be of great value to the Empire as a whole in giving a new purpose to the concept of the British Commonwealth. There were political dangers in sending undergraduates to Britain where they might develop radical attitudes. The alternative system of external degrees was not suitable for the conditions in these countries.[1]

These were new attitudes which influenced colonial educational

[1] Report on Higher Education in the Colonies, *UKA/File GMC/14.*

policies, especially with regard to higher education in Africa and the Sudan.

When the Asquith Commission was set up on 18 August 1943 to inquire into the development of higher education in the colonies, the Sudan Government received official notification from the Colonial Office that the commission would be prepared to include the Sudan in its inquiries. The Sudan Government had realized from the start that the full success of its plans depended on the outcome of the Asquith Commission.[1] Professor Channon, Professor Duff and Mr. B. Muat-Jones, three members of the Asquith Commission, were invited to visit the Sudan, and advise on the future of higher education. Mr. B. Muat-Jones advised on technical education and the future development of the schools of science and engineering.

The Asquith Commission report in 1945, like the De La Warr report, gave further necessary guidance and inspiration to the Sudan Government in developing higher education. As the main problem was financial, aid was sought from the British Government. An endowment of £1,000,000 was suggested in October 1945 as an appropriate sum which would enable the plans to be carried out, and which would secure the necessary financial independence.[2]

In December 1945 the college council decided to apply to the Senate of London University for admission of the college to the scheme formulated on the advice of the Asquith Commission. The scheme of special relationship made it possible for the students to enter for the London degrees with special conditions and syllabuses adapted to the circumstances in the Sudan. In 1947 the first students were entered for the London Special Relation degrees.

Thus by the end of 1945 the ground was prepared for the next stage in the development of the Gordon Memorial College, that of a University College. Higher and secondary education entered a new phase as from 1946.

Education in the south did not, in the meantime, undergo fundamental changes, either in quantity, quality, or policy. The 1938-46 educational plan emphasized consolidation and reorganization, rather than expansion or fundamental changes. Education was to continue under missionary control, and the limited participation by the government was advocated, not on grounds of desirability, but

[1] Minutes of the thirteenth meeting of Higher Schools Advisory Committee January 1944, *UKA*.
[2] Letter from Tothill, J. D., to Christopher Cox, 29 October 1945, *UKA*.

as an experiment in areas where the missions had failed to establish schools, such as in the Dinka area, and as an answer to the critics of the missionary system who urged that no such experiment had yet been made. The plan provided for an addition of only two elementary schools for boys between 1936 and 1944. No increase in the number of girls' schools or village schools was contemplated. It was suggested that the system should be reorganized by establishing elementary and intermediate schools, with a six-year course for each; a system similar to that in Uganda. The village schools, which were the only means of reaching the vast majority of the population educationally, were to be integrated into the system. Since the missions were to retain their control, the plan proposed the strengthening of missionary personnel by encouraging the employment of trained educationalists and the training of native teachers through increased subsidies and grants.

In the following years these proposals were the subject of discussion between the Director of Education and the various missionaries. The need for co-operation between government and different missions in the educational field was essential for the implementation of the plan. The three aspects which received particular attention were the grants-in-aid, girls' education, and the language problem. The financial difficulties faced by the missionaries during the war years necessitated an increase in the subsidies, and accordingly the grants-in-aid increased from £E9,155 in 1937 to £E26,650 in 1946.[1]

Girls' education was the subject of an commission appointed by the Sudan Government and the Church Missionary Society in March 1939. The Commission consisted of Miss N. E. Ainley and Mrs. M. C. Warburton. Its terms of reference were: 'to examine and report upon the possibilities for development of the education of girls in the area occupied by the Church Missionary Society in the Southern Sudan, and to make recommendations as to future policy'.[2] The report stated that although there was a keen desire for women's education on the part of missionaries because of its importance in building up a Christian community, and the important role played by women in the life of southern Sudanese, there were difficulties in providing education for women. Some tribes had their prejudices. In the Azande tribe, for example, it was contrary to custom for

---

[1] Appendix I, Table x.
[2] Ainley, N. E. and Warburton, M. C., Report on Women's Education in the Southern Sudan, 1939, *EDA*.

B E D

women and girls to attend schools taught by male teachers. The
Azande were also opposed to anything in the form of co-education.
The Moru tribe objected to girls attending schools taught by males
and were also against co-education, and classes had to be held at
different times for boys and girls. The Dinka did not object to co-
education, but their nomadic life made it impossible for boys and
girls to settle in one place for any length of time, to make schooling
possible. The missionaries had their prejudices too. The majority did
not favour co-education. The lack of trained women teachers and
the lack of continuity, due to a lack of European missionary teachers
able to give the girls' schools their undivided attention, were major
factors in the backwardness of girls' education.[1]

After a review of the educational facilities and difficulties, the
report recommended that education for girls should be in the closest
possible relationship with actual life, and therefore, besides the three
R's and religious instruction, the schools should teach hygiene,
agriculture, and care of animals, nature study, arts and handicrafts.
The report emphasized the need to appoint European women
teachers and the training of southern Sudanese women teachers on
a salaried basis.[2]

But this educational policy, which emphasized reorganization and
consolidation of elementary and village schools, was hampered by
the language problem. The adoption of a group language instead of
the local vernacular meant that in certain areas boys and girls were
to be taught in a language as foreign to them as Arabic or English.[3]
The alternative, that of teaching and producing literature in all the
different languages, was impossible to implement. There was no
answer to the problem except that more emphasis should be laid on
English, which was being taught from the elementary level. The
Governor-General's Council agreed in 1943 to pay an allowance to
members of the army and police force for literacy in English, in order
to encourage the adult learning of English.[4]

Thus the growth of education in the south compared to the north
was slow during this period.[5]

The Roman Catholic Verona Fathers achieved during this period

[1] Ibid., pp. 8–9.
[2] Ibid.
[3] Letter from Resident Inspector, Southern Education, to Director of Education, 3 February 1941, *EDA/File DE/SCR/1.1.17.*
[4] *EDA/File DE/SCR/1.1.17.*
[5] Appendix I, Table xi.

a greater increase in schools at all levels of education compared to other missions, in spite of the difficulties brought on by the war. The only two teachers' training centres for village schools were established by them in Equatoria in 1946.

The government participation proposed in 1938 did not materialize until 1944, when a village school was established in Tong in Bahr al Ghazal for the Dinka, and a central school established at Abwong in the Upper Nile province. In addition to these the only other government institution was the post-intermediate training centre started in Juba in 1942 for the training of medical assistants, sanitary overseers, laboratory assistants, agricultural assistants, clerks, and accountants. The duration of the course was two years, except for medical assistants, whose course lasted three years. The output of the centre during 1942–4 was as follows:

	1942	1943	1944
Clerks and accountants	9	9	9
Medical assistants	12	—	7
Sanitary overseers	2	I	—
Laboratory assistants	—	I	—
Agricultural assistants	2	—	5

These limited facilities for training and the slow progress of education resulted in a slow development of southernization of the government service. The position during 1938–44 was as follows:[1]

	1938	1941	1944
I *Clerical staff:*			
(a) Total number of staff employed by government departments in southern Sudan	159	198	267
(b) Number of southerners employed by government departments	100	81	136
(c) (b) as percentage of (a)	63	41	51
II *Technical staff:*			
(a) Total number of staff employed by government departments in southern Sudan	228	916	809
(b) Number of southerners employed by government departments	106	405	369
(c) (b) as percentage of (a)	46·5	44	45

[1] Despatch from the Governor-General to His Britannic Majesty's Ambassador in Cairo No. 89, 4 August 1945, *EDA/File DE/SCR/1.1.17.*

The 1938–46 educational plan did not bring radical changes in southern Sudan. It laid the foundations for future changes by its insistence on consolidation and reorganization. The two parts of the country remained separated by two different educational systems with different aims, arising from different administrative and political plans. The unification of the two systems and their coming nearer to each other had to wait for a change in these policies.

CHAPTER X

Nationalism, Politics and Education, 1936–1946

THE LESS reactionary attitude towards the educated class, and the more liberal attitude towards education after 1934, encouraged the growth of Sudanese nationalism. More educational facilities meant more educated Sudanese. More liberalism meant more vocal and public criticism of government policies by members of this class. Problems of education received more attention than other problems because of the belief that education was the key to progress, whether for individuals or for the nation. An article in *Al Fajr*, the literary and political magazine founded in 1934, criticized the contents of education and the new policy which aimed at ruralization and the production of government officials only. It urged the government 'to revise the aims and contents of education in the Gordon Memorial College with a view to promote it to a proper secondary school similar to those in England'.[1]

Another article with the title, 'Give us Education',[2] criticized the government for the reduction of the intake at the Gordon Memorial College, especially, as from 1932, for altering the curriculum by limiting it to a short study of commerce and business correspondence, and for discontinuing the practice of sending selected teachers to the American University in Beirut. The article urged that what was needed was an increase in the number of students in the Gordon Memorial College and the development of the curriculum, 'to prepare the students for University education and at the same time to be sufficient in itself as a last resort. The Comboni and Coptic secondary schools should be open for Sudanese as well as other communities. The missions to Beirut University should be continued and, if possible, must not be limited to teachers only.'[3] The establishment of schools of law, agriculture, and engineering was seen as essential for the future of the country and the creation of more opportunities for Sudanese in the administration of their country. The article concluded:

[1] Mahjob, M. A., 'Fi al Talim', *Al Fajr*, i, no. 11 (November 1934), 471–7.
[2] *Al Fajr*, i, no. 22 (16 June 1935), 1065–6.   [3] Ibid.

The government has embarked on giving us education, but does not seem to aim at any further steps. The danger in this lies in the fact that once education is started in a country it must be continued and developed, failing this, the people will cry out and ask for more education, because it becomes to them as essential as food, water and light. Mr. J. H. Oldham, as quoted by Professor Julian Huxley in his book *African View*, says that the fundamental business of governments in Africa is education. Our government is surely in favour of such an opinion, and would not fail to carry out its fundamental business: 'Give us education and leave us alone' is our slogan.[1]

The rise and growth of a sense of nationalism reflected itself in the organization of a Debating Club, a Social Service Club, a Dramatic Society, and a College Magazine by the Gordon College students. The Sudan Schools Graduates' Club in Omdurman became an active centre for literary and social activities, and discussion groups. The educated came to look upon themselves as 'the living articulated portion of Young Sudan'[2] aspiring to acquire 'the necessary qualifications for self-government'.[3] To them native administration was a form of government 'based on tribal prejudice and religious aristocracy'[4] and 'liable to be a failure so long as it is in the hands of the ignorant'.[5] Tribalism and illiteracy were seen to be the main enemies of progress[6] and because of this the question of education was high on the list of activities of the Graduates Congress formed in February 1938.

Problems of education were the most discussed problems, and by concerning itself with this problem it was reflecting not only the public demand for more education but also the public's fear of a growth in missionary education. Public demand was reflected in the growth of non-government education. The number of non-government elementary schools for boys and girls grew from two in 1932 to seven in 1935. The Ahfad School was transferred from Rufaa to Omdurman in 1932, and an intermediate section was added in 1933. The number of pupils in the Ahfad School grew from 200 in 1933 to 450 in 1939. The number of boys in the Omdurman Ahlia School grew from 120 boys in 1935 to 193 in 1938.

The number of missionary schools, and Sudanese boys and girls attending them, in northern Sudan grew during this period as follows:[7]

---

[1] Ibid.   [2] *Al Fajr*, i, no. 21 (1 June 1935), 1018–19.
[3] Ibid.   [4] Ibid.   [5] Ibid.
[6] *Al Fajr*, i, no. 12 (16 November 1934), 535–7; i, no. 15 (1 January 1935), 659–64.   [7] *E.D.R. 1935–6, 1937, 1938*.

	1935	1936	1937	1938
(a) Number of Roman Catholic schools	4	5	5	5
(b) Number of Sudanese boys and girls in (a)	?	65	77	134
(c) Number of American Mission schools	3	3	3	3
(d) Number of boys and girls in (c)	265	304	364	401
(e) Number of Church Missionary Society schools	10	13	13	13
(f) Number of Sudanese boys and girls in (e)	425	524	603	634

Although these schools met a growing demand for education, there was an uneasy feeling about them. The policy of the American Mission, which had schools in 1938 in Omdurman, Khartoum, and Geraif, with 401 Sudanese boys and girls, was to refuse to admit pupils whose parents objected to religious instruction.[1] It was reported in 1931 that a Sudanese girl attending Khartoum North American Missionary School was converted to Christianity. Although it was found that both father and mother were Ethiopian Christians converted to Islam, the incident was publicized and exploited by the graduates, and later by the Graduates Congress, to urge the establishment of national schools as an alternative to missionary education.

These demands and fears were expressed in a Note on Education addressed to the Sudan Government. Work on the Note started in April 1938, two months after the foundation of the congress. A committee consisting of leading members of the congress was instructed to examine the educational system, with a view to making recommendations to the government. Among the members of the committee were Ahmed Mohamed Salih, Mohamed Osman Mirghani, Mirghani Hamza, Mohamed Salih Al Shingetti, and Abdul Majid Ahmed, all graduates of the Gordon College.[2] The visit of the De La Warr Commission and the publication of its report added further impetus to the importance of the committee's work. The congress's views on education were not, however, submitted until July 1939. The congress expressed 'gratitude to the Government for accepting

[1] Note on American Missionaries' Attitude to Religious Instruction, *MIA/File CS/SCR/46.A.2.*
[2] Personal information from Mirghani Hamza and Mohamed Salih Al Shingetti.

all the proposals for educational expansion contained in the 1938–46 plan'.[1]

The Graduates Congress was also 'indebted to Mr. C. W. M. Cox, the Director of Education, for his great and untiring efforts in the work of reform and expansion of education since his arrival in the country'.[2] The Note supported the government policy of the reorganization of the Gordon College and raising its standard, of establishing another secondary school, and of expanding girls' education. It described the educational conditions in the south as disgraceful. The congress wished it to be known that 'it did not in any way underestimate the contribution which the missions had made to education in the South'.[3]

The Note argued that unless elementary education was made available for all or most of the boys in the Sudan, no progress could be achieved. The role of education in southern provinces was viewed as the only instrument through which the population would be taught the value of money and thereby achieve progress.[4]

It suggested that education should be oriented towards the Arab and Islamic, but not African, culture, because the Sudan had much in common with 'the Arabic countries of Islamic Orient'.[5] The improvement of education in the south could not be achieved through a missionary system subsidized by the government, but through the opening of government schools, similar to those in the north, and where the Arabic language would provide the *lingua franca*. One way of improving education in the south, the Note suggested, was to open it unconditionally to the northerners.[6] It also suggested that the policy of gearing education to employment should be rejected in favour of a policy which would aim at the complete removal of illiteracy, at expansion and improvement of all stages of education, at the maintenance of a higher standard and at creating the spiritual happiness of the individual and the community.[7]

In addition to these general principles and recommendations, the following proposals were made:

(a) The reduction of the age of entrance into the elementary school to six years for boys and five years for girls.[8]

[1] Note by the Graduates Congress on Education in the Sudan, July 1939 (typescript), University of Khartoum Library, Appendix V.
[2] Ibid.
[3] Ibid.   [4] Ibid.
[5] Ibid.   [6] Ibid.
[7] Ibid.   [8] Ibid.

(b) The reform of the curriculum so as to raise the standard at all levels and overlap in syllabuses.[1]

(c) The institution of practical training in the elementary and intermediate schools with a view to preparing the school-leavers who did not proceed to higher levels of education for work.[2]

(d) The provision of courses abroad for the training of secondary school teachers.[3]

(e) The formation of advisory councils for the secondary schools and the University College, in which Sudanese would be represented 'in order to advise on matters relating to the work of the welfare of the schools'.[4] The representatives, the Note stated, should be from among the educated and 'not from the so-called notables as is done in other countries'.[5]

One other educational problem which had received the Congress's particular attention since its establishment, was the problem of the Omdurman *Mahad Ilmi*. As Sudanese nationalism was closely connected with the Pan-Islamic and Arab Nationalist movement, the development of Islamic and Arabic culture was one of the aims which it tried to achieve. Because of the support the *Ulama* had among the population, it would promote the aims of the congress if their support could be obtained. Thus both principle and self-interest urged the congress to pay special attention to the problem of religious education in general, and to the *Mahad* in particular. The *Mahad* had, during its life of thirty-nine years, grown from a mosque school comparable in nature with mosque schools in the provinces into an institution of considerable size, supported by a substantial contribution from the government amounting to more than half the total grant-in-aid to all the mosques in the Sudan. It was becoming increasingly clear that, although it was still the Omdurman mosque, it had, in the public estimation, achieved more than a purely local status, and was regarded as the central religious institution *par excellence* for the whole country. The number of its students increased to 787 in 1935, of whom only 37 per cent came from Khartoum province. The rest of the students faced problems of living and accommodation. Its teachings were governed by conservatism and the educated were critical about this aspect of education, which did not qualify its graduates for an active and positive contribution to the life of the country. The standard of education did not rise to the

[1] Ibid.   [2] Ibid.   [3] Ibid.
[4] Ibid.   [5] Ibid.

level of that of Al Azhar, nor did it inspire that religious reform and
liberalism which the educated class wanted to see as an ally in their
efforts to spread national feeling.

The congress's memorandum on the Omdurman *Mahad Ilmi*
reflected these problems and aspirations. The government was asked
to increase its subsidy substantially so as to provide for teaching of
secular subjects, Azhar-trained principal and teachers, the reform of
the primary and secondary stages of the curriculum, a graduation
certificate equivalent to that of Al Azhar, a hostel for students, and
the constitution of a governing body which would advise and
administer its work. The memorandum further suggested that if the
Sudan Government was unable to meet these demands, an appeal
should be made to Al Azhar in Cairo to take over its management
and financing.[1]

These same demands were made in two letters, one by pensioners,
merchants, and notables of Khartoum and Omdurman, and the other
by twenty *Ulama*.[2]

Since the government had, from the beginning, welcomed the
congress's aim of contributing its services to the country, and engaging
in philanthropic activity, and assured it that its communications
would receive careful consideration as a contribution to the development of the country by progressive elements,[3] both notes were
welcomed and viewed as constructive suggestions. Most of the
proposals contained in the memorandum on the *Mahad* were
accepted.[4] It was decided to reorganize its administration by con-
stituting a council to control finances and appoint teachers, to improve
the teaching staff by seconding Azhar graduates, and to increase the
government subsidies. The proposals for affiliation to Al Azhar and
the establishment of hostels were rejected.[5] Certain proposals on
education had already been implemented or agreed to in principle
since the De La Warr report and the educational plan for 1938-46.
Proposals which were in direct conflict with government policy, such
as those on southern education and expansion of intermediate schools,
were rejected. But the value of the memorandum was in providing the

[1] Graduates Congress, Memorandum on Omdurman Mahad Ilmi, 20 April
1939, *SGA/File LS/SC/11.4*.
[2] Petition on Omdurman Mahad Ilmi, 26 April 1939, *SGA/File LS/SC/11.4*.
[3] Letter from Civil Secretary to the Graduates Congress, 22 May 1938,
SGA.
[4] Henderson, K. D. D., *The Making of the Modern Sudan*, p. 537.
[5] Note by Legal Secretary, 21 May 1939, *SGA/File CS/SC/11.4*.

government with a comprehensive view of the Sudanese intelligentsia on the educational system.

Congress interest in educational problems did not weaken, in spite of its involvement in politics after 1941. The congress's political memorandum of 1942 did not concern itself with the political issues only, but also with education. Of the twelve points made, two were directly concerned with education. These were:[1]

(a) the formation of a Higher Educational Council composed of a Sudanese majority, and the allocation of 12 per cent of the budget to education.

(b) the cancellation of subventions to missionary schools, and the unification of educational syllabuses in northern and southern Sudan.

Other demands relating to giving priority to Sudanese in government jobs and the reservation of a reasonable proportion of posts in companies and commercial houses for them were, in fact, demands for more educational facilities and more training opportunities.

The Graduates Congress activity was not limited to the sending of memoranda expressings its views. In 1939, its members gave active support and participated in the collection of funds to establish the Omdurman Piastre Orphanage. The suggestion came originally from Abdul Fatah Al Maghrabi, a member of the congress and a teacher in the Gordon College, in a series of articles. The aim was to establish a workshop and a hostel for orphans, where they would be given technical instruction. The success of this project, and the support which it received, encouraged the congress to institute in 1941 an Education Day, whereby voluntary contributions would be made by the citizens to establish national schools. The object was to focus the public's interest on the development of education.[2] Every year a certain day was designated to collect funds for a congress Central Educational Fund from which schools would be helped, and nation-wide support was mobilized for the projects. At the beginning it was the object of the congress to co-operate with the government in helping to establish schools where it was agreed that a demand existed, and to open local *khalwas* or congress *kuttabs* staffed by graduates of Omdurman *Mahad Ilmi* and to which a certain amount of the Education Day Fund would be contributed.[3] This attitude

[1] Henderson, K. D. D., *The Making of the Modern Sudan*, p. 541.
[2] *Al Nil* newspaper, Khartoum, 20 January 1940.
[3] Letter from Director of Education to Civil Secretary, 12 March 1941, *EDA/File 9/8.65.*

changed later and it concentrated on the opening of intermediate schools. During the period 1941–7 congress grants to *Ahlia* intermediate schools amounted to £E10,641 excluding other grants made to elementary and sub-grade schools and *khalwas*.[1] Intermediate schools were established from the Education Day Fund in 1943 in El Obeid and Omdurman. In 1944 other intermediate schools were opened in Atbara and Goled. By emphasizing and encouraging intermediate education, the congress was in fact registering its disagreement with the government attitude of limiting intermediate education. On the other hand, it was meeting the wishes of parents who considered that intermediate education was the door to employment or higher education. Secondary education was expensive and difficult to administer by a voluntary organization. Finance and support for the congress mainly came from towns, and intermediate schools were established in them. Members of the congress were in the towns and could therefore easily administer and supervise the schools. Intermediate schools further provided employment for some of those who were retrenched in 1931 or dismissed as a result of the Gordon College strike, or who later lost their government jobs as a result of their political activities. Some able teachers resigned from the department of education to become headmasters and teachers in these schools. By doing this they assured the parents that their boys would not get inferior teaching in the non-government schools. These same teachers became active members and officers of the congress's local committees and thereby furthered its aims. The Education Day thus helped the congress to forge strong links between itself and the population.

The government was at first reluctant to support such activities because of their educational and political implications. Its attitude, however, began to change in 1941 when the Director of Education questioned the wisdom of regarding the financing of a school by citizens 'as reactionary or retrogressive . . . as long as that school fulfils the reasonable demands which the government is likely to impose'.[2] He was in favour of private enterprise in education because 'education of the people and for the people is a laudable enterprise'.[3]

The application of the *Ahlia* and *Ahfad* Schools in Omdurman to

[1] Note on the Foundation, Financing and Staffing of Non-Government Schools, 19 March 1947, *EDA/File 9/8.61.*

[2] Letter from Director of Education to Civil Secretary, 12 March 1941, *EDA/File 9/8.65.*

[3] Ibid., 30 April 1941, *EDA/File DE/9/8.65.*

start secondary courses were resisted at first for fear of creating an unemployed educated class. The Director of Education again advised against the rejection of these applications because the 'production of more secondary boys will go to swell the number of those who clamour for office chairs upon which to park their persons'.[1] He argued that 'for some time we have been assiduous in preaching the separation of education from employment, while the process of finding their own levels as regards employment has already begun, the secondary schoolboy now takes on tasks which have hitherto been performed by the intermediate boys and so on down the scale'.[2]

Permission was granted and the *Ahfad* secondary section was started in 1943 while the *Ahlia* secondary section was started in 1944. It was not, however, until 1945 that this attitude changed and the system of grants-in-aid was extended to those schools which conformed to the prescribed regulations laid down by the non-Government Schools Ordinance of 1927 and attained the necessary standard.[3]

The voluntary movement was finally accepted as an integral part of the education system. During the period 1941–52, 31 *Ahlia* intermediate schools were established in different parts of the country.[4] By 1956, 4 *Ahlia* secondary schools were established.

This keen interest and desire for education did not only act as a pressure on the Sudan Government to provide more educational facilities to meet nationalist aspirations, but also invited Egypt to contribute to this field. Until 1931, the four Coptic Community Schools in Atbara, Khartoum, Khartoum North, and Karima did not admit Sudanese boys and girls. By following the Egyptian educational system, they did not provide an education suitable for employment in the Sudan and were therefore not attractive to Sudanese. From 1932 onwards a limited number of Sudanese boys and girls were admitted with government permission. In 1936 the number of the schools grew to seven at Atbara, Khartoum, Khartoum North, Omdurman, El Obeid, and Port Sudan, with 1,737 boys and girls of whom 345 were Sudanese. This increase in admission of Sudanese reflected a growing demand for education rather than a preference for the type of education provided or a change in basic government policy, which viewed the trend as politically harmful.

[1] Letter from Director of Education to Civil Secretary, 30 April, 1941, *EDA/ File DE/9/8.65*.   [2] Ibid.
[3] Letter from Director of Education to all Governors, 23 March 1945, *EDA/File SCR/9.1.1*.
[4] Appendix I, Table XII.

When the Anglo-Egyptian treaty of 1936 restored Egypt's position in the Sudan, the educated class tried to make use of the new situation by playing Egypt and England against each other, and by appealing to both to help the Sudanese to obtain more education. The editor of *Al Sudan* newspaper, in his article 'The need for sending Educational Missions Abroad',[1] hailed the Egyptian Government for admitting forty-four Sudanese students into its schools and hoped that England, the other partner in the treaty, would do something similar for the Sudan. The article suggested that Sudanese students should be given a chance to receive higher education in England. It argued that unless this was done 'the theoretical priority for government employment agreed to in the treaty would not be realized'.[2]

Al Nil newspaper[3] wrote that England had done a lot for education in the Sudan, and although Egypt had also done a lot, its contribution was of a general nature. It appealed to Egypt 'to raise in the Sudan a permanent visible monument, a Farouk Institute, a Nahas College, a Tousoon Orphanage'.[4]

The Anglo-Egyptian treaty of 1936 helped to create a new situation regarding the Coptic Community schools in the Sudan, especially that of Khartoum. Since 1934 the Ministry of Education in Egypt had begun to interest itself in the Khartoum Coptic school, paid an annual subsidy of £E820, and sent an annual Board of Examiners. It tried to control the school but the local Coptic Church which was in control of the school and other Coptic schools resisted these efforts.

Sudanese appeals and invitations to Egypt to contribute to education, coupled with a desire from the Egyptian Government to expand the Coptic Community schools and bring them under its control, led the Egyptian Government to set out on a policy of providing educational facilities in the Sudan for Sudanese, and of encouraging the Sudanese to join schools in Egypt. In 1938, it declared its intention of establishing a secondary school in Khartoum. The Under-Secretary at the Egyptian Ministry of Education visited Khartoum in December 1938, and formally proposed to the Sudan Government the establishment of an Egyptian secondary school, financed by the Egyptian Government. Although the official statement declared that the school

[1] *Al Sudan* newspaper, Khartoum, 19 October 1937.
[2] Ibid.
[3] *Al Nil* newspaper, Khartoum, 5 October 1937.
[4] The reference is to King Farouk, Mustafa el Nahas Pasha, Egyptian Prime Minister at the time, and Prince Omar Tousoon of the Royal Family, who was known in the Sudan for his support for the Sudanese.

would be open only to students of Egyptian nationality, this was soon abandoned by the Egyptian authorities. Their scheme changed from a school for Egyptian boys in the Sudan to a large school with a capital cost of £E51,000 and provision for 400 boys, Sudanese as well as Egyptians.[1] The Sudan Government, which suspected the political aims of the project from the beginning, but had no grounds for refusal as long as the new school limited its entry to Egyptian nationals, objected to this change.

The Sudan Government had from the beginning feared that the proposed school would be 'a sort of centre of Egyptian cultural influence directed from Cairo'.[2] It did not want to see two rival educational systems in the same town undermining each other. Its plans to improve the secondary system as a step towards the establishment of higher schools would be frustrated and unstable if an alien system of education was allowed to interfere. It was argued that the admission of Sudanese to the Egyptian secondary schools would attract those who could not proceed to the Gordon College, give them doubtful certificates because of the Egyptian policy of emphasis on quantity rather than quality, and therefore lead only to white-collar unemployment, and create jealousy and competition for posts in Sudan government service between Sudanese products of the Egyptian schools. As it was likely that the Egyptian school would charge no fees and might therefore attract the cream of the Sudan intermediate schools, it would be difficult to raise the standard in the Gordon College. It would also be difficult to prevent the sons of those Egyptian officials and traders domiciled in the Sudan from squeezing out Sudanese from Sudan Government jobs.[3]

In order to discourage the growth of Egyptian education, the government had laid down from the beginning that preference for government posts would only be given to those trained in Sudan schools, because 'the most suitable education for Sudanese doing government work in the Sudan is likely to be that which from the elementary stage right through to the post-secondary has been specially devised, with much thought, patience and expense, by the Sudan Government to meet the Sudan environment'.[4] In addition to this, it was decided that non-government schools, including the

[1] Note on Proposed Egyptian Secondary School in Khartoum, 15 November 1939, *EDA/File 17.D.1.*   [2] Ibid.
[3] Letter from C. W. M. Cox to Director of Education, 7 October 1939, *EDA/File 17/O/1.*   [4] Ibid.

Egyptian school, would not be allowed to undercut the Sudan
Government schools by charging only small fees or no fees at all,
and those who planned to join the Sudan higher schools by virtue
of an Egyptian school certificate obtained in the Sudan, or in Egypt,
would be charged full fees.[1] It was also decided to step up the plans
to develop university education and to encourage national intermediate schools, so as to dissuade more Sudanese from seeking
Egyptian education.[2]

The Egyptian Government's point of view was different. Although
it did not officially declare that its intention was unlimited entrance
for the Sudanese, its economic expert and official representative in
Khartoum, Abdel Qawi Pasha, privately assured the Graduates
Congress of this intention. The provision of education for the
Sudanese would, in Egypt's view, create an educated and public
opinion favourable to its political interests in the Sudan. No final
decision was taken and when the war broke out in 1939 the plans
were shelved until 1944, when the Farouk secondary school was
established.

In the meantime, plans for providing educational facilities in
Egypt were being prepared. Already in 1937 forty-four Sudanese
students were accepted free of charge by the Egyptian Ministry of
Education, through the instrumentality of Ali el Berair, a Sudanese
merchant in Cairo identified with the national movement in the
Sudan, and later chairman of the Congress Committee in Cairo.[3]
These were either sons of Sudanese resident in Egypt, or students
who went at their own expense, mostly from the Halfa and Dongola
regions. In 1938, a second group of thirty students was admitted.
The Sudan Government was not consulted. Probably there was
protest because of official representation. The Under-Secretary of
State in Egypt informed the Sudan Government in 1939 that it would
in future be asked to recommend names of Sudanese planning to
join Egyptian schools in Egypt, and laid down certain conditions.
These were:[4]

(a) Parents of selected students should be able to provide food,
clothing, and lodging for them in Egypt.

(b) Acceptance of such students in secondary schools would be
limited to those intending to proceed to the Egyptian University, and
to those possessing Egyptian primary certificates.

[1] Ibid.   [2] Ibid.
[3] *EDA/File 9.1.55.A.*   [4] Ibid.

(c) As few as possible would be accepted for secondary schools, and technical, agricultural, and commercial schools would be preferred.

(d) The maximum number admitted in any year would be thirty students.

The Sudan Government welcomed the proposal and interpreted the information as a change of policy, although nothing came of it. But this assurance soon gave way. Selection in 1940 was made by Abdel Qawi Pasha without consulting the Sudan Government. In 1942 the selection was entrusted to the Graduates Congress. The conditions regarding limitation of number to a maximum of thirty students per year and the necessity of having an Egyptian primary certificate were removed. It was made possible for Sudanese with a certificate from the Sudan to proceed to Egyptian secondary schools. These changes, in addition to entrusting selection to an unofficial body such as the Graduates Congress, which was unpopular with the Sudan Government, led to protests from the latter.[1] The Graduates Congress, however, welcomed the opportunity to act as a representative of, and a spokesman for, the interests of the people, and every year more than thirty students went to Egypt under its auspices to join Egypt's different educational institutions. In the Sudan, not only were Sudanese admitted in increasing numbers into Egyptian Government-controlled schools, but more were admitted to the Coptic Community schools. Egyptian Government grants-in-aid were extended to all the schools following the Egyptian system of education, so as to enable them to take more Sudanese students. The number of boys and girls in these schools increased from 1,737 with 345 Sudanese, or 20 per cent, in 1936 to 3,000 with 1,495, or 50 per cent, Sudanese in 1946.[2] In 1943 the number of Sudanese students attending Egyptian educational institutions in Egypt was 594, of whom 36 were following university courses, 95 in secondary schools, and the majority of the rest in Al Azhar. In 1945 a Sudan House was established in Cairo by the Egyptian Government for the residence of Sudanese students in Cairo.[3]

Fear of political implications of Egyptian education was partly responsible for the growth of non-government education and the change in the government's policy of limited encouragement to one of active encouragement and support.[4]

[1] *SGA/File 9.1.55.A.*   [2] *E.D.R., 1936* and *1945.*   [3] *EDA/File 9.1.55.A.*
[4] Letter from the Director of Education to all Governors, 23 March 1945, *EDA/File SCR/9.1.1.*

11   BED

The number of Sudanese attending non-government schools in northern Sudan controlled by missionary societies, the Egyptian Government, Coptic Community, and Sudanese nationals, grew during the period 1935–46 as follows.[1]

	Number of Boys	Number of Girls	Total number	Number of Sudanese
1933	2,005	1,966	3,971	1,340
1935	2,793	2,288	5,081	1,579
1936	3,152	2,195	5,347	2,200
1937	3,732	2,478	6,210	2,092
1938	4,397	2,622	7,019	3,345
1946	8,707	3,560	12,267	8,700

This represented an increase in the percentage of Sudanese attending these schools from 33 in 1933 to 41 in 1936 and to 71 in 1946.

While the number of Sudanese in these schools had increased during the period 1936–45 by about 400 per cent, the number of Sudanese boys and girls attending government schools during the same period increased from 17,750 to 34,630, i.e. about 200 per cent. Out of the total number of Sudanese boys and girls attending all levels of education, non-government schools provided places for about 20 per cent of the school population.

The growth of Sudanese nationalism and the reassertion of Egypt's position in the Sudan had therefore been major factors in the expansion of both government and non-government education. Egypt's political interests in the Sudan, and its desire to co-operate with Sudanese nationalism, led to the opening of a new source of education, both inside and outside the country. In 1945 the Sudan Government changed its attitude and decided to give Sudanese who had qualified from Egyptian schools a fair chance of employment in Sudan Government jobs.[2] Egyptian education, like the voluntary movement in education, was fully accepted by 1946 as a valuable source for the education of the Sudanese.

[1] *E.D.R.*, *1933–46*.
[2] Letter from Civil Secretary to all Heads of Departments, 30 May 1945, *EDA/File 9.1.55.A.*

CHAPTER XI

Educational Development, 1946–1956

THE LAST ten years of the Condominium rule in the Sudan were years of rapid advances and changes in the educational field. The educational progress in the previous years had generated yet more educational progress in the following years, and economic, political, and administrative changes again created an even greater demand for further education. Education was both a promoter and a result of these changes.

In 1937 new local government ordinances were passed and in May 1944 the Advisory Council for northern Sudan was established. Although local government was, to a large extent, still built round tribalism, and the Advisory Council of Northern Sudan was composed of a large proportion of tribal chiefs, these two developments marked the beginning of the end of native administration as it had been known and practised since 1922.

The system which had been in force for some years, whereby the sons of tribal leaders were given special privileges with regard to entrance to intermediate and secondary schools, was abolished with the coming of local government. From the government's point of view, tribal leaders no longer needed to be persuaded to send their sons to schools. There was doubt whether by pressing for privileges for this class the government was acting in the best interests of local government development. On the other hand, criticism of the policy as one of partiality to a certain class could not be defended at a time when democratic institutions were replacing traditional authorities. It was felt that, with the emphasis on local government and its requirements for efficient educated officers, and that in spite of the fact that the tribal leaders in some parts of the country would continue for a long time to wield great influence, places in schools should be given to those who qualified for them irrespective of their background. A 'special' place for a son of a tribal leader meant keeping out another boy with greater intelligence.[1]

The foundation for the development of local government in the modern sense and the association of educated Sudanese with the

[1] Letter from Director of Education to Civil Secretary, 24 April 1952, *MIA/ File SCR/27, vol. II.*

central government was thus laid. The second educational plan prepared the ground for the development of a comprehensive system of education reaching the highest level and therefore making these administrative changes both necessary and possible.

Although the Second World War had retarded development as a result of the shortage of manpower and the priority placed on the defence of the country against the threatened Italian invasion, its effects were not wholly bad. First, it stimulated political thinking. Secondly, it created an economic boom. The effect of this was to produce among the educated class an impatience with the pace of educational development and to make money available for expansion. The Graduates Congress was rebuffed in 1942 as a result of its memorandum of 3 April 1942, but this did not lead the government to slow down its policy of associating the Sudanese with the administration of the country or delay their participation in the various branches of government work.

As far back as 1942 Sir Douglas Newbold, the Civil Secretary, was convinced that the Sudan Government could not conduct 'for long a progressive or happy policy without the co-operation of the educated class'.[1] He was also convinced that a denial or delay in their effective participation would lead to discontent which would turn 'into despair, and despair into revolt'.[2]

The importance of education as a prerequisite to economic development, and its role in bridging the gap between the rural and the urban areas, was recognized by the policy-makers at both the central and provincial levels.[3]

This new attitude was not only a result of the local political and administrative changes. British imperial policy had undergone a major change since the beginning of the Second World War. The concept of trusteeship which had dominated British policy since the end of the First World War gave way to a concept of partnership and self-government. The two Colonial Welfare and Development Acts of 1940 and 1945 were manifestations of this new attitude. Through them it became possible to implement some of the principles advocated by the Advisory Committee on Education in the Colonies

[1] Newbold, Douglas, Note on Further Association of Sudanese with Local and Central Government submitted to the 502nd Meeting of the Governor-General's Council, 14 September 1942, *SGA/GENCO/3/49*.

[2] Ibid.

[3] Minutes of the meeting of the District Commissioners held at El Obeid on 23–27 December 1946, *SGA/File SCR/27, vol. II.*

since 1925. In its 'Mass Education in African Society' the committee emphasized that prosperity could only be secured and maintained if the whole mass of the people had a real share in education and had some understanding of its meaning and purpose.[1]

Educated Sudanese shared these views, but differed with the government and within their own ranks with regard to the means of obtaining independence and the pace of political development. One group chose to co-operate in the planned constitutional institutions and work for their aims from within these institutions. The other group chose to work for their aim from outside and through co-operation with Egypt. The successful establishment of intermediate schools through voluntary efforts gave them confidence and made them move into a new area of education. The *Ahlia* national secondary school, the Congress secondary school and the *Ahfad* secondary school were established through voluntary contributions and assistance from the Egyptian Government.

There was similar expansion in Christian Missionary and Egyptian schools. The number of the non-government schools was larger than schools controlled by the government. The position in 1954, for example, was as follows:

Government and Non-Government Education 1954[2]

	Government education		Non-government education	
	Number of schools	Number of pupils	Number of schools	Number of pupils
Boys' education				
Intermediate	30	5,001	42	7,823
Egyptian intermediate	—	—	15	3,153
Secondary	7	2,037	5	970
Egyptian secondary	—	—	2	836
Girls' education				
Intermediate	6	732	3	820
Egyptian intermediate	—	—	2	269
Secondary	1	128	3	209
Egyptian secondary	—	—	1	70

[1] Advisory Committee on Education in the Colonies, *Mass Education in African Society, Colonial No. 186*, H.M.S.O., London 1943.
[2] Sudan Government, *Report of the International Education Commission on Secondary Education*, Khartoum, February 1955, p. 38.

As the non-government schools were situated in most cases in urban areas, the inequality between the urban and rural areas in educational opportunities increased. In 1952, for example, 42·8 per cent of the boys completing elementary education in Khartoum province found places in intermediate schools compared to 14 per cent in Darfur.[1]

The number of Sudanese students in Egypt also increased. The delegation of Sudanese political parties to Egypt in 1946 urged the Egyptian Government to open more opportunities for Sudanese education in Egyptian universities and schools. In 1949, 789 Sudanese were receiving their education in Egypt. Their distribution was as follows:[2]

Fuad University	246
Farouk University	52
Institutes of Education	20
Al Azhar University	466
Other higher institutes	5
	789

The discussions in the Advisory Council for Northern Sudan stimulated further interest in education and its expansion. These discussions drew attention to the fact that education was the one service for which there was the biggest demand. Its lagging behind political development was alarming because the shortage in educated manpower was used to argue against political independence. On the other hand, the increased educational activities by Egypt, although meeting unfulfilled demands for education, were suspect. Those who did not sympathize with Egypt's political aspirations in the Sudan looked upon these activities as means to win Sudanese support and strengthen its supporters among the political parties.

Non-government education was not free from administrative and educational problems. Many school boards were inefficient, standards were generally low, and the teachers' salaries were low compared with those paid by the government.

Thus from 1946 onwards a note of urgency, coupled with a sense of need to expand and reform the system of education,

[1] Ibid., p. 34.
[2] *EDA/File 9.1.55*. A.

dominated the internal scene. These problems of education were dealt with in two educational plans for the north and two for the south and a number of administrative decisions concerning education.

A second ten-year plan for education (1946-56) was presented to the Advisory Council's fifth session in 1946. Unlike the first ten-year plan it was concerned with education in the north only. The plan's basic assumption was that self-government would be attained within twenty years.[1] While recognizing the urgent need to expand higher education so as to meet the requirements of self-government, the plan emphasized expansion of elementary education. It was held that this last emphasis was necessary on both economic and administrative grounds. Economic expansion required a public which was receptive 'for economic expansion and development projects'.[2] Political and administrative changes required a public 'trained to civic responsibilities'[3] and school-leavers capable of understanding 'the changes which are going on around them'[4] and capable of playing 'a useful part in the life of the community'.[5] These aims were to be achieved through the development of adult education, the establishment of youth clubs, and production of suitable literature for adults. The other emphasis of the plan was to reform intermediate and secondary education so as to improve the standard of admission to the post-secondary higher education, raise the cultural and academic standard of the secondary schools, and provide a balanced education of varying types for the majority of intermediate school-leavers who did not have an opportunity for further education and therefore enable them to contribute to 'the development of the social and economic life of the country'.[6]

The means to achieve this was the Brown Plan,[7] which proposed a new ladder for education consisting of four years elementary, followed by two years intermediate, and then four years junior secondary or six years senior secondary. This was in essence the

---

[1] Sudan Government, Plan for Educational Development in the Northern Sudan 1946-1956, *Proceedings of the Fifth Session of the Advisory Council for the Northern Sudan*, pp. 51-5.

[2] Ibid., p. 24.   [3] Ibid.
[4] Ibid.   [5] Ibid.
[6] Ibid., p. 25.

[7] The plan was called after Mr. L. Brown who was Headmaster, Hantoub Secondary School, and before that Science Master in the Gordon Memorial College and Principal, Junior Secondary School, Bakht er Ruda.

Corbyn Plan of 1926 in a new form. It aimed at producing boys with technical and practical abilities, as opposed to academic and literary, who would be needed as technicians and administrators. According to the Brown Plan the ordinary level school certificate would be examined at the end of the fifth form in the senior secondary school so that the final and sixth year would be devoted to the advanced level work preparing boys for university education. The junior secondary school, on the other hand, would be of a vocational nature, preparing boys for careers in agriculture, commerce, and industry. As these schools would provide the main source for middle-grade employees the plan suggested a revision in the terms of service so as to attract boys to them. The alternative suggestion of a system of six years elementary followed by four or six years secondary was rejected on the grounds of impracticability owing to the great increase it would entail in both staff and expenditure.

The ten-year plan provided for an increase in annual expenditure from £E412,000 or 5·4 per cent of the total budget in 1946 to £E931,000 or 6 per cent of the estimated budget in 1956. Expenditure on personnel, teachers, administrators, and advisory staff, which represented a major cost of education in previous plans and budgets, amounted to 48 per cent of the recurrent expenditure compared to 73 per cent in 1936. This decrease was mainly due to the decrease in the overhead costs per unit of education. The acceleration in the Sudanization of the administration coupled with an increased number of Sudanese employed in secondary schools made this possible. A new expenditure item was training courses abroad for Sudanese; £E12,952 was allocated in 1946 for this purpose, rising to £E16,000 in 1956. Since 1932, only two Sudanese had been sent abroad on training courses. Grants to non-government education, excluding missionary schools, amounted to £E4,580 in 1946 and £E20,000 in 1956. Capital expenditure over the same period amounted to £E2,500,000.[1]

The plan aimed at achieving by 1956 the targets of the number of schools tabled on the next page.

Like the 1938–46 educational plan, the proposals, when published, were not welcomed by Sudanese inside or outside the Advisory Council. Both groups questioned the assumptions on which it was based and criticized its emphasis on expansion of elementary education and reform at a time when priority should be given to higher

[1] Plan for Educational Development, pp. 44–7.

Educational Plan 1946-1956[1]

	Position in 1946 (number of schools)	Target in 1956 (number of schools)
Boys' schools		
Sub-grade schools	192 (for the year 1945)	469
Elementary schools	187	244
Intermediate and preparatory two-year schools	13	21
Junior secondary schools	2	5
Senior secondary schools	2	3
Technical schools	4	?
Girls' schools		
Elementary schools	69	150
Intermediate schools	3	6
Secondary schools	—	1

education and expansion.[2] The plan's aim of creating places for 36 per cent of boys at school age in 1956 was rejected by a member of the Advisory Council as inadequate because 'the people expected enough schools by the end of ten years to educate all boys of elementary school age'.[3] Members of the council from rural areas felt that the needs of their areas were neglected in favour of urban areas. The general feeling was that the plan fell short of Sudanese aspirations and needed a revision of its basic assumptions and details. This task was given to a special committee of eight Sudanese members of the council.[4] The special committee's report submitted in May 1947 was in fact the result of continuous work, research, and consultation made by its chairman, Mirghani Hanza. The report set out to achieve four main aims:

(*a*) A change in the educational policy from one emphasizing education for employment to one emphasizing the education of

[1] Sudan Government, *Proceedings of the Fifth Session of the Advisory Council for the Northern Sudan*, p. 43.
[2] Personal information from Mirghani Hamza.
[3] *Proceedings of the Fifth Session of the Advisory Council for the Northern Sudan*, p. 46.
[4] Members of the committee were: Mirghani Hamza (chairman); Surur Ramli; Mekki Abbas; Ali Bedri; Ahmed Caman el Qadi; Ahmed El Sid Elfil; Abu Shama Abdel Kahmoud; Yacoub El Hilu; ibid., p. 55.

individuals by developing their character and inculcating in them a civic sense and a sense of responsibility and self-reliance, adventure, and initiative.[1]

(*b*) The provision in the shortest possible time of universal elementary education in all parts of the country; intermediate schools in all the major towns, and secondary and higher education to provide the necessary numbers required for employment in government and non-government services.

(*c*) Decentralization of the administration of education so as to enable local government authorities to assume more responsibilities and allow them to adapt educational policies and programmes suited to their particular needs.

(*d*) Reduction of the costs of education through cheaper buildings, employment of more Sudanese teachers in secondary schools, larger classes in schools, and less expenditure and effort on research and experimentation.[2]

The last of these aims reflected the impatience of the educated Sudanese with the government's policy of slow progress and their suspicion of Bakht er Ruda's methods of training, experimentation, and research. This was due, not to ignorance of the value of research, but to a desire to see quicker results for research[3] and a less expensive way than that of Bakht er Ruda for training teachers.[4] The Brown Plan, which represented the cornerstone of reform, was rejected for the following reasons:

(*a*) The committee believed that 'reorganization should take place after, and not before, the expansion'.[5]

(*b*) It would limit the number of boys proceeding to secondary and higher education, and would therefore restrict the number of those attaining a higher cultural level.

(*c*) The early selection to secondary education as proposed by the plan would be impracticable and educationally harmful.

(*d*) The change of the educational system would entail extra expenditure and efforts which needed to be directed into other channels of a more urgent nature.

(*e*) Non-government schools would be thrown into confusion.

[1] *Proceedings of the Seventh Session of the Advisory Council for the Northern Sudan*, May 1947, p. 27.
[2] Ibid., pp. 26–9.
[3] Personal information from Mirghani Hamza.
[4] *Proceedings of the Seventh Session*, p. 30.
[5] Ibid., p. 48.

Non-government intermediate schools would find it difficult, if not impossible, to adapt to the new system.

(*f*) Expansion of sub-grade schools was a doubtful method of attaining good results in elementary education.[1]

As the expansion of education should be the main target, the committee recommended an increase in the annual expenditure to £E922,000 in 1951, and to £E1,265,000 in 1956. This represented an increase of 50 per cent on the amounts proposed in the original plan. Education should, in its view, receive 15 per cent of the total expenditure even if this was to mean extra taxes.

The reform of the *Mahad al Ilmi* at Omdurman was one of the major deliberations and recommendations of the committee. The problems of the *Mahad* had already been discussed by the Advisory Council during its sixth session. Since 1940 reforms had been introduced in its organization and curriculum. A council under the chairmanship of the Grand Kadi was formed to advise the Legal Secretary on the *Mahad* affairs and exercise control over its finances. Its budget became separate and government contribution was raised. Sheikh Abu Shama Abdul Mahmoud, who became President of the Board of *Ulama* in 1943, introduced a number of reforms aiming at the improvement of the secular side of its work. A committee from the department of education recommended in 1945 further reforms in the curriculum and the appointment of qualified teachers to teach the secular subjects. The result of these reforms was an immediate increase in the number of students from 577 in 1941, to 652 in 1946, of whom 77 per cent came from outside Khartoum province. There was a similar increase in the number of local *Mahada*. During the period 1943–55 local *Mahads* were established at Nuri (1943), Karima (1945), Kosti (1947), Halfa (1949), Masho (1950), Argo (1950), Shendi (1951), Al Damar (1953), and Tengasi (1955). All of these, except one, were in the northern province, where religious education originated and spread in the past. It was the rise in the numbers of students in Omdurman which attracted the attention of the committee, as no lodgings were provided and most of the students were forced to live with other families. They were thus exposed to the influences of town life unsuited, from the authorities' point of view, to future leaders of religion,[2] as they became involved in the

[1] *Proceedings of the Seventh Session*, pp. 35–6.
[2] Sudan Government, Legal Department, *The Omdurman Mahad Ilmi*, Khartoum 1946, p. 4.

political movements and students' strikes. On the other hand, the increase in the number of students in both Omdurman and the provinces created problems for future employment. The graduates of *al Mahad*, who in the past were employed in the local *khalwas* as teachers, became aspirants for other jobs as secular and modern subjects were introduced and expanded.

The deficiencies on the modern side of the curriculum, however, handicapped them from getting employment in government, commercial or other vocations. While a small number of *Mahad* graduates were finding employment in the expanding intermediate schools and *Mahads* as teachers, and in the *Sharia* courts as clerks, the majority of them did not find employment suitable to their training and background. In view of the fact that the *Mahad* had grown from a local mosque school to a national institution with a number of educational problems, the Advisory Council recommended the transfer of its supervision from the legal department to the education department.[1] The special committee's report endorsed this last recommendation and appealed for 'drastic measures of reform'[2] to be introduced to enable the *Mahad* and its branches to have 'effect on the life of the country'.[3] The first step towards reform in the committee's view was the reform of syllabuses and methods of teaching, and the introduction of modern subjects at all levels and on a large scale.[4]

Although education in the south was outside its term of reference and *ultra vires* the Advisory Council as constituted, the committee stated its objections to the southern educational policy. It urged that southern educational development should be accelerated so that the south would be able, in a short time, to catch up with the north and enable southerners to attend the secondary and higher schools of the north until such schools were provided for them in the south.[5] It also recommended that Arabic should be introduced in southern schools with an increased government participation and direct responsibility for education with a view to establishing a unified educational policy and system for the whole country.

The committee's recommendations were accepted by the Advisory Council and the department of education was directed to revise its original programme accordingly and re-submit it. This was done in

---

[1] *Proceedings of the Sixth Session of the Advisory Council for Northern Sudan January 1945*, pp. 12–13.
[2] *Proceedings of the Seventh Session, May 1947*, pp. 42–3.
[3] Ibid.   [4] Ibid.
[5] Ibid., p. 28.

1949 when a new plan for the years 1949-56 was presented to the Legislative Assembly.

In the meantime, southern educational policy had not changed. The factors which made for changes and pressures in the north did not operate in the south; therefore political, administrative and economic changes in the north did not influence events in the south. It remained isolated and unexposed to outside influences, except to those of the missionaries and a few northern traders. The Second World War with the upheavals it brought everywhere did not generate a political movement or a national consciousness comparable to that in the north or in neighbouring countries. The second educational plan for the south (1946-50), approved by the Governor-General's Council in 1945, did not, therefore, provide for major reforms, but only minor changes 'to suit the changing circumstances'.[1] The major feature of the plan, however, was its provision for an increase in the share of the south in the education budget from $7\frac{1}{2}$ per cent in 1938 to 21 per cent in 1950. Capital cost was estimated at £E150,000 and recurrent cost at £E95,000 in 1950.[2]

The missionary societies were to continue to be the main agencies for education in spite of objections from the northern educated class and a few political officers and administrators. Dr. Pridie, a member of the Governor-General's Council, objected to the continuation of the southern educational policy and warned that 'an advance in educational expenditure in the south, which was mainly provided by the north, might have unfortunate repercussions and not of itself be justifiable'.[3] The assistant director of education in the south doubted the wisdom of entrusting education to the missionary societies. According to him, missionary societies had only succeeded in producing 'some inferior clerks, or, at best, some clerks in inferior positions, a few agricultural demonstrators, foresters, post-office officials, a few medical dressers, and a handful of station officers without power or status, and a host of appallingly bad schoolmasters'.[4] Missionary schools were, in his view, inefficient and with low standards, and were not supported by the chiefs, who

[1] Educational Plan for the Southern Sudan 1946-1950, Minutes of the Governor-General's Council Meeting on 24 November 1944. *SGA.*
[2] Ibid.
[3] Despatch from the Governor-General to His Britannic Majesty's Ambassador in Cairo No. 89, 4 August 1945, *EDA/File DE/SCR/1.1.17.*
[4] Letter from Hibbert, D. H., to Director of Education, Juba, 2 September 1945. *EDA.*

preferred government-controlled schools. But these objections and warnings were not heeded. The government had already committed itself to the missionary societies and reached a decision whereby it agreed to increase the subsidies to the societies, to enable them to employ more British missionary educationalists.[1] The government agreed to raise the subsidy from £E350 to £E700 per annum for qualified men teachers; and from £E225 to £E345 per annum for qualified women teachers. The Roman Catholic missionaries and the American Presbyterian missionaries were not, however, included in this scheme because they were held to be in a better financial position.[2] In addition to this, the agreement provided increases in salaries of locally employed teachers. A proposal to establish a teachers' training centre to be run by a joint board of government and missionary representatives was turned down by the Church Missionary Society on the ground that training of teachers for its schools should continue to be under its own supervision and in no way interfered with by the government.

The society feared that such a step might lead to secular education. Co-operation with the Roman Catholic societies in teachers' training was unacceptable.[3] It finally agreed to the establishment of two training centres, one Protestant and the other Roman Catholic, independent of each other and with no government control.

Although the missionary societies continued to be the main agents of education, the plan provided for the establishment of a government intermediate school in the Upper Nile province, a village agricultural school in Yambio, and a vocational training centre at Juba. Elementary education was left entirely to the missions with a direction that the elementary school course be lengthened to six years, and that of the village school to three years.

Political and administrative development after 1946, however, necessitated a revision in the plan. In 1946 a new southern policy was initiated. This new policy rejected the idea and practice of separate development for the north and south, and instead advocated a policy which would gradually bind the south to the north.[4] The southern Sudan, according to the new policy, would no longer be

[1] Note by Director of Education on Proposed Increase in the Amount of Staff Grant paid to Church Missionary Society, 29 November 1948. *MIA/File SCR/9.9.7.1, vol. IV.*   [2] Ibid.

[3] Note by Director of Education, 9 May 1945, *EDA/File DE/SCR/9.2.*

[4] Note by Civil Secretary on Southern Sudan Policy. CS/SCR/1.C.1, 16 December 1946, *SGA.*

looking outside to Uganda or East Africa nor remain isolated from the north. This implied the encouragement of Arabic and its teaching in schools, the education of southerners in the northern secondary and higher schools, and a more active participation by government in education so that the south could catch up with the north. The reaction of the southern Sudanese consulted on this new revolutionary change was one of approval.[1] The missionary societies on the other hand did not readily accept or support the new policy.

The new policy of secular education and government control made possible the spread of Arabic and Islamic culture in the south, and therefore put an end to the monopoly which missionaries had enjoyed over education since the beginning of the century.

The new southern policy thus marked a new phase in education for the south. Its effects in the educational field were not, however, felt until 1949 when a Legislative Assembly for both north and south was established. The first Sudanese Minister of Education informed the members of the Assembly from the north and the south that ' as the Sudan is one country sharing one set of political institutions it is of great importance that there should be one language which is understood by all its citizens. That language could only be Arabic, and Arabic must therefore be taught in all our schools.'[2] In another policy statement he declared that the policy 'is to weld the system of education hitherto in use in the Northern and Southern provinces respectively into one harmonious whole designed to meet the needs of pupils in all parts of the Sudan'.[3] As regards missionary educational activities, the minister declared that the government would continue to give 'full support to existing missionary schools, and where necessary to upgrade them',[4] but future expansion and development of education would be the responsibility of the government. In these government schools religious instruction would be guaranteed for the different Christian groups, but pagans, who would not be excluded from attending the government schools, would be guaranteed, for the first time, freedom to abstain from classes where religious teaching was conducted.[5] For the first time pagans in

[1] Minutes of the Juba Conference, 12–13 June 1947, *SGA/Equatoria/File EP/SCR/1.A.51.*
[2] Sudan Government, *Proceedings of the Legislative Assembly, 18 November 1949.*
[3] Ibid., 20 November 1950.   [4] Ibid.
[5] Note on Religious Instruction in Government Schools in the South, Juba, 4 January 1949, no. *ADES/SCR/1/K.513, MIA/File SCR/17.A.*

southern Sudan were given the opportunity to attend schools without being compelled to be Christians.

The Legislative Assembly approved two educational plans for the north and south which fulfilled the new aims. The plan for the north (1949–56) took into consideration recommendations made by the special committee of the Advisory Council, the Sudanization Committee and the Technical Education Committee. The Sudanization Committee constituted by the Governor-General on 11 March 1947 had recommended that 62·2 per cent of senior and middle administrative and technical posts should be filled by Sudanese by 1962.[1]

Technical education had been investigated and reported on by a committee appointed by the Director of Education in June 1943.[2] The need for more technicians had grown as a result of economic development during and after the war. The demand for foremen and artisans was growing. The development of the school of engineering and the disappearance of the old Gordon College engineering section created a gap between the highly trained engineer and the unskilled worker. Although the supply was far less than the demand, parents or school-leavers did not readily apply for technical schools. Their reluctance was due to a number of factors; positions of authority in the country were in the hands of the administrators and not the technicians. As long as better-paid jobs went to the non-technical school-leavers and the salaries of craftsmen and artisans were low compared with those of clerks and accountants, parents and boys were not going to prefer technical to liberal education.[3]

The Technical Education Committee recommended action which would make salaries and wages of technicians more attractive, and the institution of new technical schools. Thus the new plan for the north, after taking the reports into consideration, recommended that recurrent expenditure should rise from £E841,320 in 1949 to £E1,049,900 in 1950, and £E1,500,000 in 1956. Capital expenditure amounted to £E2,593,110 during the same period.[4] The emphasis

[1] Sudan Government, *Report of the Committee on the Sudanization of the Civil Service*, Khartoum 1948, p. 19.

[2] Members of the committee were: W. B. de la M. Jameson (Education Department); W. N. Allen (Irrigation Department); M. H. Lees (Public Works Department); G. K. Wood (Sudan Railways), and Ibrahim Ahmed (Education Department).

[3] Letter from Director of Education to Mekki Abbas, 6 June 1947, *EDA/File DE/SCR/9.7.1*.

[4] Sudan Government, *Proposals for the Expansion and Improvement of the Educational System in the Northern Provinces, 1949–1956*, Khartoum, p. 16.

on technical education in the plan led to a new major development in technical education—the establishment of a technical institute in Khartoum in 1950. The aim of the institute was to provide full-time courses in various branches of technology, commerce and art, leading to standards at a sub-professional level, and part-time and evening courses of a similar type.[1]

The plan for the south, on the other hand, took into consideration the new objective declared by the first Sudanese Minister of Education —unification of the two systems. Twenty-six government elementary schools for boys were planned—an increase of 500 per cent on the number of government elementary schools already established. Recurrent costs were estimated at £E665,200 in 1956, and capital costs during the plan period at £E907,952. The Institute of Education at Bakht er Ruda was made responsible for teacher training in the south. A Publication Bureau, the purpose of which was to prepare suitable Arabic material for schools and to assist in the conduct of mass literacy work in the south, was established at Juba.[2] Grants-in-aid to missionary schools rose from £E109,209 in 1949 to £E314,000 in 1956.

The financing of the two programmes was made from internal resources. When the two development programmes were approved in 1946 and 1951, education was allotted 10 per cent and 15 per cent respectively.[3]

Current expenditure on education rose from £E1,702,717 or 7·8 per cent of the total national budget in 1951–2 to £E3,907,230 or 11·8 per cent of the total budget in 1955–6.[4]

The establishment of a Ministry of Education in 1948 made it necessary that some sections of the Non-Government Schools Ordinance of 1927 be revised so that the powers which had been until then in the hands of the Governor-General and the Director of Education might be transferred instead to the Executive Council and the Minister of Education. The Minister of Education suggested that the Governor-General's powers should be transferred to him. This was rejected because the Civil Secretary insisted on retaining his powers especially in relation to the opening of missionary schools in

[1] Sudan Government, *Report of the International Education Commission*, p. 78.
[2] Sudan Government, *Proposals for the Expansion and Improvement of the Educational System in the Southern Provinces*, 1951–56, Khartoum, pp. 10–17.
[3] Appendix I, Table XIII.
[4] Appendix I, Table I.

the north and south, and the opening of non-government Muslim schools in the south. The Civil Secretary argued that Christian missionary bodies in the Sudan had external affiliations and their activities could not therefore be considered as purely local education matters. He also argued that the opening of Muslim non-government schools in the south must be referred to him on political grounds because of the administrative problems which might arise.[1]

When the matter was referred for legal advice, the Advocate-General advised that the Governor-General could not delegate his powers to the Minister of Education. The ordinance was amended to give the Executive Council and the Minister of Education the previous powers enjoyed by the Governor-General, but a clause was added to the effect that in the case of schools opened by religious bodies or by non-Sudanese, joint approval of the Minister of Education and the Civil Secretary should be obtained.

The tempo of expansion and change in education was further accelerated by the political development in 1953 when the Anglo-Egyptian agreement of 12 February 1953 was signed. The deliberations of the Sudanization Committee, which was constituted in February 1954 as a result of the agreement to put into effect the measures to complete the Sudanization of the Administration, the Police, the Sudan Defence Force, and other government posts which might affect the freedom of Sudanese in determining their future, revealed the lagging of education behind the political development. In 1954 there were 133 Sudanese in senior administrative posts compared to 108 British officials, and 8,915 Sudanese in non-administrative posts compared to 1,156 British. The majority of Sudanese in the first group had no university, higher or post-secondary education. The majority of those in the non-administrative posts had no education beyond the intermediate schools. The lack of trained and qualified Sudanese did not, however, prevent the Sudanization Committee from going ahead with its task and declaring that 647 posts held by British officials out of 1,069 and 87 posts held by Egyptian officials out of 153 should be Sudanized. Many British officials whose posts were not intended for immediate Sudanization, especially in the technical departments, demanded compensation and left the service, and by July 1955 only 150 remained. This created a shortage of qualified teachers at all levels, especially in the secondary

[1] Letter from Civil Secretary to Minister of Education, Khartoum, 27 November 1949, *EDA/File No. 9/8.*

and intermediate schools. Expansion in secondary education necessitated the transfer of intermediate teachers to the secondary schools.
The resignation of expatriate teachers from the secondary schools
and the educational administration necessitated more transfers from
the intermediate to the secondary schools. The situation was further
aggravated by the new policy adopted by the Gezira Scheme Board.
When the latter was nationalized in 1950 many teachers were recruited
for work as field staff and inspectors. The establishment of three
branches of the Institute of Education in Deling, Shendi, and Maridi
for the training of elementary school teachers, and an Intermediate
Teachers' Training College at Bakht er Ruda in 1949 had contributed
to a partial solution of the problem, but not to its final solution.

Sudanization had brought to many ex-teachers extra benefits and
privileges, while the status and the salary of those remaining in the
profession were unchanged. Graduates of the University College
preferred other more lucrative jobs, and the small number of
graduates who used to join in past years were attracted away by the
new openings in other fields. In spite of all this, expansion continued,
but tended to produce a general lowering of the standard in the
whole educational system.

Two other factors which contributed to the lowering of standards
were the expansion of non-government education without having the
adequate means for training or employing qualified teachers, and
the political strikes.

In March 1946, the students of the University College staged the
first political demonstration in Khartoum since 1924. This was
followed by similar demonstrations and strikes in six other schools
in Khartoum and Omdurman. During the period 1946-56 there were
no less than 120 incidents of strikes and demonstrations by schools
of different levels in different parts of the country. Not all of these
were political demonstrations or strikes, but most of them were
aimed at supporting the national movement and the political parties
in their demands for independence. As the number of schools increased and the student body became a considerable force in the
formation of political public opinion, political parties started to
seek the support of the student body for their programmes. The
concentration of students in towns and semi-urban areas enabled
the political parties to establish contact easily with them. The students
responded to these efforts and became involved in politics. Sudanese
students studying in Egypt, and who had been involved in the

Egyptian students' political movement, gave a further impetus to
political action by students in the Sudan. The growth of a militant
trade union movement which resorted to strikes and demonstrations
as a means of achieving recognition and better wages set an example
to the students. Trade unions did not confine their activities to the
industrial field alone, but also became involved in politics. The
students, like the trade unionists, looked upon political action as a
national obligation as long as it was directed towards a foreign
government which was responsible, in their view, for the backwardness of the country. They were unhampered by family responsibilities
or established careers, and were therefore quick to respond to the
encouragement of the political parties. Not only were nationalist
ideals dominant, but also socialist ideologies. The illegal Communist
Party, formed in 1946 under the name of the Sudanese Movement
for National Liberation, became the dominant party among the
students in the secondary schools and the University College. Its
success in attracting them was due to the fact that it was associated
with modernism, anti-colonialism, economic development, and
equality. The involvement of students in politics had therefore
become a real problem and it was thought to be a factor in the
lowering of standards in the schools. There was an urgent need to
review the whole system of education with a view to guarding the
standards and laying the foundations of a new system suitable to
the latest requirements of political and economic development. An
International Education Commission was invited, in 1955, to do
this job.

With the exception of its secretary there was no Sudanese member
on the commission.[1] The names of its British members were recommended by Sir Christopher Cox to the then Sudan Minister of
Education.[2] Its terms of reference were to

inquire into and make recommendations to improve secondary education
in the Sudan with particular reference to:
(a) The low standards of secondary schools and the problem of producing
adequate numbers of young men with prerequisite qualifications to enter
the University College of Khartoum.

[1] Members of the commission were: K. G. Sayedin (India—chairman); Miss
L. L. Charlesworth (Britain); Dr. H. F. Abu Hadid (Egypt); Sir Charles Morris
(Britain); Dr. Abdul Aziz El Sayed (Egypt); Mr. W. Abbot (Britain); L. C.
Wilcher (the Principal of the University College, Khartoum); and Dr. Ahmed
El Tayib (Sudan—secretary).
[2] Personal information from L. C. Wilcher.

(*b*) Inter-relationship of different types of secondary schools.

(*c*) The contents and methods of selection at the lower stages and how they affect this standard.[1]

With these wide terms of reference the commission was able to investigate and report, not only on secondary education, but also on all other levels of education. Its final recommendations dealt, therefore, with the whole system and its problems, except those pertaining to the University College. The report laid new objectives for education in the Sudan, and stated them as follows:

The country has emerged from the stage of colonization into political freedom and is on the way to developing democratic institutions. It is beset with many difficult economic problems. It has to fight poverty and raise the living standards of the masses, and for this purpose it must develop its potential resources with the help of modern science and technique. In order to do so and also to deal with its growing problems of administration and social services which must now be handled by the Sudanese themselves, it must find and train efficient men (and women) for the various Government Departments as well as other national needs and activities. They must not only be 'efficient' in the technical sense but also as the nation's servants on whose character, integrity and devotion the nation may rely at this time of particular urgency and difficulty.

On the social side it has to deal with a number of very difficult and complicated problems, like the unification of the people—particularly as between the North and the South, bridging the social, cultural and economic differences which exist between the different regions, securing equality of opportunity, eradicating customs and traditions which are reactionary or out of harmony with the new shape of things. While in the solving of all these problems education has obviously a vital role to play. These problems must themselves largely determine the pattern of education and educational objectives. It has to be remembered that in the final analysis, the character of a people accounts for more than its material resources, and it is here that a sound system of education can make its impact most powerfully.[2]

These new objectives, setting for the first time a new role for education in the Sudan, could be achieved, in the commission's view, through a general reorganization of education, its expansion and the improvement of its quality. In order to achieve this the commission recommended:

(*a*) The re-orientation of secondary education with a view to

[1] Sudan Government, *Report of the International Education Commission on Secondary Education*, Khartoum, February 1955, p. 6
[2] Ibid., p. 20.

developing the character, personality, intellectual and technical ability of the young Sudanese so as to enable them to participate actively in the democratic institutions of the country and its intellectual and economic life. This education for democracy meant, in its view, educating them to be tolerant, co-operative, disciplined, self-denying, and respondent to the needs of the community. In addition to these values it should lead to the improvement of technical efficiency and a respect for labour. The absence of a sense of dignity of labour and respect for manual work among the educated class was, in the commission's view, the result of 'the undue emphasis that has been placed between schools and productive work of various kinds'.[1]

(b) The diversification of secondary education so as to provide suitable educational curricula and activities for students of varying abilities.[2]

(c) The institution of a better system for selection to secondary schools and the reform of the secondary school syllabus to enable the student to sit for the ordinary level school certificate at the end of the third year in the secondary school, leaving the final year for specialization and work at the advanced level.

(d) Expansion of education at all levels, especially at the elementary level, not only because this was consistent with the idea of education for democracy, but also because this would make it possible to select, not only better but also a larger number of candidates to secondary schools.[3]

(e) The institution of a local certificate examination notwithstanding the benefits derived from an external examination with regard to the standards.[4]

(f) The establishment of two committees: one consisting of local experts and educationalists to revise the syllabuses and curriculum according to the national needs; and the other consisting of educationalists, industrialists, and other interested bodies to advise on technical education.[5]

(g) The establishment of a Department of Education in the University College to undertake post-graduate training for teachers or, as an alternative to this, either a Teachers' Training College as part

[1] Sudan Government, *Report of the International Education Commission on Secondary Education*, Khartoum, February 1955, p. 21.
[2] Ibid., p. 14.
[3] Ibid., pp. 32–3.
[4] Ibid., p. 42.   [5] Ibid., p. 92.

of the University College, or one which was independent of the latter.[1]

The commission's most important recommendations were in connection with language teaching and southern education. In the commission's view, English should be discontinued as a medium of instruction in the Sudan schools, because teaching in a foreign language below university level was both 'harmful and wasteful',[2] and the reasons justifying this in the past were no longer valid. As for education in the south, the commission recommended that schools should be taken over by the government so that southern Sudanese would be provided with an education which would make them citizens of the country and able to take part in its development. In the meantime, and until enough schools were provided by the government, missionary societies should be asked to broaden the scope of their education. On the question of language the commission found 'little argument in favour of English being particularly suitable as the medium of instruction in the south'.[3] Arabic, being already the *lingua franca* of the south, would be easier to teach and consistent with the policy of national unity which was an objective of the educational system and policy. Teaching in the vernacular was rejected because 'it would be a waste of time and energy to try to teach the children of the south in their own vernacular in which they will not be able to pursue any reading after they leave school. Such vernaculars have no literature and cannot be used as cultural media.'[4]

The report and recommendations of the commission were, therefore, a dissection of the problems of education, and suggestions for remedies, respectively. It was an evaluation of the new role which education should assume in a country moving fast into a new political and administrative set-up. The only field which it did not pronounce on was higher education because it was outside its terms of reference, but this did not mean that there was no concern with its problems or its important role. A similar search for new organization and targets was being undertaken by the University College Council and Senate.

The establishment of the Special Relation Scheme between the University College and the University of London in 1947 marked the beginning of a new development in higher education. Degree

[1] Ibid., pp. 64-7 and 108.
[2] Ibid., pp. 17, 51-2.
[3] Ibid., p. 53.   [4] Ibid., p. 54.

Courses for selected students who reached a high standard at the intermediate level were started. The award of local diplomas to those who did not qualify for the degree courses was continued. This latter arrangement, not followed by other university colleges in special relation with the University of London, enabled the college to admit increasing numbers of students without lowering the standards required by the University of London. The decision to retain the diploma courses was made in spite of the pressure from certain members of the expatriate staff to abolish it as being sub-university work.[1] The introduction of degree courses persuaded many candidates who would otherwise have sought education in Egyptian universities to remain in the Sudan for this purpose. Another significant decision was to defer appointing professors until 1951. The field to draw upon was limited and the opportunities for research work were small. The immediate need was to get the basic equipment, organize the syllabuses and curriculum and develop all parts of the university to a higher level. Priority was thus given to transforming the higher schools into a proper University College serving the immediate needs and taking into consideration the conditions of the Sudan, both economic and political, without losing sight of the ultimate goal. Perhaps the close association of Sudanese with the University College by being on its council and members of the administration had made this possible.[2]

The second step in the development of higher education was taken when the ordinance establishing the University College of Khartoum came into force on 1 September 1951. The ordinance brought the Gordon Memorial College and the Kitchener School of Medicine into a single institution under one common management. The new college was constituted as a statutory public corporation vested with legal powers and responsibilities. Its constitution was worked out with the help and advice of the Inter-University Council and the Senate of the University of London.[3] Although the special relation with London had allowed a measure of freedom in adapting syllabuses, guaranteed the standard of degrees, and helped to attract teachers from abroad, it was not a satisfactory arrangement from the national point of view. The relation resembled that of a dependent territory and was out of step with political developments. In 1953

---

[1] Personal information from L. C. Wilcher.
[2] Personal information from L. C. Wilcher.
[3] *GMCR, 1951.*

Dame Lilian Penson, representing the Senate of the University of London, advised that the college should consider the possibility of breaking its connection with the University of London and becoming an independent institution.[1] This was, from the point of view of some of the staff, a risk which should be avoided. There was a fear that the degrees awarded independently of the University of London might not be recognized by the international body of universities. There were qualms that the recruitment of expatriate staff would be affected if the relation with the University of London was not maintained. The national feelings and political considerations were, however, so pressing that changes were inevitable. The first Sudanese Government had already announced that it was expecting the University College 'to co-operate wholeheartedly with the government in the implementation of national policy',[2] to do its utmost to produce graduates in both numbers and quality, to hasten Sudanization, to speed the Sudanization of its own staff, and to take the necessary steps to ensure that the latter were recruited on an international basis.[3]

The Special Relation Scheme did not include any of these requirements in its objectives nor allow for freedom of action in these fields. The concept of Sudanization of the institutions in form and content was spreading to the University College. The Academic Board therefore decided to recommend that the University College should seek 'to obtain full university status by 1 July 1955, or soon after'.[4] This was endorsed by the Council soon after that. A scheme of scholarships for Sudanese graduates to enable 'one or more students overseas each year for further training' was also approved. This decision marked the beginning of the creation of a nucleus of Sudanese scholars and university lecturers.

The academic development of the University College to suit the new conditions was the subject of two reports submitted to the Council in 1955. Dame Lilian Penson and Dr. J. W. Cook were invited to inquire into the problems of admission and the introduction of honours degrees. On the problem of admission they did not propose changes in the requirements but directed attention to the weakness in the educational structure as a result of the small number

[1] Minute 104 of fourth meeting of the Council of University College, Khartoum, 7 April 1953, *UKA*.
[2] Sudan Government, *Weekly Digest of Proceedings of Senate, Second Session*, Khartoum, 1954, p. 164.   [3] Ibid.
[4] Minute 136 of sixth meeting of the Council of University College, Khartoum, 6 April 1954, *UKA*.

of secondary schools.[1] On the question of honours courses they recommended their introduction, and directed attention to the need of strengthening the faculties of arts and science.[2]

The second report was submitted by L. C. Wilcher, the principal of the college. His memorandum discussed a number of suggestions relating to new faculties, departments, and courses. The memorandum rejected the proposals of establishing a faculty of commerce and departments of education, geology, archaeology, and the teaching of foreign languages other than English, on the grounds that the demand for these courses by future employers was doubtful. The proposal to establish a department of pharmacy was also rejected on the ground that it was not a university subject. Extra-mural studies were not to be given priority in development, although a report in 1948 had recommended their establishment, because of the considerable need and demand for educational and cultural courses conducted by the university.[3] The report was rejected on the ground that its recommendations were not in keeping with the demands at the time. The University College authorities wanted a scheme which would provide evening classes and courses in subjects of interest to the government officials.[4]

The memorandum proposed that priority in academic development should be given to architecture, philosophy, anthropology, and African languages. The Academic Board and Council, however, decided to give priority to architecture, philosophy, geology, and political science. The first three of these were established in 1956.

In the meantime the plans for another university, to be financed by the Egyptian Government, were being discussed in October 1955. A branch of Cairo University was established in Khartoum and 286 students were admitted to its faculties of commerce, arts, and law. The degrees awarded were those of Cairo University, and the teaching was done in the evening only. It was accommodated in Khartoum Egyptian Secondary School. As the requirements of entry were lower than those of Cairo University or the University College of Khartoum, it was possible to admit those who did not qualify for either; and as the teaching was carried out in the evenings only, many of its students were government officials combining work and study. The

[1] Minutes of the ninth meeting of the Council of University College, Khartoum, 6 April 1955, *UKA.*
[2] Ibid.
[3] Hodgkin, T., Report on Extra-mural work, Khartoum, 1948, *UKA.*
[4] Personal information from L. C. Wilcher.

establishment of the Khartoum branch of Cairo University was a further contribution by Egypt to the education of the Sudanese.

Although political events during 1955 had promoted expansion and the search for reform in education, and the number of pupils attending different levels of education in the north in 1956 more than doubled compared to 1948,[1] they caused a setback in education in the south.[2]

The educational policy which had been followed since 1949 had not been welcomed by the missionary societies, nor by the southern educated class. The missionary societies were afraid that the new policy would open the way to Islam and Arabic culture. The Catholic Mission, in particular, opposed the policy on principle. It claimed that 'it is the right of the Church and of Catholic parents to educate their children in schools in which religious and cultural progress go hand in hand'.[3] The southern educated class, themselves products of missionary schools, suspected that the aim of the northerners was to spread Islam and Arabic culture. Sudanization of the civil service and administration, because of the lack of qualified and trained southerners, meant in fact that the British administrators were replaced by northern administrators. The two groups, each a product of a different educational system, lacked confidence in each other. The mutiny in August 1955 by the Equatorial Corps of the Sudanese Defence Force was partly a result of the new educational policy.[4] Educational progress in the south was hindered and lagged further behind educational progress in the north.

The educational policy of the Condominium Government lay at the root of disparity and antagonism between the south and the north. The new southern educational policy, initiated by the Sudanese Government, failed to uproot these disparities and establish a unified system of education which would create national unity.

[1] Appendix I, Table xiv.
[2] Appendix I, Table xv.
[3] Letter from the Catholic Mission to the Minister of Education in Juba, 5 June 1954, *EDA.*
[4] Republic of the Sudan, *Southern Sudan Disturbances*, Khartoum 1956, pp. 5, 7, 21.

CHAPTER XII

Conclusion

THE SUDAN, which became independent in 1956, inherited from the Condominium administration an educational system of great complexity in quantity and quality. Educational facilities were limited and unequally distributed between the different regions, and between male and female. According to the first population census carried out in 1956, the literacy rate among the population at the age of five and above stood at 14 per cent. Only 2·2 per cent of those who were literate had attended secondary and post-secondary schools, 6·9 per cent had eight years of education, and the remaining 90·9 per cent had elementary education of one sort or another.[1] The literacy rate among females was much lower than that among males. While the number of males over 10 years in 1956 was 3,461,000 and the number of females was 3,389,000, the literacy rate among the first group was 22·9 per cent, and among the second group only 4 per cent.[2]

There was a similar disparity between education in the north and the south. While the proportion of employable population over the whole Sudan claiming to have attended school among adults of 15 years and above was 12 per cent, the average for the six northern provinces was 30 per cent and for the three southern provinces only 7 per cent. The provision of education for both males and females in the Upper Nile and Bahr al Ghazal provinces was the least compared to other provinces. Kordufan and Darfur provinces were in a similar situation to those of the northern provinces.[3]

Education was most widespread in the north-east regions of the Sudan—Blue Nile, Kassala, and Khartoum provinces—and least in the southern provinces. Khartoum province had the most widespread elementary education and next to it came the Northern province. In Darfur, elementary education was less advanced than it was on the average in the south.

There were also differences in the geographical distribution of

---

[1] E. S. Crosby and the Education Division Staff, *Sudanese Manpower 1956–1965*, Education Division U.S.O.M. to Sudan (Khartoum, 1960), p. 23.

[2] Appendix I, Table XVIII.

[3] E. S. Crosby, *Sudanese Manpower*, p. 24.

persons with post-elementary education. Though Khartoum province, for example, had about one-twentieth of the total population of the Sudan, it contained about half of the men and two-thirds of the women with education higher than elementary. By contrast to this, Darfur province, which contained about one-seventh of the population, had a very small percentage of the educated population.[1]

On the other hand, education was closely related to the level of economic activity. Though only about 8 per cent of the Sudan's population was classified in the census as urban, nearly half the men and nearly two-thirds of the women with elementary education were found in the urban groups. There was a greater concentration in urban areas of persons with more than an elementary education and a much greater concentration of persons with secondary education.

The second feature of Sudan education in 1956 was its varied sources. A traditional system of Moslem education, a Christian education provided by missionary societies, schools, and institutions following the Egyptian system of education, and a network of modern 'Western'-type schools established by the Sudan Government or voluntary agencies—all existed side by side. Each of these had its own objectives. The products of these different systems did not have a common educational background; and had, therefore, different attitudes and capabilities.

When the Condominium administration came to an end on 1 January 1956 the number of Sudanese in the civil service was 1,152 compared to 7,860 in 1953. Twenty-seven per cent of the posts in the directorship and highest grades were held by Sudanese.[2]

The Sudan's two major requirements in 1956 were economic progress and national unity. The implications of these two requirements for education, although difficult to set out in detail, seemed to have been obvious. First, the narrow, but practical, aims laid down by Currie in 1900 and later modified to suit the economic, political, and administrative development were no longer suited to the new conditions. Secondly, it was obvious that manpower requirements at the highest levels were beyond the capacity of the University of Khartoum (which became independent in 1956) and other higher institutes. Thirdly, the expansion of education at all levels, particularly

[1] United Nations, *Population Growth and Manpower in the Sudan*, Department of Economics and Social Affairs, Population Studies, no. 37, United Nations (New York, 1964), pp. 108–9.
[2] Halim, M. A., The Sudan Civil Service, *The Proceedings of the Conference on Tradition and Change*, Khartoum, 1960.

at the elementary level, was necessary. Economic development depends ultimately on people; unless the educational system provides the required numbers and levels when needed, economic development will not be achieved.

Finally, it was clear that the disparity in education between males and females, and between north and south, had to be progressively eliminated for the interests of both economic development and national unity.

It was with these aims in mind that the Akrawi Committee, the Kadhim Committee and the Educational Investment Programming Mission were invited to discuss and report on the educational system. In 1958 a committee of 11 Sudanese educationalists was appointed under the chairmanship of Dr. Akrawi, a Unesco expert. In 1960 Dr. Kadhim was invited for the purpose of advising on the implementation of the Akrawi report and suggesting any modifications if necessary.

Like the International Commission report of 1955, neither of these reports was comprehensive in its scope. 'The reports were not based upon a close analysis of the economic needs of the country, upon the potential manpower resources and requirements and upon the financial resources upon which it would be reasonable to rely.'[1]

Nevertheless, some constructive suggestions were made. Both reports agreed that sub-grade schools should be eliminated, that the elementary schools should be of six years duration and that eleven was too early an age for a child to cease his education.[2] The Akrawi report proposed an elementary stage extending over 6 years and a secondary stage, subdivided into general and higher stages. In the higher stage, two types of schools were recommended: one predominantly academic and the other predominantly vocational. The latter were to be diversified into technical, agricultural, commercial, and home economic schools.

The Kadhim report, while in general agreement with the basic conclusions of the Akrawi report, did not agree with its proposals regarding the latter, or the organization of education. Its alternative proposal was the provision of a four-year elementary education for every child, and that every child should be allowed to proceed, without the need to surmount an examination hurdle, to the intermediate school.[3] At the end of the second year intermediate, the

[1] Unesco: *Educational Investment Programming Mission Report*, p. 123.
[2] Ibid.   [3] Ibid., pp. 124–5.

pupils would pass an examination before being allowed to go further. Those who did not pass the examination would not be allowed to continue. The intermediate school would be followed by a four-year secondary education of one of the following types: academic (literary and scientific divisions), technical, commercial, vocational, agricultural, teacher training, and home science.

Thus the two reports agreed that the structure and organization of the schools system should be changed.

As regards the curriculum, the Akrawi report drew attention to the fact that the elementary school did not prepare the children for life as individuals, citizens, or workers. The aim of the new six-year elementary school proposed should not be, according to the Akrawi report, 'to turn out a skilled craftsman but a more lively, interested and active human being'.[1] To achieve this end the report recommended:

(1) The introduction of agricultural activities in the schools in rural areas and trade activities in the schools of the urban areas.

(2) That special emphasis should be laid on health education, handwork, and the teaching of Arabic, which should be made the language of instruction in the whole of the Sudan up to the end of the secondary school.

In order to avoid lowering the standards it was recommended that the teaching of English should start in the fourth year of the new proposed primary school. For the proposed general secondary school the report advocated a curriculum which should emphasize broad academic and practical work. While the general secondary school should lay the foundations for higher studies, it should be complete in itself since the majority of boys and girls attending would go no further in their formal education. The senior secondary school, too, should offer a variety of courses and subjects, but not all courses and subjects would be available in all schools.

On the medium of instruction the report had this to say: 'Teaching in a foreign language retards the progress of students so that a change to Arabic should ensure a much higher standard in the same period of time and avoid the anomaly of preventing the very able students from qualifying for University admission because of inadequate expression in English in the examinations.'[2]

The Kadhim report, while agreeing that there was lack of co-ordination between the different stages of education, repetition in

[1] Ibid., pp. 124–25.   [2] Ibid., pp. 126–7.

the syllabuses, and over-emphasis on theoretical studies, drew attention to the fact that most of the deficiencies were due to the shortage of trained teachers at all levels. The Akrawi report proposed a four-year course following upon the proposed general secondary school for those who would be teachers of the proposed six-year primary stage. For those teaching in the general secondary or senior secondary school, the report suggested that they should have obtained a university degree or its equivalent. The Kadhim report agreed to these proposals but suggested certain modifications, especially with regard to the training of primary school teachers.

Both reports suggested some changes in the administration of education. The Kadhim report, in addition, suggested the establishment of a number of advisory committees to advise on teacher training, adult education, and distribution of textbooks, teaching aids, and school inspection.

The Akrawi report, the Kadhim report, and the International Commission report, provided a review and detailed criticism of the educational system of the Sudan which had been developed over nearly sixty years of Condominium administration. None of them proposed a total dismantling of the whole system. This would have been impossible and not constructive. All three proposed major changes and in some cases far-reaching changes.

The need for a new educational policy which would promote unity between the north and south, bridge the gap between male and female education, and suit the new political, administrative, economic, and social conditions was recognized. The Condominium administration had laid the foundations and developed a modern system of education. Its policy and action in the field of education was influenced by internal and external factors. It was guided mostly by its immediate requirements. None the less it had left behind a network of schools and institutions which the Sudanese—masters of their own destiny—could build on and develop.

PART FOUR
APPENDICES

APPENDIX I

TABLE I

Annual government revenue and expenditure and annual expenditure on education (in Egyptian pounds), 1899–1956

Year	Revenue (1)	Expenditure (2)	Expenditure on education (3)	(3) as percentage of (2)	Remarks
1899	126,596	230,238	?	?	
1900	126,888	331,918	?	?	
1901	242,300	407,335	1,075	0·3	
1902	270,226	516,945	3,577	0·7	
1903	462,605	616,361	6,118	0·9	
1904	567,013	628,931	8,552	1·3	
1905	665,411	681,881	12,806	1·9	
1906	780,858	793,657	19,958	2·6	
1907	923,630	960,918	28,880	3·8	
1908	924,832	1,109,774	36,936	3·3	
1909	982,302	1,100,620	39,615	3·6	
1910	1,104,873	1,158,562	43,936	3·8	
1911	1,236,446	1,286,120	43,936	3·8	
1912	1,355,635	1,421,334	57,493	4·0	
1913	1,568,352	1,533,063	58,057	3·7	
1914	1,543,549	1,531,346	?	?	
1915	1,495,227	1,462,934	58,146	3·9	
1916	1,857,856	1,745,320	58,090	3·3	
1917	2,195,355	1,901,941	62,243	3·3	
1918	2,774,689	2,336,315	66,520	2·8	
1919	2,992,792	2,720,513	?	?	
1920	4,425,340	3,564,848	85,159	2·4	
1921	4,069,235	3,900,242	93,241	2·4	
1922	3,498,595	3,496,999	99,568	2·8	
1923	3,766,133	3,392,470	99,448	2·9	
1924	4,298,856	3,453,273	96,855	2·8	
1925	4,866,883	4,375,670	96,508	2·0	
1926	5,857,988	5,482,388	104,294	1·9	
1927	5,929,944	5,504,890	137,918	2·3	
1928	6,646,833	6,045,287	157,991	2·3	
1929	6,981,590	6,610,274	179,609	2·7	
1930	4,693,623	4,693,623	160,000	3·3	
1931	4,396,180	4,396,180	119,450	2·7	

Table I (*continued*)

Year	Revenue (1)	Expenditure (2)	Expenditure on education (3)	(3) as percentage of (2)	Remarks
1932	3,853,798	3,853,798	116,434	2·3	
1933	3,639,570	3,521,957	112,393	3·1	
1934	3,774,911	3,794,488	119,086	3·1	
1935	4,098,413	3,993,113	12,885	3·3	
1936	4,402,309	4,204,917	88,388	2·9	Expenditure on Wellcome Research Laboratories not included as from this year.
1937	4,748,302	4,457,784	94,197	2·2	
1938	5,131,635	4,857,784	103,448	2·1	
1939	5,053,765	4,857,784	?	?	
1940	4,632,351	4,543,790	?	?	
1941	5,379,277	5,047,160	147,274	2·9	
1942	5,814,165	5,337,991	165,212	3·3	
1943	5,861,944	5,601,790	173,990	3·9	
1944	6,578,769	6,529,662	196,127	3·0	
1945	7,763,078	7,548,186	272,751	3·6	Expenditure on higher schools not included as from this year
1946	8,288,985	8,207,802	301,688	3·6	
1947	10,141,495	9,534,668	482,862	5·0	
1948	12,697,809	11,318,589	652,989	5·8	
1949	19,172,548	13,964,007	?	?	
1950/1	41,867,359	23,596,510	?	?	
1951/2	46,299,658	21,531,991	1,702,717	7·8	
1952/3	30,295,657	25,658,747	1,866,680	7·3	
1953/4	35,436,422	27,611,034	2,189,065	7·9	
1954/5	38,110,530	30,588,642	3,780,618	12·3	
1955/6	42,322,551	32,097,705	3,907,230	11·8	
1956/7	45,869,401	32,698,857	4,436,247	13·5	

Sources: Sudan Government, *Annual Budgets 1899–1956*, and Annual Budgets of Education Department 1901–56.

TABLE II
Sudan Government capital expenditure: sources and distribution, 1899–1918

| Item of expenditure | Capital expenditure in Egyptian pounds | | | |
	From Egyptian loans and grants	From Sudan reserve fund	Total	Percentage
Transport	5,968,000	348,000	6,316,000	76·3
Telegraphs	61,000	117,000	178,000	2·1
Agriculture	—	150,000	150,000	1·8
Miscellaneous, including education	537,000	1,096,000	1,633,000	19·8
Total	6,566,000	1,711,000	8,277,000	100

Source: Abdu, O. M. Osman: Ph.D. thesis, University of London, 1960, p. 249.

TABLE III
Education taxes, 1906–1913

Year	Amount paid in Egyptian pounds	Remarks
1906	350	The tax was paid in the Blue
1907	2,355	Nile, Dongola, Khartoum,
1908	2,464	Sennar, and White Nile prov-
1909	2,215	inces only, and discontinued
1910	4,177	in 1913
1911	4,606	
1912	?	
1913	5,293	

Source: Sudan Government, *Annual Budgets 1906–13*.

TABLE IV

Classified posts held by Sudanese and non-Sudanese in the
government service in 1920

Department or province	British	Egyptian	Sudanese	Syrians	Others
Governor-General's office	5	3	1	—	—
Sudan Agency	4	6	—	3	—
Agriculture	18	14	30	—	1
Forests	7	23	31	—	1
Civil Secretary's office	10	4	5	—	1
Customs	12	41	36	6	4
Education	31	53	282	4	5
Finance	10	119	10	54	4
Central Economic Boards	7	—	7	1	—
Intelligence	7	1	3	5	8
Legal	17	62	141	10	6
Medical	15	41	9	34	—
Posts and Telegraphs	18	358	143	2	2
Public Works	43	27	10	2	10
Railways and Steamers	148	444	142	17	40
Slavery	4	5	4	—	—
Stores	2	23	5	1	1
Surveys	13	14	53	—	3
Veterinary	20	20	4	1	—
Bahr al Ghazal	9	25	29	3	—
Berber	7	35	44	1	—
Blue Nile	5	48	60	1	1
Darfur	11	23	45	—	—
Dongola	3	50	57	2	—
Halfa	2	29	14	2	—
Kassala	5	36	27	2	2
Khartoum	19	71	65	1	3
Kordufan	10	47	63	2	—
Mongalla	8	33	23	3	—
Nuba Mountains	5	24	20	—	—
Red Sea	12	30	36	4	2
Sennar	7	36	53	1	—
Upper Nile	6	9	22	2	—
White Nile	6	30	39	—	—
Total	506	1,795	1,523	166	102
Sudan Irrigation	29	29	21	1	6
Total	535	1,824	1,544	167	108

Source: Memorandum on the Sudan, *Milner Papers*, in the Bodleian Library, Oxford.

TABLE V

Educational development in Northern Sudan (government education), 1922–1932

	1922	1923	1924	1925	1926	1927	1928	1929	1930	1931	1932
Number of boys in assisted *khalwas*	?	889	2,700	5,444	8,422	13,077	17,280	21,060	28,669	?	?
Number of boys in elementary schools	8,815	8,410	8,296	7,852	8,196	8,057	7,836	7,827	8,388	9,342	8,943
Number of boys in primary schools	1,153	?	?	?	1,153	1,296	1,286	1,280	1,276	1,315	1,059
Number of boys in Gordon College higher schools	191	207	211	235	303	370	442	510	555	?	436
Number of boys in Teacher Training section	36	15	?	?	?	?	?	?	55	?	?
Number of boys in technical schools	255	283	247	215	332	351	361	370	387	?	213
Number of girls in elementary schools	353	360	344	397	555	694	1,075	1,248	1,905	2,045	2,316
Number of girls in training colleges	20	19	21	28	22	22	30	36	61	?	?

Source: *Annual Reports of the Education Department*, 1922–32.

200

TABLE VI

Gordon Memorial College secondary school—number of pupils and province of origin, 1934–1946

Province of origin	1934	1935	1936	1937	1938	1939	1940	1941	1942	1943	1944	1945	1946
Khartoum	194	175	146	151	166	211	275	285	290	270	233		
Northern	88	85	63	86	94	100	116	111	120	124	143		
Blue Nile	51	39	43	47	55	67	82	78	80	89	95		
Kordufan	12	10	14	15	21	20	16	18	11	19	17		
Kassala	14	11	5	8	9	13	19	21	21	18	20		
White Nile	22	21	16	14	11	—	—	—	—	—	—		
Darfur	1	1	1	1	—	—	—	—	—	—	—		
Somali	2	2	3	3	1	—	—	—	—	—	—		
Aden	—	—	—	—	—	—	—	2	2	3	6		
Total	384	344	291	325	357	411	508	515	524	523	514	517	528

Source: *Annual Reports*, G.M.C. and Education Department.

TABLE VII

Gordon Memorial College secondary school—number of pupils according to occupation of fathers, 1935–1944

	1935	1936	1937	1938	1939	1940	1941	1942	1943	1944
Government officials	169	147	171	189	202	255	257	263	248	243
Army officers	16	11	14	13	16	17	14	15	12	12
Farmers	61	49	46	51	63	74	75	73	70	71
Tribal chiefs	1	1	5	3	5	12	9	13	16	13
Merchants	78	64	59	72	85	100	100	112	110	112
Craftsmen	19	18	30	29	40	50	60	58	67	63
Total	344	291	325	357	411	508	515	524	523	514

Source: *Annual Reports*, G.M.C.

TABLE VIII

Higher education: number of students, 1942–1956

	1942	1943	1944	1948	1951	1952	1953	1954	1955	1956	Remarks
School of arts	57	73	58	100	112	152	144	183	175	187	
School of agriculture	12	11	11	7	6	37	35	40	40	33	
School of law	?	?	?	36	27	39	84	67	82	99	Numbers for 1942–4 included with arts
School of engineering	17	19	19	14	12	29	39	44	35	46	
School of medicine	21	22	29	32	47	50	70	82	71	128	
School of science	38	31	44	92	100	170	149	185	167	213	
School of veterinary science	3	5	2	9	13	15	10	10	10	16	
Total	148	161	163	290	317	492	531	601	580	722	

Source: *Annual Reports*, G.M.C.

TABLE IX
Number of graduates from the higher schools, University College and K.S.M., 1935–1956

Faculty	1935	1936	1937	1938	1939	1940	1941	1942	1943	1944	1945	1946	1947	1948	1949	1950	1951	1952	1953	1954	1955	1956
Agriculture	—	—	—	—	—	—	—	3	—	—	8	—	4	—	5	—	—	8	8	—	13	10
Arts	—	—	—	—	—	—	—	9	13	—	10	16	30	20	13	9	35	26	1	24	40	35
Engineering	—	—	—	—	—	—	5	—	—	6	4	6	—	7	—	—	—	8	5	6	1	8
Law	—	—	—	—	—	—	—	—	6	1	—	—	—	7	1	—	10	3	4	—	16	—
Medicine	9	4	6	1	7	7	1	—	6	—	4	8	—	6	—	4	—	10	5	12	1	14
Science	—	—	—	—	—	7	—	8	—	—	4	—	5	5	4	2	4	7	—	9	6	14
Veterinary science	—	—	—	—	—	—	3	—	—	3	1	2	—	—	1	—	1	6	—	—	1	1
Total	9	4	6	1	7	14	9	20	25	10	31	32	39	45	24	17	50	68	23	51	78	82

Source: Republic of the Sudan, *Educational Statistics for the Academic Year 1958–9*, Ministry of Education, Khartoum 1959, Table 32.

TABLE X

Grants-in-aid to missionary education in the Southern Sudan, 1933–1946 (in Egyptian pounds)

Year	Upper Nile province	Bahr al Ghazal province	Mongalla province	Equatoria province	Total for Southern Sudan	Remarks
1933	1,150	2,275	4,180	—	7,605	
1934	1,240	2,370	4,180	—	7,810	
1935	1,240	2,380	4,200	—	7,720	
1936[1]	1,540	—	—	6,670	8,210	[1] The provinces of Bahr al Ghazal and Mongalla became Equatoria
1937	1,690	—	—	7,465	9,155	
1941	1,975	—	—	11,875	13,850	
1942	2,276	—	—	13,068	15,344	
1943	2,536	—	—	13,645	16,181	
1944[2]	2,477	—	—	14,390	16,867	[2] Building grants excluded from these figures
1945[2]	3,105	—	—	16,249	19,354[3]	[3] In addition to these totals £E2,000 were allocated in 1945 and in 1946 under miscellaneous expenditure as a pool from which all missionary societies in the south could draw for emergency purposes
1946[2]	3,656	—	—	23,000	26,650[3]	

Source: Annual Budgets of the Education Department, Khartoum

	Equatoria province				Upper Nile province			
	1938		1946		1938		1946	
	Number of schools	Number of pupils	Number of schools	Number of pupils	Number of schools	Number of pupils	Number of schools	Number of pupils
Church Missionary Society								
Boys' elementary education	7	808	8	963	3	141	3	148
Girls' elementary education	3	175	4	330	—	—	—	—
Boys' intermediate education	1	95	1	133	—	—	—	—
Boys' technical education	1	18	1	23	—	—	—	—
Total	12	1,096	14	1,449	3	141	3	148
American Presbyterian Mission								
Boys' elementary education	—	—	—	—	2	121	3	266
Girls' elementary education	—	—	—	—	2	65	1	18
Total	—	—	—	—	4	186	4	284
Roman Catholic Mission								
Boys' elementary education	16	1,619	18	2,405	4	100	4	184
Girls' elementary education	12	458	8	537	—	—	—	—
Boys' intermediate education	2	175	2	333	—	—	—	—
Boys' normal education	2	88	—	—	—	—	—	—
Boys' technical education	2	89	2	86	—	—	—	—
Elementary teachers' education	—	—	2	112	—	—	—	—
Total	34	2,429	32	3,473	4	100	4	184
Grand total	46	3,525	46	4,922	11	427	11	616

Source: *Annual Reports of the Education Department.*

TABLE XII

Non-government education: *Ahlia* intermediate schools

Place	Date of opening
Omdurman	1927
Omdurman (Ahfad)	1933
Medani	1941
Omdurman (Hay Alarab)	1943
Port Sudan	1943
Obeid	1943
Goled	1944
Atbara	1944
Atbara (Congress)	1944
Berber	1945
Rufaa	1945
Fasher	1945
Kamlin	1946
Kosti	1946
Nuhud	1946
Halfa	1946
Shendi	1946
Khartoum	1947
Kassala	1947
Atbara (Workers')	1947
Gedarif	1948
Omdurman (Beitalmal)	1948
Omdurman (Wadnabawi)	1949
Hassa Heissa	1950
Al Kosh	1950
Medani	1951
Massalamya	1951
Omdurman (Beit Alamana)	1951
Omdurman (Nahda)	1951
Omdurman (Girls')	1951
Khartoum North	1951
Dalgo	1952
Tokar	1952
Singa	1952

TABLE XIII
Development expenditure 1946–1951 and 1951–1956
Percentage allocation between different sections of the economy

	1946–51	1951–56
Production schemes	35·6	16·8
Social services	13·6	11·8
Education	10·0	15·5
Administration	23·3	13·8
Communications	8·5	26·8
Public liabilities	7·5	13·4
Miscellaneous	1·5	1·9
	100%	100%
Total in million pounds	14·6	45·1

Source: Republic of the Sudan Ministry of Finance and Economics.

TABLE XIV

Educational development in the northern Sudan (government education)
Number of pupils attending schools in 1936, 1944, 1948 and 1956

	1936	1944	1948	1956
Higher education	?	163	306	722
Secondary education—boys	291	514	801	1,700
Junior secondary education—boys	—	221	191	280
Intermediate education—boys	1,072	1,847	2,255	4,675
Elementary education—boys	12,402	19,381	26,074	76,996
Teachers' training for elementary schools	62	149	217	438
Sub-grade education	—	12,738	25,640	53,500
Subsidized khalwas	22,400	10,133	7,328	5,000
Technical education—boys	175	221	295	609
Teachers' training—girls	29	90	130	265
Elementary education—girls	2,927	6,681	?	26,581
Intermediate education—girls	—	114	313	1,288
Secondary education—girls	—	—	37	265

Source: *Annual Reports, Education Department.*

TABLE XV

New schools opened in the North and South, 1951–1956

	1951/2	Per- centage	1952/3	Per- centage	1953/4	Per- centage	1954/5	Per- centage	1955/6	Per- centage
Total number of new sub- grade schools opened	49	100	17	100	26	100	114	100	44	100
Share of northern provinces	40	83	6	35	8	31	39	34	44	100
Share of southern provinces	9	17	11	65	18	69	75	66	—	—
Total number of new elemen- tary schools opened	65	100	47	100	83	100	69	100	93	100
Share of northern provinces	61	94	40	85	72	87	41	59	93	100
Share of southern provinces	4	6	7	15	11	13	28	41	—	—
Total number of new inter- mediate classes opened	2	100	4	100	10	100	17	100	4	100
Share of northern provinces	1	50	4	100	10	100	16	94	1	25
Share of southern provinces	1	50	—	—	—	—	1	6	3	75
Total number of new secondary classes opened	2	100	2	100	3	100	5	100	8	100
Share of northern provinces	2	100	2	100	3	100	5	100	7	87
Share of southern provinces	—	—	—	—	—	—	—	—	1	13

Source: *Annual Reports, Education Department.*

TABLE XVI

Classified posts in the Sudan Government service held by Sudanese and non-Sudanese, 1939–1955

Year	Clerical posts				Supervisory and middle grade				Super and directors' posts			
	Total number of posts	Sudanese	Non-Sudanese	Percentage Sudanese	Total number of posts	Sudanese	Non-Sudanese	Percentage Sudanese	Total number of posts	Sudanese	Non-Sudanese	Percentage Sudanese
1939	4,249	4,029	157	96	408	26	382	6	60	—	60	—
1945	5,516	5,416	100	98	518	35	463	10	72	—	72	—
1948	7,367	7,243	124	98	683	109	574	16	92	5	87	5
1950/1	8,193	8,046	147	98	820	180	640	22	107	9	98	8
1954/5	10,646	10,299	347	97	1,156	467	689	40	168	45	123	27

Source: Ministry of Finance and Economics, Khartoum.

TABLE XVII

Educational attainment of the Sudanese population, 1956 (in thousands)

Age groups	Total population above 15 years		Sub-grade schools		Elementary schools		Intermediate schools		Secondary schools and beyond		No school at all	
	Males	Females	Males	Females	Males	Females	Males	Females	Males	Females	Males	Females
15 to 19	560	545	93	14	52	15	14	4	8	2	393	510
20 to 24	468	454	78	8	31	10	7	2	6	1	346	433
25 to 34	709	684	121	4	36	5	8	1	4	1	540	673
35 to 44	479	461	70	2	18	2	5	—	2	—	384	457
45 to 54	307	302	22	—	7	1	3	—	1	—	274	301
55 to 64	175	182	7	—	1·5	—	1·5	—	1	—	164	182
65 and over	101	115	2	—	0·5	—	0·5	—	—	—	98	115
Total	2,799	2,743	393	28	146	33	39	7	22	4	2,199	2,671

Source: Republic of the Sudan, *Educational Statistics for the Academic Year 1959-60*, Ministry of Education, Khartoum, 1961, p. 9.

TABLE XVIII

Literacy and illiteracy in the Sudan, 1956 (in thousands)

Age groups	Population above 10 years		Literate people		Illiterate people		Rate of literacy	
	Males	Females	Males	Females	Males	Females	Males	Females
10 to 14	662	646	207	71	455	575	31·3	11·0
15 to 19	560	545	166	32	394	513	29·6	5·9
20 to 24	468	454	120	18	348	436	25·6	4·0
25 to 34	709	684	165	10	544	674	23·3	1·5
35 to 44	479	461	92	2	387	459	19·2	0·4
45 to 54	307	302	31	1	276	301	10·1	0·3
55 to 64	175	182	9	—	166	182	5·1	—
65 and over	101	115	1	—	100	115	1·0	—
Total	3,461	3,389	791	134	2,670	3,255	22·9	4·0

Source: Republic of the Sudan, *Educational Statistics for the Academic Year 1959–1960*, Ministry of Education, Khartoum, 1961, p. 9.

APPENDIX II

Letter addressed by Lord Kitchener of Khartoum and Aspali to the public press on the 30th November, 1898[1]

Sir,

I trust that it will not be thought that I am trespassing too much upon the goodwill of the British Public, or that I am exceeding the duties of a soldier, if I call your attention to an issue of very grave importance arising immediately out of the recent campaign in the Sudan. The region now lies in the pathway of our Empire, and a numerous population has become practically dependent on our race. A responsible task is henceforth laid upon us, and those who have conquered are called upon to civilize. In fact, the work interrupted since the death of Gordon must now be resumed.

It is with this conviction that I venture to lay before you a proposal which, if it met with the approval and support of the British public and of the English-speaking race, would prove of inestimable benefit to the Sudan and to Africa. The area of the Sudan comprises a population of upwards of three million persons, of whom it may be said that they are wholly uneducated. The dangers arising from that fact are too obvious, and have been too painfully felt during many years past for me to dwell on them. In the course of time, no doubt, an education of some sort, and administered by some hands, will be set on foot. But if Khartoum could be made forthwith the centre of an education supported by British funds and organized from Britain, there would be secured to this country indisputably the first place in Africa as a civilizing power, and an effect would be created which would be felt for good throughout the central regions of that Continent. I accordingly propose that at Khartoum there should be founded and maintained with British money a College bearing the name of the Gordon Memorial College, to be a pledge that the memory of Gordon is still alive among us, and that his aspirations are at length to be realized.

Certain questions will naturally arise as to whom exactly we should educate, and as to the nature of the education to be given. Our system would need to be gradually built up. We should begin by teaching the sons of the leading men, the heads of villages and the heads of districts. They belong to a race very capable of learning, and ready to learn. The teaching, in its early stages, would be devoted to purely elementary subjects, such as reading, writing, geography and the English language. Later, and after these preliminary stages had been passed, a more advanced course would

[1] Source: University of Khartoum Archives.

be instituted, including a training in technical subjects, specially adapted to the requirements of those who inhabit the Valley of the Upper Nile. The principal teachers in the College would be British, and the supervision of the arrangements would be vested in the Governor-General of Sudan. I need not add that there would be no interference with the religion of the people.

The fund required for the establishment of such a college is one hundred thousand pounds. Of this, ten thousand pounds would be appropriated to the initial outlay, while the remaining ninety thousand pounds would be invested, and the revenue thence derived would go to the maintenance of the College and the support of the staff of teachers. It would be clearly impossible at first to require payment from the pupils, but as the College developed and the standard of its teaching rose, it would be fair to demand fees in respect of this higher education, which would thus support itself, and render the College independent of any further call upon the public. It is for the provision of this sum of one hundred thousand pounds that I now desire to appeal, on behalf of a race dependent upon our mercy, in the name of Gordon, and in the cause of that civilization which is the life of the Empire of Britain.

I am authorized to state that Her Majesty the Queen has been graciously pleased to become the Patron of the movement. His Royal Highness the Prince of Wales has graciously consented to become Vice-Patron.

I may state that a General Council of the leading men of the country is in course of formation. Lord Hillingdon has kindly consented to accept the post of Hon. Treasurer. The Hon. George Peel has consented to act as Hon. Secretary, and all communications should be addressed to him at 67 Lombard Street, London, E.C. Subscriptions should be paid to the Sirdar's Fund for the 'Gordon Memorial College at Khartoum', Messrs. Glyn, Mills, Currie & Co., 67 Lombard Street, London, E.C.

Enclosed herewith is a letter from the Marquis of Salisbury, in which he states that this scheme represents the only policy by which the civilizing mission of this country can effectively be accomplished. His Lordship adds that it is only to the rich men of this country that it is possible for me to look, yet I should be glad for this appeal to find its way to all classes of our people.

I further enclose a letter from the Baroness Burdett-Coutts, whose devotion to the cause of Africa has been not the least of her magnificent services. I forward besides an important telegram from the Lord Mayor of Liverpool, and letters of great weight from the Lord Provost of Edinburgh and the Lord Provost of Glasgow. I would venture to address myself to the other great Municipalities of the Kingdom.

Above all, it is in the hands of the Press of this country that I place this cause. I look with confidence to your support in the discharge of this high obligation.

I have the honour to remain,

Yours faithfully,

(*Signed*) KITCHENER OF KHARTOUM.

APPENDIX III

Notes on the Kitchener Memorial Medical School[1]

1. *History*

This project originated with Lord Kitchener when he revisited the Sudan in 1911. He then pointed out that it was necessary to found a Medical School at Khartoum to provide the doctors that would be necessary to carry out the medical and hygienic precautions that would be essential to the intensive economic and agricultural development of the Sudan. He also looked on this school as a further, and the most important step in the completion of the educational system which he initiated when he founded the Gordon Memorial College.

The foresight and imagination shown by Lord Kitchener in the founding of the Gordon College in what was at that time a wasted and depopulated desert, has been more than justified by the results. The wonderful recovery made by the Sudan in the ensuing years could not have taken place without the agency of this Training College and the educational system of which it was the centre.

When Lord Kitchener's death was announced in the Sudan, the people who have an enormous veneration for him expressed a desire that some permanent memorial to him should be established at Khartoum.

After careful consideration it was decided to carry out as a memorial this project, which Lord Kitchener himself had proposed.

The Sudanese, who are very interested in education, and who, above all, are anxious to have young men of their own race trained as doctors, received this proposal with enthusiasm and subscribed a large sum of money. Further large sums have been subscribed by the European community in the Sudan and also from outside sources.

The present position is that all the capital expenditure has been met, and in addition a sum of £20,000 has been subscribed towards an endowment fund.

The buildings for the Medical School will be completed by November next, and the first medical students will commence their training in January of next year. These young men will be selected from the most promising of the final year students of the Gordon College.

[1] The notes, with no date, were prepared and printed for limited circulation. They were marked 'Not for Publication'. Source: *University of Khartoum Archives*. Probably written in 1924.

2. *The need for the school*

(*a*) *Economic reasons*

The Sudan is being widely opened to economic developments. A dam is being built across the Blue Nile about 170 miles south of Khartoum, and 300,000 acres of the fertile Gezirah plain will shortly be brought under perennial irrigation for cotton cultivation.

The railway is also being pushed through to Kassala so as to link up this potentially rich country with Port Sudan, thus enabling large areas of the fertile Gash Delta to be brought under cotton cultivation on a profitable basis. The cotton-growing areas of the Sudan can be extended almost indefinitely. In the Gezirah alone a million acres of ideal cotton-growing land await development, and there are further enormous areas in Kassala province and up the White Nile and the Sobat Rivers, which will gradually be brought under cotton cultivation.

There is just sufficient manpower to meet the needs of this development but none to spare. It is essential that there should be no wastage of manpower, and that there should be a steady increase of the population to meet the progressive development foreshadowed above.

The whole success of this development therefore depends on adequate hygienic and, in particular, anti-malarial measures being carried out.

These hygienic measures must be directed to the main objects:

1. To keeping the present population healthy and fit to work, and to preventing wastage of population through disease.

2. To ensuring a steady increase of the population to meet the needs of further development.

The great enemy to industrial efficiency and the great cause of wastage of the population is malaria, but this disease is seconded by two other diseases, Ankylostomiasis (Hookworm disease) and Bilharziasis. These two latter diseases debilitate those whom they attack and lower their resisting power to malaria.

The two great enemies to a healthy increase of the population are (*a*) Malaria, a very common cause of abortion and infantile death, and (*b*) Venereal diseases.

Given a sufficient number of doctors these diseases can be stamped out or enormously diminished, but an adequate supply of doctors is essential.

There are other diseases of great importance in the Sudan and in some cases of dangerous urgency, such as sleeping-sickness in the extreme south, and in Kala Azar on the upper reaches of the Blue Nile, Syphilis and Tuberculosis everywhere, but the four diseases mentioned above are the especial enemies of economic development in the Sudan.

To establish the medical and hygienic conditions necessary to successful economic development it is necessary to provide a large and steadily increasing supply of doctors carefully trained in tropical medicine and hygiene.

It has been decided, after very full investigation, that the only way to ensure this supply is to found a Medical School at Khartoum to train young Sudan-Arabs as doctors.

(b) *Civilization and pacification*

It is found that a doctor stationed in a partially pacified country will obtain far more influence, and be a greater power for order and civilization than will a political officer, even though he has a body of troops at his disposal.

The African negroid races are too apt to look on government representatives as people who want to get something valuable from them, i.e. taxes, and who have nothing which they, the natives, value to give in exchange.

He looks on the doctor in an entirely different light; here, he says, are men with remedies of immense value to offer, and who want very little in exchange.

The doctor begins by being a man with supernatural power for good and evil; he is then seen to be disinterested, and in consequence his advice is asked for on every kind of question, and he thus becomes a great power for peace and order.

The quickest and surest way to pacification and civilization in Central Africa is to enormously increase the number of doctors.

(c) *Political reasons*

While the spirit of nationalism has spread through nearly all the native races of the world, the natives of the Sudan have remained intensely loyal, and this in spite of a great deal of anti-British propaganda from outside sources. During the war the Sudanese not only remained loyal, but they subscribed to the Red Cross and other war funds to an extent out of all proportion to their material wealth. It is, therefore, very desirable to anticipate in good time all legitimate aspirations by training them to take an increasing share in the administration and the development of their country.

In no way can this be done more usefully to the country and more gratefully to the people than by training them as doctors.

It is difficult to think of any way in which such far-reaching results can be obtained in return for such a small financial expenditure . . . so much suffering relieved, so much work done towards enabling the great potential wealth of this country to be developed.

3. *General remarks*

In any consideration of Sudan questions a few main facts should be borne in mind.

i. That Khartoum is over 1,000 miles from Cairo, four days by train and boat, and that it is the capital of an entirely separate country,

differing from the Egyptians in physical characteristics, and in ideals,
history, and origin.

ii. That between Egypt and the Sudan there is a physical barrier of nearly
300 miles of arid waterless desert, bridged only by a single river fringed
by a few yards of very sparsely populated cultivation, and that the
natural outlet of the Sudan is by Port Sudan and the Red Sea.

iii. That with the exception of the extreme south, the Sudan is occupied
by an Arab race crossed to a varying degree with pre-Arab and Negroid
races, and that this race is quick, intelligent, and eager for education.
It is intensely loyal to the British connection.

APPENDIX IV

Note on education in the Northern Sudan
by G. C. Scott[1]

1. *The Need for Education*

There are so many who think that education for the Sudanese is wrong or unimportant, that it seems worth while to try to make a case for it by collecting and applying to the Sudan some of the ideas produced during the last dozen years by many administrators and educationalists.

The ancient manner of life of the Sudanese is picturesque, but it is squalid, poor, and barbarous. It is so picturesque that one may easily forget its nature, the sweaty wringing of necessities out of a barren country, the brutish torpor that succeeds it. But since the Occupation the Sudanese have been given a sight of ease, riches, and civilization; and to some now, and all eventually, the sight is alluring and disturbing. As they turn from the old ways of life they also turn from the old values, traditions, and religion; and as they take up the new they take up foreign things, little understood. If education means unrest, a discontent with old way through an acquaintance with new, then the Sudanese are being educated whether we will or no.

It may be said—admitted that this education by contact is unsettling, but school education is more so, as history proves. Why add a second factor of unrest? Further, it is futile; though change cannot be stopped it must be gradual; the centuries cannot be jumped. The Sudan, again is a poor country, which will not support that higher standard of life for which school education increases the desire. The great uneducated do not feel their squalor; let us leave them in their torpor while we spend all our energies in the bettering of their material life. In fine the function of the Education Department should be to produce a just-sufficient quantity of clerks for the government offices, and for the rest not to promote but to delay education until such time as the minds of the people and the means of the country are capable of receiving it.

There is falsehood as well as truth in these arguments. History has not proved that the education of backward peoples is unsettling: what it has proved so far is the contact of backward peoples with civilization aided by a certain type of education. It is inevitable that the centuries be jumped, and the native be torn from his values and traditions; education might help him to keep his feet, and to grasp new values that will take the place of the old. It might make a poor country richer. It might lessen squalor,

---

[1] Personal communication from G. C. Scott, May 1932.

and create the capacity for recreation to take the place of torpor. The improvement of material conditions cannot be accomplished except by schemes which destroy the ancient associations of family and tribe, unless by education we can substitute adaptation for destruction.

These may be aspirations, not arguments; but there remains an argument that is indisputable. The Sudan Government is committed to a policy of education. The opinion of civilized peoples and its own need for clerks compelled it to found a system of schools. The opinion of civilized peoples and the will of its clerks and their children compel it to continue. For the Sudan Government to allow itself to be dragged unwillingly along the path of education is a policy unworthy of a race that claims to rule, leading admittedly to disaster, and with a streak of barbarism. Since education is a strong and dangerous influence that cannot be destroyed or indefinitely suppressed, it is necessary for the government to take the only alternative course of guiding and inspiring it. Thus it may follow a creative policy worthy of Britain's traditions, may prove itself benevolent and enlightened and may change a powerful cause of sedition into one of progress and contentment.

The need for a strong educational policy and the broad lines which it should follow, become clearer when connected with the guiding principle of Sudan Government policy—Native Administration. Only a few, still imagining to themselves the golden age of the noble savage guided by wise and fatherly British officials, or mistaking the static descriptions of the anthropologist for prophecies binding on the future, now believe that Native Administration can find a permanent foundation in ignorance. But many do not realize that that foundation is already inadequate to bear the structure. Peace and economic development have even now to a great extent undermined the old traditions and organizations, and have made powerless old methods and abilities. In the centre the Great Men of the Three Towns and the giant modernity of the Gezira Scheme, in the north the influence of trade and of Egypt, in the east the dock labour and commercialism of Port Sudan and the cotton cultivations of Kassala and Tokat, the gum-trade in the mid-west and cotton again in the south; throughout the country tribesmen learning that their own ways are not the only ways, labourers at work far from their families, and landless effendis begetting occupationless children. And the thing will spread, even to the Kababish. It may be true that so long as the Kababish remain in their own country their civilization is economically impossible but can they be trusted to know it? The noble savage cannot be kept savage, and will not permanently pose either for the anthropologist or for the sentimentalist. It is no good pretending that Native Administration as we mean it is an old thing, as old as the tribal system. The tribal system will not keep the peace in Arabia or in the Sudan. To weld it into a comprehensive system of stable government neither Mohamed's methods nor Ibn Sa'ud's are practicable; the method of education remains to be tried. There is a need for native rulers whom a wise education has enabled to understand the new conditions, and to adapt their aims and methods. The rulers need servants to whom education has supplied the means of service without robbing them of sympathy for their people, or belief in their traditions.

But probably most important of all is the elementary education of the masses; and that for three reasons. First, since the Arab, the peasant, the herdsman, and the villager are proverbially conservative, the Native Administration must be able through a widespread system of elementary schools to guide its subjects to a peaceful and profitable appreciation of changing conditions. For the child unlike the adult is not incorrigible. Secondly, only by elementary education is it likely that we can avoid a great and well-understood danger. The secondary and higher education of the effendi-class exists and must continue; and we may learn from India the wisdom of combining that with the ignorance of the many. The uneducated country people may live happily for years in their model administrations under the benevolence of the government. But sooner or later arrives a man or a party who is both educated and knows how to appeal to the uneducated. The peasant, the herdsman, the villager, understanding little outside their own primitive environment, and knowing nothing of the aims and methods of government, have nothing to set against, nothing by which to judge, the striving glorious call to a fight for independence; and educated and uneducated perish together. Thirdly, it has been said that there is no room in the Sudan for a middle class; but that this is only true in that up till now 'middle class education' has been too much developed in proportion to 'lower class education'. An educated middle class needs a partly educated lower class on which to live. By first improving and then increasing elementary education we may form a demand for those services which only more advanced education can give, and may thus find occupation for those 'effendis' that we cannot help but continue to turn out. To those who fear the unsettling effect of elementary education on the masses it may be replied that there is no historical evidence that such education leads to sedition: on the contrary, the seditious movements in England, France, Russia, Egypt, India, all took the form of an educated middle-class leading ignorant masses against an aristocracy.

Education, therefore, is a necessity to administration, and there is no need to add that it alone can cure the crudities of many kinds that not only make the people unhappy, but hinder the government, and dirty its name—indifferent agriculture, fanatical Mahdism, disease-carrying dirt, female circumcision, and all the cruelty and barbarity of a backward people. Native Administration means administration by natives, and the Sudan native can neither administer nor be peacefully administered unless he progresses. Native Administration without education is a broken cart without a horse.

2. *The Present Supply of Education*

It is better, however, to be stationary in a broken cart than to be careering to destruction in a lorry; and this is what will happen if our schools supply the wrong type of education. A survey of the schools, their aims and their results, is therefore necessary. But it may be supposed in advance that the outcome of such a survey is unlikely to be encouraging; for since the present educational system was built, ideas have changed. To say this is in no way to depreciate the past work of Sudan educationalists and teachers. Not only were former conditions infinitely more difficult than they are now, not only was there no foundation on which to build, but the importance of the new ideas on the education and government of backward peoples was not yet known. Inevitably, just as government was based on direct administration, education was based on westernization. Even had the educationalists immediately devised and put into effect the means for bringing educational policy into line with the new administrative policy, the time has been too short for any great results to be evident. Actually, one obvious fact must make us doubt whether our present education system is the right one—the bitter and almost united opposition of the educated classes to Native Administration. Either our education system or Native Administration is wrong.

Quantity of Education

As to quantity, the survey is soon made. If we accept the solution of the assisted *khalwas* as reliable, and if we consider the assisted *khalwa* courses to be a kind of education, then some $11\frac{1}{2}$ per cent of the boys of school age are receiving some kind of education (taking the figure of 300,000 boys of school age in Northern Sudan from the Education Department Annual Report for 1930). But we know better than to accept *khalwa* statistics, and the truth is nearer 9 per cent. If we deny the assisted *khalwa* course the name of education, then some $3\frac{1}{2}$ per cent of the boys of school age are receiving at least an elementary education. Boys will grow up and marry, and even in the Sudan they will listen to their wives. But no more than $\frac{2}{3}$ per cent of the girls of school age are being educated.

Quality of Education

In assessing the quality of the schools there is no space here for details; but the judgements are based on the opinions of many who know them, and though there may be some disagreement I think that the general picture will be accepted as a true one.

Unassisted Khalwas

The unassisted *khalwas* cannot be considered as part of the school system. Some exceptional boys succeed in getting a little education from them, but in general while they may supply 'baraka' they do not supply education.

Assisted Khalwas

The assisted *khalwas* differ from the other schools in that they are aided, not owned, by government, and that the system was inspired by the same class of ideas that inspired a policy of Native Administration. But the main difficulties, which are two, have proved greater than was expected. First, there is the ancient Arab tradition—in the crude environment of the Sudan made even more poisonous—that education consists of learning gibberish by rote. And secondly, the short period of training proved quite inadequate for the weak teachers available. Most of them had been *fekis* and ex-pupils of unassisted *khalwas*, and were too firmly set in the old ignorance to be much affected by a two or three months' course and an occasional inspection. The remainder were youths with a *Khalwa* education; but while they carried with them from the *kuttab* a better idea of the three R's, they brought away also not only an undimmed faith in the gibberish method, but just those 'academy manners' that it was one of the main objects of the *khalwa* system to exclude. The best *khalwas* (a minority) need two or three years to bring their boys to that standard which in the preparatory class of the *kuttab* is reached in one. To enable a clever boy to read and write simple correspondence and to figure moderately, six to eight years at the average *khalwa* are needed—and few boys stop as long. Not only do the majority of the *khalwas* fail to teach reading, writing, and arithmetic; many, if not most of them, fail to inspire the child's mind and body. To sit for 7 to 9 hours out of the twenty-four—some of them at night—in a dark and dirty hovel, flies buzzing round one's gummed eyelids, to learn double-Dutch by heart and be beaten at intervals by a lazy and stupid assistant—it is hard for a child of six to ten years old, even though he be a Sudanese. The assisted *khalwas* of the three northernmost provinces are better. They were better originally; and more time, care, and money have been spent on their improvement. Most of them do succeed in teaching simple reading, writing, and arithmetic to a majority of their pupils, though at the expenditure of infinite labour. But the boys' minds are deadened by the rote system as much as elsewhere.

Boys' Kuttabs

Though the rote system—learning by heart without understanding—is not carried in the *kuttab* to such absurd lengths as in the *khalwas*, nevertheless in the *kuttab* also it pervades everything. It is in the blood of the people, and the indifferent training which most of the teachers have received has not eradicated it. In the *kuttab*, too, there is an additional reason for it, directly due to the system on which government schools were founded. The *kuttab* (in spite of circulars) is looked upon as the beginning of the road to government employment, the gate to the primary school, the workshops and the *arifs'* school, but only those boys who excel in their examinations can pass out along the longed-for path. The examinations therefore are the ends to which all energies are directed, and the surest way of passing an examination—at any rate to the Sudanese mind—is to learn off all possible questions and answers by heart. Here the first great fault of the *kuttab* is connected with the second: centralization. It is a sound rule that there can be no reality or life in any new idea that is dispensed to the people ready-made rather than planted like a seed in the local soil. But *kuttab* education (again in spite of circulars) is dispensed ready-made from Khartoum. And it is administered to the accompaniment of those 'academy manners' above mentioned—a legacy, through Egypt, from the old English elementary school.

The faults of the *kuttab* have long been recognized, and attempts have been made to cure them. But little impression has been made. The attempt to decentralize and localize the *kuttabs* by placing them partly under the control of District Commissioners, with or without native individuals or boards to assist them, has in most districts met with little success. Most District Commissioners are too busy, and children's education is to them an art too unfamiliar for their influence in the schools to be great. The local sheikhs on boards, being for the most part uneducated, find the work still harder. At most *kuttabs* where they have been appointed—and at every *kuttab* where the District Commissioner does not take an exceptional interest—they have taken no action at all beyond a pious resolution or two on their first appointment. Nor must it be forgotten that however competent the District Commissioners and the boards may be, they will still have to deal with teachers who were themselves educated in the old way, and cannot change their whole outlook for an occasional inspection, recommendation or resolution. It is easier to form a new educational policy than to put it into effect. So the centralized outlook, the academy manners and the rote system remain for the most part unchanged, though here and there fine and whole-hearted work has let in some rays of light. While of recent years a new hindrance has appeared. Before the introduction of the *khalwa* system the *kuttab* received many of its pupils straight from home, or after a comparatively short time at the *khalwa*. Now that at most *kuttabs* the *khalwas* take the place of the preparatory class, the *kuttab* receives its boys already deadened and set by the rote system at its worst.

Girls' Kuttabs

Girls' *kuttabs* are a small but delightful oasis in the desert of Sudan schools, and the reason is obvious. Everything depends upon the teachers, and the teachers of the girls' *kuttabs* have from first to last been scientifically and sympathetically trained. For girls' *kuttabs* two difficulties do not exist—*khalwa* education and the lure of government employment. But they have two at least as great—the impossibility of using mature or permanent teachers, and the general prejudice against girls' education.

Primary Schools

It would be surprising if we found education in the primary schools untainted by the rote system; for their pupils come straight from *kuttabs* and their teachers are either exceptional men of the old 'alim' type, or young men who themselves started their education in a *khalwa* or *kuttab*, and continued it under the influence of that vicious circle which originated there. Moreover, entrance into the Gordon College and to government employment are even stronger lines to the primary school than is the primary school itself to the *kuttab*. Consequently, though some very great improvements have been achieved by the better training of the newer teachers, the primary schools remain to a large extent cramming-shops for the Gordon College. The majority of the boys, however, cannot but fail to enter the college, and used in the past to get minor government and commercial posts. Now they return home with a foreign, second-rate, half-finished, vocational education, which has dissatisfied them with their home life and has fitted them only for work which is not available.

The Gordon College

The British staff of the Gordon College know well that it needs reform, and they are doing what they can. But two things are clear. First the college is in essentials what the *kuttabs* and primary schools make it; and all reforms at the college will be merely palliative unless reform can first be established lower down. And the second point arises out of the first. The Gordon College and the schools on which it depends, have been built up on the old idea, that only through westernization could efficiency and civilization be attained. Now, the old policy has been recognized as wrong by the British. But it has taken a generation to make the Gordon College what it is, and it will take at least a generation to change it.

The Aims of Reform

It may be said that the disadvantages of parrot-education can be over-estimated, that many a British schoolboy had the same and got over it. But the British schoolboy came from a cultured home in a civilized land, and had the traditions of a thousand years behind him. All that the poor Sudanese boy knows of the light is what he gets at school; and he learns it all by heart so that he may be as good as the English. Here is no jumping of the centuries—merely the reciting of a new *Koran*, as unintelligible as the old. Just as the essence of the policy of Native Administration is that the native should, instead of learning by rote ill-understood phrases, be enabled to develop a real mind and character of his own. It is more than a parallel; it is an identity of principle, the applications of which in school and country must be closely woven together if either is to succeed. Judged by this principle, the schools of the Sudan are not only inadequate, they are dangerous. If they are to satisfy either the educationalist or the administrator, if they are even to produce efficient government clerks, they must be able so to base western knowledge on native values that it may act as both a stimulant and a means to the creation of a native culture.

[1] The aim of reform is not to increase the number of subjects or of facts taught, but to have them taught in a sounder manner. Education does not consist solely in providing the child with better gadgets for the business of life—literacy for the greater convenience of written communication, arithmetic for the calculation of prices and profits, geography for the direction of wholesale trading, or all the subjects for the passing of examinations and the getting of jobs. That is purely technical education —a useful and necessary part. But if we forget that it is only a part, and attempt to make it a whole, not only do we miss all that a higher element in education can give, but the very absence of that higher element makes impossible the effective teaching of the first. The higher element in education is the development of the child's mind and character, his conversion from a barbarous and isolated little individual into a member, however humble, of the society of men. Through literacy he may learn to conceive, develop, and express his own ideas and to understand those of others; through arithmetic he may learn tidiness of mind and the application of fact; through geography and history he may get a glimpse of the meaning of causality and of the unifying principles that bind into a whole the isolated details of the world, and may begin to understand his own comparatively humble relation to that whole in place and time. Through all his studies, he may be led to understand that truth derives its authority not from books or from its statement by the teacher, but from its agreement with the facts of experience, material or spiritual; and thus, if we can succeed in presenting 'eastern' knowledge to the Sudanese in such a manner, he may be able, because he will appreciate its meaning, to use it to build up a culture of his own on a foundation of his own values. The stimulus will be foreign, he is shaken out of his passivity; the means will be foreign, he is presented with implements made by Westerners; but the plan or the work will be native, and will be real. Or we can leave Sudan education as it is, and laugh at the Sudanese as at parrots saying their piece, trousered monkeys aping men. We can do that, if we are ready to shoot them down when they think they have learnt our magic and want to work it, if we are happy to damn them by destroying their faith and giving them nothing in its place, and if we are justified in refusing them the heritage of civilization which we owe to others.

3. Reform

It seems probable that from the political point of view the reform of elementary education is the most urgent. From the educational point of view it is evident that no reform can be real that does not begin at the elementary school. For each government-trained native teacher in the

[1] This paragraph was suggested by Mr. Griffiths.

kuttabs, the primary schools and the Gordon College must spend the most susceptible years of his scholastic career as a *kuttab* pupil and usually as a *khalwa* pupil too. And it is the quality of the education that he receives there that determines to a large extent his subsequent outlook and achievements, and through him influences the many hundreds of his pupils. It is submitted therefore that the reform of elementary education must come first, and that if necessary other branches of education should be stinted in order to achieve it. Extension of elementary education should come second, only when it is reasonably certain that the new schools will not repeat the errors of the old.

From ten to fifteen years must pass before the new boy in *khalwa* becomes himself a teacher in *khalwa* or *kuttab* or primary school; and at least another ten must pass before his pupils in their turn can begin to show in life the results of their education at school. If we must wait twenty years for results, let us begin now.

It is easy to state aims and to urge action, much more difficult to suggest the means. Educationalists are not agreed as to methods in the older problem of education in Europe; although there the results of countless experiments are already available for guidance. Much has been written recently on the education of backward peoples, and particularly on African education, and many experiments are being made; but the results of those experiments will not be fully available for many years, and no certainty is possible. Even were these methods proved to be practicable and beneficial elsewhere, they would not be wholly applicable in the Sudan, where conditions differ. In order therefore that the Sudan educationalist may discover the paths to his goal, he must not only have a full knowledge of what is being tried out in countries where some conditions are similar— East Africa, Nigeria, Palestine, Syria—but he must also have adequate machinery for practical experiment in the Sudan. New educational research by practical experiment can only be carried out in the Sudan at the present time by British headmasters of schools, or at least by British inspectors in close and continual contact with a limited number of schools.

What opportunity is there at present for such research? The two British inspectors are required to visit between them over a hundred schools annually (not to mention 600 or 700 assisted *khalwas*). In addition they are required to do work at headquarters and to act for the Assistant Director when he is on leave, which reduces them in effect from two to one and a half full-time inspectors. This time is quite insufficient for normal inspection, let alone research. The Gordon College staff includes ten British (recently eleven) but it is submitted that there are three things wrong with this arrangement. First, the College staff normally includes some British who are unsuited to research work owing to their lack of experience, and to the fact that they are looking forward to leaving the Education Department very shortly. Secondly, it is a comparative waste of experienced personnel if outside schools are short, to concentrate so many British in one school, where the work that is normally expected of British officials—originality within an approved policy, the inspiration and guidance of native staff—must necessarily be in the hands of one man. Thirdly, as stated above, reform in secondary education is neither of first urgency nor practicable. It is to elementary education that the maximum available force of British personnel should be applied. What other British staff is there available for research? Under the command of the Secretary for Education and Health there are 35 British already engaged in research of some kind; they include bacteriologists, chemists, entomologists, a geologist, botanists, pathologists, and veterinary research officers; but (outside the Gordon College) not one educationalist, not even a psychologist, or an anthropologist. The care of the bodies of the Sudanese may be more important than the care of their minds; but not more important by thirty-five to naught.

Finally, research and reform in Sudan education demand from the educationalist more than practical ability in school management, more than a knowledge of pedagogy and of modern ideas on native education, more than a practical sympathy with the people and a vague if sincere vision of their future. Since it is the first necessity of our education that it should be firmly based on native values, and since the Northern Sudanese are a people whose most important values derive from Muslim and Arab origins, the Sudanese educationalist requires also an adequate knowledge of Islam, and of Arab history, literature, and traditions. Not every schoolmaster need or can have this knowledge, but there must be one expert who has it, and whom a knowledge of the Sudan enables to apply it. There is no such expert in the Education Department, nor has any member of it the time to learn.

The proposals which follow are put forward, therefore, not as affording a solution of the problem of creating a real education in the Sudan, but as suggestions for preliminary steps which might make it possible for others to find that solution. For this reason they are concerned not so much with the purely educational side as with matters affecting organization, appointments, and expenditure. The proposals are neither new, nor the nostrums of any particular person. Though I am responsible for their selection and presentation, most of them are the ideas of other members of the Education Department. They are arranged in order of convenience, not necessarily that of importance.

Proposal One
Recruitment of British Staff

i. It is submitted that the method of recruiting British officials to the Education Department might be improved. Sufficient skill and duration are not as a rule found in the young men waiting to be appointed to the administrative service, nor yet in the older District Commissioner who later joins the Department without educational bent or knowledge; nor yet in the educationalist void of practical experience with backward peoples. It is submitted that in future candidates should be specially selected at home for their previous educational training, including practical experience in teaching, and for the likelihood, so far as it can be judged, that they will be able and willing to devote their time to the cause of Sudan education; and that on their arrival in the Sudan they should be appointed for at least two years as assistants to selected District Commissioners, so that they may get some of that general knowledge and experience which is essential to their doing any good in the Education Department. The Political Service would thus be burdened with a slightly increased number of inexperienced men, but the harm thereby done would probably be small in comparison with the advantages reaped in better education. It is not suggested that transfers from the Political Service should be ruled out, but that they should be exceptional; and that they should only occur when there is a District Commissioner available who already has a knowledge of and an interest in educational matters, and is willing to be permanently transferred.

Proposal Two
Increase of Inspecting Staff

ii. It is submitted that at the end of 1932 the British Inspectorate (the title of Chief Inspector, always an empty one, may well lapse) in the Northern Sudan should be divided into the same number of educational districts, with an educational inspector in charge of each, responsible to the Director, but in close touch with the Governors and District Commissioners. That no inspector should have any headquarter work, and that all should go on leave together during the summer holidays. It would only be by such an arrangement that an inspector could get to know his schools, their staff and the parents of their pupils, and could do work of any value in research experiment and reform. Four educational districts are not enough; but the number is put forward as a minimum made necessary by the shortage of money and personnel, and to be increased when practicable. It is further submitted that these two new appointments should be made if necessary by reducing the British staff of the Gordon College. If that were done, the standard of teaching in the College would fall; but this would be a price well worth paying for improvement in the more important field of the elementary schools. It is mainly the teaching of English in the College which would suffer; and if a temporary drop in the standard is at any time allowable, now is the time for it when the government is requiring no new employees. As for discipline and morals, recent changes in the College organization seem to show that the native teacher is capable of taking over from the British tutors more of such duties than he has been allowed to do in the past. As a final inducement, the appointment of two native housemasters would be a welcome and harmless step to a vociferous party.

Proposal Three
Reorganization of H.Q.

iii. The last proposal included the condition that the inspectors should be free of all headquarter work. But this would not necessarily involve a return to the old system whereby the Director does the Assistant Director's work while the latter is on leave. It should not be either difficult or undesirable to get a stop-gap to sign routine work and postpone the rest, during a period of three months annually when all schools are closed, and the Director, the Assistant Director, and all inspectors and teachers are on leave—not to mention all those high officials in other departments who are likely to raise matters affecting educational policy. But the Director and the Assistant Director need sufficient time for visiting the districts to supervise and to keep in touch, and for considerable periods of study leave, and this may be found difficult if the District Inspectors are to give no assistance at headquarters. If so, it would be necessary to have a fifth inspector at headquarters; and it is submitted that in that case he also should be stolen from the Gordon College, if he cannot be got otherwise. But it is suggested that there are three ways in which the headquarters work will be lessened. First, every year will not be an economy year. Secondly, a great mass of the work which at present comes to headquarters will be dealt with by the inspectors in their districts. Thirdly, it is admitted that the routine work at headquarters takes up far too much of the Assistant Director's time owing to faulty office organization. Whatever reorganization were required might be completed by the end of 1932, if the new educational district were to be formed at that time.

Proposal Four
Improvement of Existing Teaching Staff

iv. The *kuttab* teachers' training school at present contains ten students in the first class, eight in the second and fifteen in the final class. It is submitted that all of the fifteen who pass satisfactorily should be appointed teachers in January 1933 (involving an expenditure in 1933 of £E 720, if all the fifteen are satisfactory), and that twenty new students be accepted for the first-year class in 1933 and in subsequent years. The object is not to increase the number of *kuttabs*, but to improve their quality, in three ways. First, the training school has been reformed this year, and further reforms are suggested in proposal 5. But there are now 242 *kuttab* teachers, and if the training school turns out only ten teachers per year it will be very many years before its improved methods have any appreciable effect. It is suggested that there should always be at the training school in addition to the normal classes of students, a class of old teachers undergoing a further course: this would involve other teachers taking their places in the *kuttabs*. Allowing for no increase in the schools, two four-month courses of twenty teachers each would teach one teacher from each school in the course of two years. Secondly, *kuttabs* can never reach the required standard so long as they have to rely on *khalwas* to prepare their boys. The experimental substitution of *khalwas* for preparatory classes has been a failure, and 60 per cent of the *kuttabs* require extra masters for preparatory classes. Thirdly, many *kuttabs* have single classes of fifty boys, and in many others masters attempt to teach two separate classes at the same time. Until such schools are given an adequate staff, they cannot, I think, provide a proper education.

Proposal Five
Improvement of Kuttab-teachers' Training School

v. The proposed teachers' class would involve an increase of one in the staff of the training school and it is submitted that he should be appointed in January 1933 (involving an expenditure in 1933 of £E84). Secondly, it is proposed to abolish the Khartoum primary school *kuttab* next autumn, and to form in its place an experimental and demonstration *kuttab* as a part of the Training School (temporary quarters are available). Thirdly, the present site and buildings of the Training School are admittedly so unsatisfactory that they seriously affect the quality of the training. It is submitted that suitable buildings should be erected on a suitable site next year, so as to be ready by January 1934. Fourthly, this school is the key-school of the whole of the Sudan educational system, and it is, I suggest, absurd that it should not be in charge of a British headmaster. Technical schools have two British heads, until recently three. The girl-teachers training school has one, and the primary school teachers section has the part-time services of the British staff of the Gordon College. Yet none of these schools has the fundamental importance of the *kuttab*-teachers' training school, which until January 1932 had a third of a native head-master and now has one native headmaster. It is submitted that a British headmaster should be appointed in January 1934. Fifthly, this British headmaster must have ample time for practical research work, to perform which he will be at once the best qualified and the best situated official in the Department. He must have time to keep in touch with the District Inspectors, and to visit their schools. If he is to do all this, as well as the work suggested in proposals 9 and 10, a further increase of two, or at least one, in the native staff will be necessary.

Proposal Six
Improvement of Conditions for Kuttab-teachers

vi. It was financially approved in 1928 that *kuttab* teachers should be pensionable. But the putting into effect of this approval was postponed owing to the expectation of the Provident Fund Ordinances. Since then no action has been taken, and the teachers are still neither under the pension nor the Provident Fund Ordinances. They feel this very strongly indeed, and it is only because of their loyal and unselfish recognition of the Government's difficulties during the past two years that they have not protested more strongly. But unless they are made pensionable shortly (the Provident Fund is, I submit, not adequate), it is probable that most of them will lose confidence in the government. If that occurs, so far from a reform of the *kuttab* being possible, there will be a deterioration equivalent to a setback of many years. It is submitted that to put the 1928 decision into effect is both just and expedient.

Secondly, prior to 1931 it has always in fact occurred that a *kuttab* teacher after serving for at most seven years has been promoted from the Special Education Grade to Grade VIII, unless he was incompetent. This promotion enabled him to receive minimal increases of £E12 per annum, compared with his previous increases of £E6 per annum, and inevitably came to be regarded by *kuttab* teachers as a normal expectation, similar to that of an assistant District Commissioner from Grade III to Grade II. From January 1931, however, the Financial Department has pointed out that according to existing financial regulations such promotions are not automatic, but can only be made to fill vacancies. Since then, there have been no vacancies in Grade VIII in the Education Department; and for many years to come their number is likely to be quite negligible. So that in fact the prospects of all *kuttab* teachers appointed after 1923 are now very much inferior to what they were previously supposed to be, and to the actual prospects of teachers appointed in 1923 or before. It is not submitted that in the present hard times this promotion ought to be as automatic as it was; but that financial approval should be sought for a fair annual proportion of promotion to Grade VIII, or the equivalent in salary. I fear that if this is not done the teachers' work will suffer, owing to a natural sense of grievance; and it is upon these younger teachers that we chiefly rely for the reform of *kuttab* education.

Proposal Seven
Agricultural Education

vii. The survey of Sudan education in section two contained no mention of agricultural education, because there is none (except the American Mission School at Gerif, which would repay careful study before the foundation of a government school). There is no government agricultural school, and the so-called teaching of agriculture in the *kuttabs* is a farce, because the teachers have no agricultural knowledge or training. The Northern Sudan is an agricultural country; agricultural education is going ahead in the Southern Sudan and in the rest of East Africa—we cannot lack interest in the matter here, nor consider that we have nothing to teach. Both the Agricultural Department and the Veterinary Department have, I understand, done a considerable amount of research work on native farming (I use the term to include stock-raising). But the government has made only weak attempts (the most successful attempt seems to have been the agricultural school at Berber, which did some excellent work; but it suffered from the government employment complex, and when its pupils failed to find employment in the Agricultural Department, and the Nile changed its course, it was allowed to die through lack of interest; the headmaster was a Copt), to interest and encourage the native, in short, to educate him. The only farming that it has seriously attempted to improve is farming for export; and its methods there have been as far as possible those of direct administration. It is suggested that it is worth the government's while to make a real attempt to get the native willingly to improve his farming, rather than to keep on ordering him to do so. It is recognized that the difficulties are very great, but the need is very great also.

It is suggested that an agricultural school should be established whose main aim would be the encouragement of Sudanese farmers (both export farmers and others) to improve their methods. It would draw its pupils from two classes, the sons of landowners or land-lessees, most of whom would return home on the completion of the course, and the sons of landless *effendis* (see appendix) for whom a land settlement scheme would be necessary. The Gezira, Gedarif District, and the Fung province might provide the land. In addition, as a necessary lure for pupils and to fill a real need, a minority of the boys might be given an extra course to enable them to be appointed as travelling teachers for the improvement of agricultural teaching in the *kuttabs*, and as assistant inspectors in the Agricultural Department and the Sudan Plantations Syndicate. That is only a rough scheme based on very inadequate knowledge of the subject. The whole matter obviously needs study by a qualified agriculturist who has knowledge of the Sudan and sympathy with the Sudanese and with education. And it is submitted that such a man ought to be found as soon as possible and set to work.

Proposal Eight
Other Technical Schools

viii. Other technical education was omitted from the survey in section two merely because it is more conveniently dealt with in a single paragraph. Our main aim here is presumably similar to our main aim in agricultural education—to give as many Sudanese as possible the desire and the means to improve their standard of living, in so far as it can be done by technical education. Up to the present, technical education in the Sudan has done comparatively little to achieve this aim. The technical workshops at Atbara perform the necessary work of supplying the railways with skilled servants, and the technical schools in Khartoum and Omdurman have filled the Three Towns with a superfluity of skilled artisans in certain trades. But in almost every Sudanese village the standard of housing, of house furniture, of agricultural and other implements, of non-government water supply, of personal ornaments, shows little if any improvement over the standards of the last century. It is not submitted that this is a matter of urgent importance, but that here is a field which will repay study and enterprise whenever the government can afford it.

Proposal Nine
Improvement of Primary and Secondary Education

ix. It is clear that reform is badly needed in the primary schools. But we cannot bite off everything at once, and it seems that no fundamental reforms can be begun at present at any rate, and that all that is possible is to continue the slow improvement of educational methods under the present system—and the burden of this work should be somewhat lightened by the proposed increase in the inspectorate. It is submitted, however, that there is one matter which requires very serious consideration, the need for a school above *kuttab* standard suitable for the education of boys who will later succeed to positions of great responsibility in the native adminis-tration. There is no need to repeat the arguments in favour of the education of the native aristocracy; nor to enumerate the reasons why the existing primary schools are unsuitable for this purpose. The institution of a school 'for the sons of sheikhs' was discussed by the Director of Education with the Civil Secretary and Governors some years ago, but no practicable way was found. Such a school would need a headmaster of unusual ability and qualifications and a considerable amount of money—neither of which, I think, is available. But there is, I suggest, a stopgap which can be used temporarily, and might eventually develop specially for this purpose. The *kuttab*-teachers' training school, though primarily existing of course to train teachers, should now be able to supply a post-*kuttab*, all-Arabic education which is not to be despised, especially if the recommendations in proposal 5 were approved. With its present staff it can deal with a small number of extra pupils, and two sons of the Sultan of Dar Masalit are actually being educated there at present.

I am not competent to speak of the reform of secondary education, and there are no comments which I can make on the proposals recently put forward for the improvement of the Gordon College, except to repeat that the fundamental quality of the College depends on that of the *kuttabs* and primary schools.

Proposal Ten
Adult Education

x. Many boys on leaving village *kuttabs* quickly lose any skill of mind or useful knowledge that they may have acquired there, owing to lack of opportunities for use. Secondly, they may have learnt there some attitudes of mind which ought if possible to be eradicated. Thirdly, a very long period must elapse before ex-pupils of reformed *kuttabs* form any considerable proportion of the Sudan population. For all these reasons it is suggested that a very useful part would be filled by two forms of adult education— travelling libraries for the literate, and travelling magic-lanterns and cinemas for the illiterate. Both the libraries and the cinemas would be expensive (it seems probable that specially photographed films would be necessary). But it appears likely that the Carnegie Trust would be willing to contribute largely for such purpose, as soon as the Sudan Government is prepared also to contribute a part. A third very real need, in many countries already catered for, is a vernacular magazine for the stimulation and help of native teachers. That this venture is practicable in the Sudan may be presumed from the marked success of the Boy Scout Magazine, whose fourth number is now being prepared. It is suggested that though all this work would certainly require a whole-time British official to run it, some of it could be started experimentally in 1934 or 1935 by the British headmaster of the Teachers' Training School (see proposal 5).

Conclusion

The above proposals are intended to do no more than to suggest some bases for reform and the most suitable points for its beginnings. For I am not capable of suggesting more. If they are unacceptable, I hope that they may be at least the occasion of the adoption of other methods more efficient. For the main object of this note is to suggest that the reform of Sudanese education is overdue, and that whatever methods are selected as the most efficient it is worthwhile to provide money for their execution, even though other important services are thereby stinted. If it is argued that it is more important to prevent war, disease and injustice, it should be replied that in the long run they cannot be prevented if the system of education is false; and that the failure in India appears in great part to be due to a system of education similar in spirit to that of the Sudan. A truer education has been shown to us, which consists neither in the dispensing of western ways and knowledge nor in government propaganda, but in the sympathetic assistance of the people to find themselves. This is what prevents sedition and creates the future. It is the identical aim of both the administration and the educationalist, and each is powerless without the other.

Appendix

UNEMPLOYMENT AMONG EDUCATED SUDANESE

It is well known that the country contains considerable numbers of 'educated' Sudanese without employment, and with no prospect of it, and that most of them are begetting and attempting to educate children, most of whom will also be without employment. Our faulty educational system has produced them, and will continue to produce them for many years to come. The dangers of such a situation affect the educational as well as the political future. For the presence of large numbers of discontented and futile educated persons is not only likely to bring education into disrepute with the Sudan and Home Governments, but creates a very real danger that the direction and pace of educational progress may be forced by these to its unsuccessful products. It is because of this bearing on educational matters that I venture to include here a matter which, as I understand, is already receiving the serious attention of the government. No doubt but that all possible opportunities are being made and taken for the absorption of some of these people into useful jobs in the Native Administration in the Sudan Plantations Syndicate, and elsewhere. But the number so absorbed must be small.

Most of these people's fathers or grandfathers were farmers; and farming is the only occupation in the Sudan which appears at present to give promise of any considerable expansion. It is submitted, therefore, that it appears advisable to get these people or their children back to the land, and that the institution of a land settlement scheme, a suggestion for which is included in proposal 7, is of considerable importance.

CORRESPONDENCE ON THE ABOVE NOTE

Strictly Confidential

22 May 1932

The Director of Education,

I submit for your consideration a note on education in the Northern Sudan. No originality is claimed for the ideas expressed which are mostly taken from books or from other members of the Education Department and the Political Service. But it seemed that it might be of value to attempt at the present time a statement of the aims and methods of Sudan education.

G. C. S.,
Chief Inspector,
Education Department

APPENDIX V

Graduates Congress Note on Education

INTRODUCTION

Foreword

Educational work in the Sudan started since the arrival of the Arabs in the Country. The main object was a religious one and reading and writing were primarily taught for the purpose of learning Koran and Islamic instructions, hence the great number of *khalwas* throughout the country which played a very good part in the way of education and general enlightenment. These *khalwas* were run by the people themselves until recently when some of them were subsidized by the Government.

Comparisons

There is no record of the number of literate in the Sudan, but it is believed that they are not over 1 per cent of the total population. There are not less than 300,000 boys of six to twelve years of age in the country of whom 19,000 only receive elementary or intermediate education in Government and other schools or about 6 per cent, while in Uganda over 33 per cent of boys of the same age actually receive similar education.

Girls' education is so backward that it cannot be compared with any other country. The number of girls receiving education is not more than 5,000 in both Government and other schools while girls in the country are more numerous than boys.

The annual expenditure on education including subsidies to Missionary Schools and other Non-Government Schools amounts to about 5 per cent of the Government budget while the cost of education in neighbouring countries ranges from 7 to 9 per cent of their budgets.

The above statistics clearly indicate that education in the Sudan is in a backward position and that even if the present number of elementary and intermediate schools is doubled in a few years time, it will still fall short of our aspirations, and far from being compared with other Arab countries it will not reach the stage achieved by the neighbouring countries.

Educational Policy

General Lines

In numerous aspects of our life we have much in common with the Arab countries of Islamic Orient which is due to our akin descent. We therefore consider that education in this country should take an Islamic Oriental character and not a pagan African one, or in other words that the Arabic Language and Religious Instructions should receive the greatest possible care in all stages of education.

Aims

Education in the Sudan has mainly been designed to supply the various Government Offices with suitable staff. This may have been inevitable in the early years for operating the Government machinery. The Government Offices having been fully equipped with the necessary staff, we think that it is high time that a new and more general policy should have been laid down.

The new educational policy should, in our opinion, aim at:

(*a*) Total removal of illiteracy and

(*b*) expansion and improvement in all stages of education with a view to maintaining a high cultural standard to ensure:

(i) creating spiritual happiness for the individual in community life;

(ii) inculcating public and co-operative spirit in the individual so that he may take an active interest in the welfare of his community, and

(iii) equipping the individual with the qualities which make for success in his struggle for existence.

Practical Training

Modern educational theories do not stop at teaching reading, writing, and arithmetic and we do not think that education in this country will serve its purpose if it fails to prepare the educated for a life more productive than that of the uneducated and induce them to impart the advantages so gained to their community.

The present educational system is primarily designed to prepare the pupil for the next higher stage of education with a view to ensure continuity of education, but it neglects the practical training for future life work of those pupils (the majority) who are not likely to receive higher education. To achieve both purposes we suggest that a special system be introduced, in both elementary and intermediate schools, whereby the pupils receive a common syllabus after which those who desire to continue their education enter the next higher school, the rest who wish to qualify for life work being given two years further training.

Centralization of Education

It is realized that for the fulfilment of our foregoing suggestion a certain degree of de-centralization will be involved owing to the expanse of the country and the geographical differences of its regions. But these differences need not affect the common spirit that should in the first place predominate education in all its stages and also its theoretical side such as mathematics, rudiments of sciences, principles of economics, languages etc. It is therefore considered necessary that the co-ordination of policy to suit the needs of various regions be vested in the General Education Centre in Khartoum.

Finance

It is noted with gratitude that the Government has accepted the Education Department's plan for expansion of education which involves a liability of £E150,000 a year, spread over a period of ten years commencing from 1936.

We are not in a position to say whether the proposals and suggestions contained in the next chapters can be carried out within the funds which will be made available during the next eight years, but it is earnestly hoped that our proposals will not be postponed for lack of funds.

PART ONE: NORTHERN SPHERE

Chapter I

PRIMARY EDUCATION

Curricula

The re-organization envisaged by the educational policy visualized above requires a thorough revision of the present curricula in all schools. We cannot go deeply into detail in the matter of school curricula for the various stages of education, as this is a subject for the experts, but there is no doubt that it cannot be too strongly emphasized that the present standard of education in all stages falls short of what the country needs at present. In the case of elementary education, great hopes are attached to the enormous efforts made at Bakht er Ruda to devise syllabuses and to prepare efficient teachers capable of removing the present defects and raising the standard of elementary education.

It is likewise of vital importance that similar efforts and arrangements be made in the way of Intermediate education.

School Age

There are two points to which we attach particularly great importance and on which depends to a great extent, the expansion of education in the country: at present boys begin their elementary schooling at the age of eight. They consequently finish their secondary education at the age of twenty which is a comparatively high average age for entering higher schools which require from four to six years of study. This will have serious results in that the students' aptitude for study may be enormously reduced. It is therefore hoped that arrangements will be made whereby the boys start their elementary education at the age of six.

Overlap

The other point is the existing overlap between the curriculum of the elementary and intermediate schools. At present the boys receive more or less, the same course in Arabic, arithmetic, and geography in the first and second years of the intermediate schools which they went through in the last two years of elementary schools. If the syllabuses are revised so as to begin intermediate schooling where elementary schooling finishes, it will be possible to remove the present overlap and to save a further year which together with a reduction of two years in the age of entry, will reduce the average age at the end of secondary education to seventeen years. The only disadvantage of this arrangement is that the boys who are not able to go beyond the elementary education will not make much use of their knowledge at the age of ten, but this will be remedied by the introduction of the system already suggested under 'Educational Policy'.

Arabic Language and Religious Instruction

These two subjects need particular attention as regards the method of teaching as well as the standards in the three first stages, viz. elementary, intermediate, and secondary. This can only be attained by the training of suitable teachers on the lines recommended by Ali Bey El Garem in his report, which if duly implemented will help to raise the standard of teaching in all the schools. Religious instruction should in our opinion be treated as a principal subject in examination and in consideration of marks.

Art and Literature

Experience in intermediate schools and in the College has shown that there is great aptitude for fine arts and literature. We therefore trust that more attention be given to it. We suggest that the Education Department provide staff for developing and directing natural aptitudes for poetry, writing, painting, and music. It is important that the teachers be well qualified for this work and we hope the possibility of introducing these subjects in schools' syllabuses will be considered.

Teaching Staff

The recruitment of teachers and training of teachers are of vital importance. It ranks above the preparation of curricula and the devising of methods. It is not a difficult task to adopt the most modern methods in education but this will be of little value unless the right men who will shoulder the great responsibility and difficult work of education are properly trained and an adequate number is provided in each school. It is noticed in this connection that the present number of teachers in each of the elementary schools is three including the headmaster, whereas the number of classes is four. This shows that one of the classes remains idle during part of the working hours. To save the boys' time it is suggested that four teachers at least be provided for each school including the headmaster.

The training centre in Bakht er Ruda is no doubt capable of producing the right type of teachers for the elementary schools. It is hoped that intermediate school teachers' standard will be raised to a relatively similar footing by continuing to make refresher courses for the existing staff and by confining new recruitment to these schools from the proposed training school for teachers in the School of Arts.

Teaching of English

It is suggested that owing to the importance of the English language in this country, intermediate school masters who will teach this language in the senior classes should be sent abroad in order to specialize in the technique of teaching English or at least receive a special course in the country for this purpose.

ELEMENTARY EDUCATION

General

Until elementary education is made available for all or most of the boys of the Sudan, it is believed that no real progress can be achieved in the development of the country. Malnutrition, bad housing, and inadequate sanitation are all factors which combine to retard progress and these can only be removed by direct education or propaganda which is not possible without the knowledge of reading and writing.

Khalwas

The main object of the *khalwas* was the teaching of the Koran and religious instruction, until the Education Department included some of them (about 700) in their educational system against a subsidy in the form of rewards to the *fikis*. The rest are still functioning on the original lines and are doing useful work.

It is now felt that Government-subsidized *khalwas* are not serving the purpose for which they were intended owing to the fact that the *fikis* absent themselves from their *khalwas* for a good part of the year in pursuit of their living. This is due to two reasons: (1) the reward given to them is scanty and does not cover their necessities, (2) the parents of the pupils ceased to offer the small contributions or fees they used to give in the past to the *fikis* for their education on the understanding that they are Government servants in receipt of regular salaries. For the same reasons the *fikis* were also deprived of the assistance they used to get from Heads of tribes and others towards the maintenance of the *khalwas* as religious institutions.

The Education Department has apparently discovered these defects and has therefore (1) reintroduced the preparatory class in the elementary schools to enable the boys to enter these schools directly from their homes without having any instruction in a *khalwa*, and (2) devised a new system of half elementary schools (sub-grade) in places where elementary schools do not exist.

Government Subsidy to Khalwas

But in view of the necessity of the *khalwas* for religious purposes and as an additional means of combating illiteracy it is suggested that the present contribution by the Government is necessary for maintaining the old

religious *khalwa* and also for encouraging the people to continue devel
oping the present Government-subsidized *khalwas* on the original lines

To remove the feeling described at the beginning of this section it is
suggested that no direct payments be made to the *fikis* but that a lump
sum grant be placed at the disposal of the Omdurman Mahad Board or
a special committee to be appointed by the Mahad Board, who may be
authorized to distribute the money at their discretion in consultation with
the local authorities.

Sub-Grade Schools

The experiments made in certain Provinces on this system have been of
great success and it is suggested that this system be furthered by sub-
stituting sub-grade schools for modernized *khalwas*. The Governor's
Educational Fund may be exclusively utilized for these schools, thus
enabling a greater number of them to be opened in the smaller villages
The present method of providing teachers for these schools by selection
from amongst the *khalwa fikis* or from graduates of elementary school
is considered unsatisfactory. The best solution in our opinion is to employ
them from graduates of Intermediate Schools who should also receive a
short course of training in the method of teaching, at the Elementary
Teachers' Training School.

Elementary Schools

The present number of schools is obviously inadequate and far short of
the needs of the country. It is understood that a plan has been drawn up
for increasing these schools but the number envisaged under the ten years
plan is not known to us. The Director of Education and Governors are
in a better position to decide the centres where such schools are most
needed but we suggest that the present number of schools be doubled
within the next ten years.

Teachers' Training Schools

The stumbling block is the training of teachers for such schools. The only
school for this purpose is the Elementary Teachers' Training School at
Bakht er Ruda. The methods taught in this school were highly praised by
the Lord De La Warr's Educational Commission who recommended the
eventual opening of a similar school in each Province. We strongly support
the Commission's recommendations but we appreciate that these recommendations cannot be implemented for some time on account of the high
expenses involved. To meet immediate needs, however, it is suggested that
the present school be extended to take double classes, each class being
increased to take twenty boys at least, thus increasing the school's annual
output to forty teachers.

It is also suggested that two other similar schools be opened during the
next ten years. The eventual total output from these three schools will
amount to 120 teachers every year who will be fully needed for strengthening

the teaching staff in all existing elementary schools as suggested above, for providing teachers for new schools and for replacement of retiring staff. It is, however, suggested that boys for these schools should in future be taken from the graduates of Intermediate Schools instead of those of elementary schools as hitherto. It is strongly believed that it is only in this manner that satisfactory standards of education can be achieved.

The arrangement at present contemplated by the Education Department by recruiting elementary school teachers from boys who had completed their elementary study after undergoing a six months course in the Teachers' Training School is excellent as a temporary measure to enable the desired quick expansion of elementary schools to be achieved within as short a space of time as possible. But it is earnestly hoped that the regular policy to be aimed at is that all elementary school teachers should be graduates of the Bakht er Ruda type of Training Schools, who have at first obtained full intermediate education prior to their admission to this school as suggested above. In course of time the teachers provided under these temporary arrangements can be gradually replaced by the product of the Bakht er Ruda standard and the former should then revert to their right place in the sub-grade schools as and when they are relieved from the Elementary Schools.

INTERMEDIATE EDUCATION

As already envisaged in the preceding section, elementary education is, in our opinion, merely a means of spreading literacy amongst the majority of the population, and a necessary step towards higher education. In fact true education starts in the intermediate schools. It is therefore necessary that these schools should not be designed only to pave the way for secondary education but also to provide the majority who will not be able to receive higher education, with some form of practical knowledge to help them in their future career. Agriculture is the foundation on which Sudan culture and education must be built and to some extent commerce. It is therefore suggested that most of the Intermediate Schools be raised from four to six years in order to give to students who do not intend to continue their education in a secondary school a practical course on Agriculture or Commerce according to the centre in which the school exists.

We are glad to know that this principle has been advised by Lord De La Warr's Commission on the lines previously proposed by Mr. Corbyn and now accepted by the Education Department.

Proposals for Expansion

The first step towards expansion of intermediate education should, in our opinion, be the completion of half schools to full schools. Great difficulties are experienced by the people in places where such schools now exist as some of the boys who complete their elementary education have to wait for a full year without schooling before they are admitted into the intermediate school. The additional expenses involved by completing these schools are not great and are fully justified.

The second step should be the doubling of classes in schools of the larger towns such as Khartoum and Wad Medani. The demand in such towns is very great and it is a pity to deprive the boys from education when they pass the examination and are prepared to pay the full fees.

It is further suggested that the new intermediate schools be opened within the next ten years in the following centres where it is expected to supply the needs of not only the town in which the school is situated but also that of a large surrounding zone as well. It is worthy of particular mention here that the ability of the population to pay school fees varies from place to place according to their economical condition and that the percentage of remission of fees should also correspondingly vary in the various localities. The opening of an intermediate school should not, therefore, be wholly measured by the ability to pay the school fees but, primarily, by the need for such education. It is undoubtedly in the interests of the country at large, that the opportunities for education are fairly distributed throughout the country as a whole, irrespective of the ability of the individual centres to meet their share of the cost of education on an equal footing with the more prosperous parts.

The suggested centres in the order of priority are:

1. Dongola	4. Fasher
2. Kassala	5. Nahud
3. Kosti	6. Singa

This will enable the present number of intermediate school boys to be doubled within ten years.

We are pleased to know that it has already been decided to raise the Omdurman Intermediate School to half a secondary school with a commercial bias. It is trusted that if the experiment succeeds, the same facilities will be extended to similar centres such as Port Sudan and El Obeid.

It is also suggested that similar half secondary schools but with agricultural bias may now be started in suitable centres in the Blue Nile, Northern and Kassala Provinces.

Boarding Houses

As some of the existing intermediate schools as well as the new ones suggested are supposed to serve a big area, and in order to encourage boys from neighbouring towns and villages to receive intermediate education, it is suggested that boarding houses be provided in schools such as Wad Medani, El Obeid, El Fasher and Port Sudan. Such facilities will have to be paid for and their provision will not therefore involve any appreciable cost and will avert the necessity of having to open additional schools in other towns which the country cannot afford at present. It is, however, trusted that boys of the poorer villages will be admitted in these boarding houses free of charge or at reduced fees, otherwise the purpose of the boarding houses will be defeated.

Chapter II

SECONDARY EDUCATION

At present there is a belief among some sections of the general public that the standard of education in some of the foreign secondary schools in the country is superior to that of the Gordon College. It is regretted to say that as things stand at present, it is at least difficult to assert that this is not a subject of argument in favour of either theory. It is, however, a strong desire of the peoples of this country to feel that the superiority of the standard of education in the Government Secondary School over that in all other foreign schools in the country is established beyond all doubt in the eyes of the public.

We are, however, pleased to learn that the Gordon College authorities were also dissatisfied with the old standards and have actually started a reorganization which aims towards the setting up of a good secondary standard capable of producing a suitable class of student for higher education. Apart from general education pertaining to a secondary school, the country is still in great need for vocational training for employment purposes in both Government Offices and Commercial Houses. The latter obtain most of their requirements, at present, from Comboni College and consider the product of that college better equipped for their purpose than the Gordon College boys.

It is therefore suggested that the aim should be to raise the standard of general education to that of a full British Secondary School as already decided, and to cater for the needs of both Government Offices and Commercial Houses by introducing a short post-graduate course at the end of the secondary school career to enable the students who are not desirous of receiving higher education to have vocational training in Book-keeping, Shorthand, Typing, etc. for one year.

Increased Facilities for Secondary Education

We are grateful to know that it has been decided to open an additional secondary school after the move of the present school to Wadi Seidna. It is trusted that these two schools will be designed to take 120 boys each, every year in order to absorb an increased number of the boys of the present intermediate schools and those which are likely to be opened in future. Apart from the requirements of the Higher Schools, which we estimate shall not be less than sixty for the Colleges already started grading up to about a hundred a year for those we hope to be brought into existence in the near future, an average number of about seventy boys will be needed for government employment and from fifty to a hundred for Commercial Houses.

It is realized that the move of the present school and the building of a second one will take some time. It is therefore suggested that in order to ease the present pressure and to satisfy the high desire for secondary education, to increase the number of classes in the Gordon College from four to six as from 1940 the number of boys in each class being temporarily increased from twenty-six to thirty until the new schools are ready, even if it necessitates the appointment of additional qualified teachers on short term contracts.

Teaching Staff

To reach the standard which we aspire for we consider that it is of the utmost importance that secondary education should be entrusted to specialists in the various subjects taught. We therefore beg to request that this principle be adopted as soon as possible, qualified teachers being sent to receive adequate specialized training in the subjects in which they are interested. As regards English we suggest that it should be entrusted exclusively to British teachers who are well versed in the technique of teaching English to foreign students.

School Vacation

It is considered that the present summer and winter vacations are too long. The total period during which the students are actually at work does not exceed seven months. This is apparently due to leave arrangements for British staff and to the holding of examinations in the winter. It is therefore suggested that the school year be altered to start in September and end in May and thus remove the necessity for a long winter vacation.

Chapter III

HIGHER EDUCATION

We have not the expert knowledge to make proposals in the professional courses to be taught in the Higher Schools and we should leave this to the Educationalists and to the experts whose advice will be sought for this and for laying the foundation of the Sudan University. We earnestly hope, however, that the general standard will not be below that of similar schools abroad, with due consideration to the country's requirements and traditions, in order to make it possible for students intending to complete their education in a British University to obtain a degree in the branch on which they specialize, until the time comes when recognized degrees could be given in the Sudan University. We also hope that these schools will not be confined to Government requirements but will include a reasonable margin for private practice especially in the schools of Agriculture, Commerce, Law, Medicine, and Engineering.

Courses of Study

In addition to the schools of applied science which have already been opened, namely School of Medicine, Engineering, Agriculture and Veterinary and the School of Arts, which we understand will be opened in 1940 for training Teachers, Lawyers and Administrative workers, we suggest the opening of a school of Commerce as soon as possible. Professional training in Economics and Accounting is, in our opinion, very essential for Government employment as well as for private work. Commercial business in the Sudan is now mainly in the hands of foreign firms and until a school of Commerce is established for those aspiring to more responsible positions in the commercial centres, the Sudanese cannot effectively participate in promoting trade in their country or enjoy the material benefit there.

Higher School for Teachers

We suggest that the Training School for Teachers may be designed to supply masters specialized in teaching Arabic and English as well as other subjects, thus implementing the recommendations of Ali Bey El Garem and Lord De La Warr in one school. Teachers specialized in the various subjects will of course receive additional instructions separately on such subjects. We wish to add in this connection that the recommendations of Ali Bey El Garem with respect to the high studies in Arabic and religious subjects are highly commendable and we consider that they form a suitable basis for the required developments in this direction. It is, however, essential, in our opinion, to look ahead from now on into the requirements of the future by the provision of a more highly qualified class of Sudanese candidates for the leading positions in the country in both subjects, e.g. for teaching those subjects in the secondary and higher schools, for Educational Arabic Inspectorate and generally for the leading of an Islamic Arabic culture and literature. We suggest that the outstanding products of the School based on Ali El Garem's proposals be sent abroad for further specialization in Egypt on the subjects themselves and some of them even further for a short period in England for studying the latest methods and technique of teaching and getting into touch with the latest developments in educational progress.

Teaching Staff

Lecturers and Professors in these colleges will no doubt be selected from highly qualified University men who had previous experience of teaching in similar colleges. In order to develop higher education in the Sudan in the right local traditional character, it is important to make early arrangements for providing Sudanese Lecturers by sending the best suited of the first products of the new Colleges abroad for academic studies for sufficiently long periods in order to obtain higher degrees qualifying them for teaching in the future University College as Demonstrators, Assistant Lecturers and then eventually as Lecturers.

Advisory Councils

Lord De La Warr's Commission have recommended the forming of Advisory Councils for both the Secondary Schools and the University College under the presidency of the Director of Education, the educated Sudanese and various communities being represented in these councils in order to advise in matters touching the work of Welfare of the schools. We strongly support this view and wish to emphasize the necessity of selecting Sudanese members from the educated and not from the so-called notables as is done in other councils.

Chapter IV

GIRLS' EDUCATION

Girls' education in this country is still in its infancy. The efforts made by the Government in this direction are greatly appreciated by all.

The Sudanese woman has always led a simple domestic life. Now both husbands and wives have felt the need for woman's education in order to fulfil her duty as a mother and home-maker and not as a wage-earner. This is witnessed by the great demand for girls' education in both towns and villages and by the efforts made by certain enterprising individuals in contributing towards this purpose by providing premises for girls' schools.

School Age

In order to attract the best girls to join the Teachers' Training College and to keep the teaching staff as long in the service as possible, it is suggested that new entrants in the elementary schools be accepted at the age of five so that the girls' age on leaving the training school will be about fourteen years which gives the mistress five or six years before she reaches the marriage age. This will also enable girls to reach intermediate schools at an early age which is of the greatest importance if intermediate education is to be entertained.

Elementary Schools

There are at present about thirty Government schools for girls all over the Sudan while the number of girls exceeds the number of boys. To further the country's progress which is, to a great extent, retarded by the ignorance of the Sudanese woman, it is essential to provide as many schools for girls as there are for boys and to raise the standard of such schools to a level that ensures the production of suitable wives and mothers capable of making a happy home and taking proper care of their children. We beg to make the following suggestions in this direction:

    i. That the present elementary school career be increased by one year which should be confined to practical training in domestic subjects and hygiene for those who are not desirous of continuing their education in the Teachers' Training College or in an intermediate school where advanced training on these subjects will have to be taught.

ii. That the number of schools be increased during the next ten years to a hundred schools at least to take from ten thousand to fifteen thousand girls, thus enabling about 5 per cent of the girls of educational age to receive elementary education.

Girls' Training College

The proposals contained in the previous paragraph will doubtless necessitate a relative improvement and expansion of the Girls' Training College at Omdurman in order to provide an adequate number of fully qualified mistresses. With this aim in view we venture to suggest:

i. The increase of school career to four years as is now done in the Elementary Teachers' Training School for boys in order to enable an improved standard to be attained.

ii. The expansion of the present college to produce forty mistresses each year and the opening of a new college of the same capacity in a suitable other centre. These two colleges will eventually produce eighty mistresses a year who will enable the additional seventy elementary schools proposed above to be opened during the next ten years and to replace those who leave the service to get married.

It is also suggested that, in due course, girls for the Training Schools should be taken from the product of the Girls' Intermediate Schools.

Intermediate Schools

We are pleased to learn that the Education Department has already decided to open an intermediate school for girls in Omdurman. We hope that similar schools will shortly be opened in other towns where there is a demand for such education. Fees will of course have to be charged but they should be reasonably low to encourage all classes of people to send their girls to these schools.

In addition to the general education subjects pertaining to intermediate schools, we suggest that special care be taken in giving to the girls advanced work in domestic subjects, hygiene and home nursing.

Teaching Staff for Teachers' Schools and Intermediate Schools

To attain the improved standard of girls' education, suggested in this chapter, it is of the utmost importance that the Mistresses of the Training Schools and Intermediate Schools should have received Higher Education and sufficient training in the methods of teaching. No Sudanese Mistresses of this standard are available and they will therefore have to be obtained from Egypt and England. Domestic Science should particularly be entrusted to a well qualified foreign mistress, otherwise no real progress can be achieved in this direction.

Boarding Houses and Transport Facilities

It is considered necessary that intermediate schools should be provided with boarding houses to enable girls from neighbouring towns where such schools exist to be accommodated and also to enable the day pupils to be kept in school all day in order to participate in housekeeping and other activities.

We also believe that lack of suitable means of transport between the house and the school discourages a great number of Sudanese girls from attending schools. The provision of a means of conveyance for day pupils is therefore essential. A big motor coach as that used by the Comboni College will suit the purpose. Girls who wish to use the coach may be charged for their transport.

Contact with Mothers

It will serve great purposes if arrangements could be made to bring together mothers and mistresses of schools as frequently as possible. This is not only useful for the welfare of the pupils but it also provides possibilities for the enlightenment of adult women. It is therefore suggested that a mothers' day be made in all girls' schools weekly or fortnightly when lectures or informal talks may be delivered by school mistresses on hygiene, home nursing and other general questions of interest to adult women.

Chapter V

TECHNICAL EDUCATION

It is most necessary that technical education in any country should advance hand in hand with scientific and economic development. Although building trades, namely: masonry work, brick-laying, painting and carpentry were started very early, training in these trades did not yet reach the standard required. This is due, in our opinion to two reasons: (a) lack of qualified instructors in vocational work and (b) difficulty of assuring apprenticeship in a suitably equipped workshop, after leaving school.

Boys receiving training in mechanical trades in the Railways Technical School are more fortunate. In the first place they receive their training from sufficiently qualified instructors; secondly, they have the advantage of apprenticeship in a properly equipped workshop and a purely mechanical atmosphere. Training in these trades was further enhanced by the provision of a section for training intermediate schoolboys as mechanical foremen.

Omdurman Technical School

In order to provide better skilled artisans in building trades, we venture to suggest:

1. The appointment of first class instructors from England or Egypt for the Omdurman Technical School in the more important trades.

2. That an arrangement be made with the Public Works, Sudan Railways and Irrigation Departments to accept boys who completed their education in this school as apprentices for two years at least. To encourage the boys to complete the period of apprenticeship they may be paid a small wage, the school leaving certificate being only given after this completion of the prescribed period of apprenticeship. Such an arrangement should not of course be confined to boys required for government employment but should be generally applied in order to produce a suitable type of artisan for private work.

Pottery

A course of instruction in pottery was given in Omdurman Technical School some time ago, but this was stopped for reasons unknown to us. There is a great demand for artisans in this craft for making roof tiles and glazed utility articles. In his report for 1936 the manager of this school has given an interesting account of his experiments with local clays which seems to be very encouraging and we earnestly hope that this section will be reintroduced to the Omdurman School. It is relevant to mention in this connection that the Piastre Orphanage Committee was contemplating to start a course of instruction in pottery but for lack of funds was unable to do so. If it is not considered possible or desirable to reintroduce this work in the Government School, perhaps the results of the manager's experiments could be placed at the disposal of the Piastre Orphanage Committee who will be prepared to start a section if the Government will help by bearing the salary of the expert instructor.

Railway Technical School

As already stated at the beginning of this chapter, the Railways School appears to us to be adequate for mechanical training. We beg to request, however, that the school be expanded to allow a greater number of both elementary and intermediate schoolboys to receive full training as now accorded to the Railway mechanics and foremen, for private work and for employment in other Departments. It is needless to say that there is ample demand in the country for this type of man which is likely to increase in future.

Training of Building Foremen

As is well known, foremen of works for the Public Works and Irrigation Departments were provided in the past from the Engineering Section of the Gordon College which has now been revised to a higher professional level. To bridge this gap and to provide foremen of works for private work, it is suggested that a higher course be given in the Omdurman Technical School for Intermediate Schoolboys. This will not involve any considerable expenditure if the school is provided with first class instructors as suggested above; the school of engineering lecturers might also help in the class work.

PART TWO: SOUTHERN SUDAN

Education in the Southern Sudan is left entirely in the hands of Missions which are subsidized by the Government. This, in our opinion, is responsible for the backwardness of education in that sphere. In saying this, we do not wish, in any way, to underestimate the contribution which the Missions have made and are making towards education in the south, but as the main object of these Missions is a religious one, the educational value of Missionary Schools is consequently low and therefore, so far, has very little effect in the life of the Southerners. Tribes still live in such a primitive and inhuman condition that would not befit the twentieth century. It is a disgrace that in most parts of the Southern Province people do not yet use any clothes, they have no proper housing, they are underfed and they consequently do not know the value of money. We think that on the latter hangs the development of the South, but unless the people feel the need for clothing, good housing, nutrition, and certain luxuries of life, they are not likely to realize the value of money and will not therefore be inclined to do any work. It is only through proper education for both boys and girls that these necessities will be known.

We therefore venture to suggest that improvement of education in the South cannot be attained by expanding and improving the present missionary schools at the Government expense but by opening entirely new schools on the lines of those in the Northern Sudan. The Arabic language will provide a suitable *lingua franca* as it is already spoken by most of the tribesmen and will thus solve the present difficulties expressed by the Director of Education in his report for 1936.

Quicker results can, however, be achieved if the present restrictions are removed and the South is opened unconditionally to the Northerners. Apart from the educational value of the continuous contact between the peoples of the North and South, the economic conditions will be improved by promoting trade and agricultural activities.

Elementary School at Malakal

It is understood that a very expensive elementary school, which will be run by a British Headmaster is being started at Malakal. It is in our opinion more useful and less expensive in the long run, to open an ordinary elementary school, especially in a place like Malakal, where the Arabic language is spoken by all the population. Other elementary schools should also be opened in other suitable centres as soon as possible.

An Intermediate School on the lines of those in the North would also appear to be badly needed not only for the Southerners but also for facilitating intermediate education to a large number of the Northerners who live in the south and who find great difficulties in educating their sons. It will also help to train teachers for the new elementary schools until a proper training school could be established.

PART THREE: NATIONAL EDUCATION

In spite of their limited resources, the people of this country, prompted by their desire to provide additional facilities for educating as many of their children as possible at a reasonable cost and to enable the poorer classes to receive free education have, by combined efforts, established a few elementary and intermediate schools which they still continue to maintain at their own expense. Some of these schools receive some help from the Education Department in the form of free issue of scholastic materials. These grants are much appreciated but it is felt that these schools deserve more substantial subsidies from the Government. Their greatest difficulty lies in the lack of qualified teachers. This is partly due to the absence of capable teachers locally and partly to the inability of these schools to offer suitable terms of service for properly qualified teachers from within or without the country. It will greatly alleviate these difficulties and also make for the raising of the standard of education in National Schools, if the Government provides such schools and at the same time extends their subsidies to all the National Schools to cover the pay of the Headmaster or one teacher at least in each as is done to Missionary Schools. This will not only help to maintain the present schools but will also enable some of the funds collected to be utilized for expanding such schools to take a greater number of boys and relieve the present pressure on Government schools.

Technical Schools

The only national technical school is the Piastre Orphanage of Omdurman. In this institution very useful and new trades are being taught, viz.: weaving, rug-making, and leather work; the school is a charitable one. It provides free education, free boarding and free clothing. Unfortunately its resources are very limited and does not therefore cover its great liabilities. Consequently great difficulties are experienced by its Committee in balancing its budget. If an annual subsidy by the Government could be made to cover the deficit, great results will be attained to the country at large, and a real industrial development will be achieved.

CORRESPONDENCE ON THE ABOVE NOTE

(A)

No. G.G.C./10　　　　　　　　　　　Omdurman, 5 July 1939
　　　　　　　　　　　　　　　　　　　P.O. Box 79

The Civil Secretary,
Sudan Government,
Khartoum.

Dear Sir,

I beg to forward a note by the Graduates General Congress on education in the Sudan for favourable consideration.

The preparation of this note was first started in April 1938 and was to be ready for submission in the following autumn while the education problems were being considered but it was necessary to collect information and to sound the public opinion in order to be able to represent the views of the intelligentsia. The long process of investigation and consideration by the various committees of the Congress has further delayed the submission of this note.

A ten years' plan has since been submitted by the Director of Education and approved by the Governor-General's Council but we trust that our proposals will be duly considered in connection with the implementation of that plan.

We beg to express our gratitude to the Government for accepting all the proposals for educational expansion submitted by the Director of Education and for placing at his disposal the necessary funds for implementing the first year's programme.

We are greatly indebted to Mr. C. W. M. Cox, the Director of Education for his great and untiring efforts in the work of reform and expansion of education ever since his arrival in the country.

We venture to express the hope that our comments will be of some assistance to his successor, who will, we trust, follow his steps.

　　　　　　　　　　　　　Yours faithfully,
　　　　　　　　　　　　　　　(*Signed*)
　　　　　　　　　　　　　　　Acting Secretary
　　　　　　　　　　　　　Graduates General Congress

(B)

No. 17.B.1　　　　　　　　　　　　　　　　11 July 1939
Strictly Confidential
Director of Education.

I forward herewith a note by the Graduates General Congress on Education in the Sudan for your information and consideration in due course.

I need not attempt at present to comment on the substance of the note, but I think you will agree that its form is very unexceptionable.

I attach a draft which, subject to your comments, I propose to send to the Secretary to the Congress.

(*Signed*) J. A. Gillan,

CIVIL SECRETARY

Education Department,
Khartoum
13 July 1939

No. 17.B.1
Strictly Confidential
Civil Secretary.

I have received your letter dated July 11th forwarding a note by the Graduates General Congress of Education in the Sudan and agree that its form is unexceptionable.

In the meantime I have no comment to make on your draft letter to the Secretary of the Congress, but I should welcome the opportunity of discussing this with you before I leave the country.

(*Signed*) C. W. M. Cox,

DIRECTOR OF EDUCATION

(C)

No. 17.B.1   16 July 1939
Dear Sir,

I have to acknowledge, with thanks, receipt of your letter of the 5th instant covering a note by the Graduates General Congress on Education in the Sudan.

At this stage I need only say that I have read the Note with great interest and have forwarded a copy to the Director of Education for his consideration. I shall further bring the Note to the notice of His Excellency the Governor-General on his return from leave.

Without entering at present into detail I am glad to assure you that I recognize the Note as a constructive contribution to a problem vitally affecting the welfare of the Sudanese.

Yours faithfully,

(*Signed*) J. A. Gillan,

CIVIL SECRETARY

Secretary,
Graduates General Congress,
P.O. Box No. 79,
OMDURMAN

BIBLIOGRAPHY

I *Unpublished Sources*

A Britain

I Church Missionary Society, London, *Précis Book* 1905–1934, Church Missionary Society Archives, London.

II Documents collected for the Information of the Special Mission, *Milner Papers*, at the Bodleian Library, Oxford.

III Public Record Office, London.

Letter from Cromer to Bishop Blyth, 8 February 1900, *PRO/FO/633/Vol. 8.*
Letter from Cromer to Sir E. Gorst, 12 November 1908, *PRO/FO/633/Vol. 14.*
Letter from Cromer to Gwynne, Cairo, 13 March 1900, *PRO/FO/633/Vol. 8.*
Letter from Cromer to Landsdowne, 9 March 1900, *PRO/FO/633/Vol. 1.*
Letter from Cromer to McInnes, Cairo, 16 May 1906, *PRO/FO/633/Vol. 8.*
Letter from Cromer to Salisbury, 22 February 1900, *PRO/FO/633/Vol. 6.*
Letter from Cromer to Sir Thomas Sanderson, Cairo, 21 December 1898, *PRO/FO/633/Vol. 8.*
Letter from Sir E. Gorst to Sir E. Grey, 1905, *PRO/FO/36.*

IV Papers of the third Marquis of Salisbury deposited at Christ Church, Oxford.

Letter from Cromer to Salisbury, Cairo, 12 June 1900, *SP/A/112.*
Letter from Jackson to Cromer, Omdurman, 15 June 1900, *SP/A/112.*
Letter from Jackson to Sirdar, Khartoum, 4 March 1900, *SP/A/112.*
Letter from Salisbury to Kitchener, 21 November 1898, *SP/A/113.*
Report by Colonel Jackson on the Omdurman Incident, *SP/A/112.*

V Sudan Archives, School of Oriental Studies, University of Durham.

Currie, J., lecture at Oxford on 3 May 1935, *SAD/243/1.*
Diary of Sir William Mather (1839–1920), *SAD/404/8/1.*
Letter from Civil Secretary to Wingate, Khartoum, 2 February 1907, *SAD/103.*
Letter from Cromer to Wingate, Cairo, 3 February 1904, *SAD/275/4.*
Letter from Currie to Wingate, 23 June 1904, *SAD/103.*
Letter from Currie to Wingate, Khartoum, 2 January 1907, *SAD/103.*
Letter from Governor Bahr al Ghazal to Wingate, 30 March 1907, *SAD/103.*
Letter from Gwynne to Wingate, Khartoum, 13 March 1907, *SAD/103.*
Letter from Gwynne to Wingate, Khartoum, 26 December 1910, *SAD/103.*
Letter from Gwynne to Wingate, 26 February 1916, *SAD/103.*

Letter from Wingate to Cromer, Khartoum, 29 December 1906, *SAD/103*.

Letter from Wingate to Cromer, Khartoum, 19 July 1907, *SAD/103*.

Letter from Wingate to Finlay, Khartoum, 20 March 1907, *SAD/103*.

Letter from Wingate to Governor Bahr al Ghazal, 3 February 1904, *SAD/103*.

Letter from Wingate to Governor Bahr al Ghazal, Khartoum, 27 December 1910, *SAD/103*.

Letter from Wingate to Gwynne, 6 April 1907, *SAD/280/4*.

Letter from Wingate to Gwynne, 17 May 1911, *SAD/300/5*.

Letter from Wingate to Kitchener, Khartoum, 26 October 1911, *SAD/301/4*.

Report on the Military School, Khartoum, *SAD/106/4*.

B   Sudan

I   Education Archives, Ministry of Education, Khartoum.

Abbas, M., Interim Report on Um Gerr Experiment, *EDA*.

Ainley, N. E. and Warburton, M. C., Report on Women's Education in the Southern Sudan, 1939, *EDA*.

Cox, Christopher, Report on Education in the South, July 1937, *EDA/File DE/SCR/9.9.9.15*.

Despatch from the Governor-General to His Britannic Majesty's Ambassador in Cairo, No. 31/I.C.I., 10 March 1938, *EDA/File DE/SCR/1.1.17*.

Despatch from the Governor-General to His Britannic Majesty's Ambassador in Cairo No. 85, 4 August 1948, *EDA/File DE/SCR/1.1.17*.

Despatch from the Governor-General to His Britannic Majesty's Ambassador in Cairo No. 89, 4 August 1945, *EDA/File DE/SCR/1.1.17*.

EDA/File 17.A.2.7.

EDA/File 9.1.55.A.

EDA/File DE/SCR/1.1.17.

Education Department, Occasional Note No. 2, *EDA/File DES/9.1.4*.

Education Department, Occasional Note No. 6, 28 October 1936, *EDA/File DES/9.1.4*.

Griffiths, V. L., Note on the British Contribution to Character Training in Sudan Education, *EDA*.

Griffiths, V. L., Summary of views on Extension of Higher Education in the Northern Sudan, 15 and 17 February 1937, *EDA*.

Letter from British Ambassador in Cairo to Rt. Hon. Anthony Eden, 11 January 1938, No. 30/84/3/83, *EDA/File DE/SCR/9.9.9.14*.

Letter from the British Mission to the Holy See to the Foreign Office, 4 August 1939, No. 127/76/22/38, *EDA/File DE/SCR/9.9.9.14*.

Letter from Catholic Mission to Minister of Interior, Juba, 5 June 1954, *EDA*.

Letter from Civil Secretary to all Heads of Departments, 30 May 1945, *EDA/File 9.1.55.A*.

Letter from Civil Secretary to Minister of Education, Khartoum, 27 November 1949, *EDA/File No. 9/8.*

Letter from C. W. M. Cox to Director of Education, 7 October 1939, *EDA/File 17/0/1.*

Letter from Director of Education to all British Officials in the Education Department, 15 November 1941, *EDA.*

Letter from Director of Education to all Governors, 23 March 1945, *EDA/File SCR/9.1.1.*

Letter from Director of Education Department, to all staff, 16 March 1939, *EDA.*

Letter from Director of Education to Civil Secretary, 3 October 1941, *EDA/File 9/8.65.*

Letter from Director of Education to Civil Secretary, 12 March 1941, *EDA/File 9/8.65.*

Letter from Director of Education to Civil Secretary, 10 January 1942, *EDA/File DE/9.1.1.9.*

Letter from Director of Education to Civil Secretary, 30 April 1941, *EDA/File DE/9/8.65.*

Letter from Director of Education to Mekki Abbas, 6 June 1947, *EDA/File DE/SCR/9.7.1.*

Letter from Foreign Office to His Majesty's Mission to the Holy See, 21 March 1938, J 835/220/16 No. 18, *EDA/File DE/SCR/9.9.9.14.*

Letter from Governor-General to His Britannic Majesty's Ambassador Extraordinary and Plenipotentiary, Khartoum, 7 December 1937, Cairo, No. 145/46.A.A., *EDA/File DE/SCR/9.9.9.14.*

Letter from Hibbert, D. H., to Director of Education, Juba, 2 September 1945, *EDA.*

Letter from Resident Inspector, Southern Education, to Director of Education, 3 February 1941, *EDA/File DE/SCR/1.1.17.*

Letter from Scott, G. C., to Lord De La Warr, 5 April 1937, *EDA.*

Note by Director of Education, 9 May 1945, *EDA/File DE/SCR/9.2.*

Note on the Foundation, Financing and Staffing of Non-Government Schools, 19 March 1947, *EDA/File 9/8.61.*

Note on Proposed Egyptian Secondary School in Khartoum, 15 November 1939, *EDA/File 17.D.I.*

Record of the Meeting held on 13 October 1936 in Foreign Office to discuss Education Policy in the Sudan, *EDA/File DE/SCR/9.9.9.14.*

Secretariat for Education and Health, *Education Policy, Northern Sudan*, Report of a Committee appointed by His Excellency the Governor-General, 7 March 1933, *EDA/File EH/17.A.1.1.*

Sudan Government, *Technical Training of Sudanese*, Report of the Committee appointed by His Excellency the Governor-General, Khartoum, 15 July 1935, *EDA.*

II   Ministry of Interior Archives, Ministry of Interior, Khartoum.

Bowers, J. B., A Note on Missions and Educational Policy in Upper Nile Province, 14 December 1942, *MIA/File SCO/46.A.I.*

Letter from Director of Education to Civil Secretary, 24 April 1952, *MIA/File SCR/27, vol. II.*

Letter from High Commissioner, Cairo, to Governor-General, 20 March 1929, *MIA/File SCO/46.A.I.*

Letter from High Commissioner, Cairo, to Governor-General, 13 April 1929, *MIA/File SCO/46.A.I.*

Letter from Ismail al Azhari, Mufti of the Sudan to the Civil Secretary, 16 October 1926, *MIA/File 17/D/21/23.*

Letter from Lord Lloyd to the Foreign Office, 19 June 1929, *MIA/File SCO/46.A.I.*

Memorandum by the Governor-General, 17 December 1929, *MIA/File SCO/46.A.I.*

MIA/File SCR/I.C.7.

Minute by His Excellency the Governor-General, 1 January 1927, *MIA/File 33.*

Note by Director of Education on Proposed Increase in the Amount of Staff Grant paid to Church Missionary Society, 29 November 1948, *MIA/File SCR/9.9.7.1, vol. IV.*

Note on American Missionaries' Attitude to Religious Instruction, *MIA/File CS/SCR/46.A.2.*

Note on Religious Instruction in Government Schools in the South, Juba, 4 January 1949, No. ADES/SCR/1/K.513, *MIA/File SCR/17.A.*

Report by Governor Upper Nile province, June 1929, *MIA/File SCO/14/A.1.*

III Sudan Government Central Archives, Khartoum.

Educational Plan 1938–1946, *SGA/GENCO/3/42.*

Educational Policy, Northern Sudan, Report of a Committee appointed by His Excellency the Governor-General, 7 March 1933, *SGA/File EH/17.A.1/1.*

Graduates Congress, Memorandum on Omdurman Mahad Ilmi, 20 April 1939, *SGA/File LS/SC/11.4.*

Hillelson, S., Report on Education in Mongalla Province, 22 April 1922, *SGA/CIVSEC/17/1.*

Letter from Al Mahdi to Ahmed Hamad al Magdoub, al Murshid ila Walhaiq al Mahdi, Numbers 508 and 509, *SGA.*

Letter from Bredin, G. R. F., to Governor Blue Nile Province, 30 July 1938, *SGA/Blue Nile/1/15/File SCR/17.D.6.*

Letter from Civil Secretary to the Graduates Congress, 22 May 1938, *SGA.*

Letter from Director of Education to Governor Bahr al Ghazal, 30 March 1929, *SGA/File SCR/17.A.1.*

Letter from Director of Intelligence to Governor Khartoum province, 23 February 1924, *SGA/File DI/LB/257.*

Letter from Governor Bahr al Ghazal to Civil Secretary, 20 January 1932, *SGA/File BGP/SCR/1.C.14.*

Letter from Governor Bahr al Ghazal Province to Civil Secretary, 22 March 1932, *SGA/File N.B.G.P./SCR/1/C.6.*

SGA/CIVSEC/1/57/File 1.P.B, vol. I and vol. II.

SGA/CIVSEC/1/9/File L.F, vol. I.

SGA/CIVSEC/File 17.A.3.

SGA/DAKHLIA/17/5/File 17.B.8.

SGA/DAKHLIA/17/6/File 17.D.6.4.

SGA/DAKHLIA/File 17.D.16, vol. I.

SGA/GENCO/1/1/File No. 6.

SGA/ND/SCR/1.C.1.

Letter from Governor Blue Nile Province to Director of Education, 1 November 1958, *SGA/Blue Nile/1/15 File SCR/17.0.6.*

Letter from Governor Khartoum Province to Civil Secretary, 7 December 1935, *SGA/CIVSEC/File 17.A.3.*

Letter from Grove, E., to the Director of Intelligence, Khartoum, 17 September 1918, *SGA/CIVSEC/File 17.A.2.6.*

Letter from Hillard, A. J., to Governor Blue Nile Province, 30 June 1938, *SGA/Blue Nile/1/15 File SCR/17.D.6.*

Letter from Hunter, N. B., to Director of Education, 12 November 1925, *SGA/CIVSEC/File 17.D.48.*

Letter from Hunter, N. B., to Director of Education, 29 January 1929, *SGA/CIVSEC/File 17.D.48.*

Letter from Lord De La Warr to Governor-General, 16 October 1937, *SGA/CIVSEC/17/3/File 17.B.1.*

Letter from Secretary of Education and Health to Northern Governors, Khartoum, 19 January 1934, *SGA/CIVSEC/17/1 File 17.A.1.6.*

Minutes of the Governor-General's Council Meeting on 24 November 1944, *SGA.*

Minutes of the 419th Meeting of the Governor-General's Council, *SGA.*

Minutes of the Juba Conference, 12–13 June 1947, *SGA/Equatoria/File EP/SCR/I.A.51.*

Minutes of the 6th Educational Conference of Mongalla Province, Juba, 16 April 1932, *SGA/CIVSEC/17/1/File 17.A.2.6.*

Newbold, Douglas, Note on Further Association of Sudanese with Local and Central Government submitted to the 502nd Meeting of the Governor-General's Council, 14 September 1942, *SGA/GENCO/3/49.*

Note by Civil Secretary on Southern Sudan Policy, *CS/SCR/1.C.1,* 16 December 1946, *SGA.*

Note by Udal, N. R., Khartoum, 1928, *SGA/DAKHLIA/17/2, File 17.A.23.*

Note by Gordon Memorial College Warden on moving the secondary school out of Khartoum, Appendix C to the 1938–46 Educational Plan, *SGA/GENCO/3/42.*

Note by the Governor-General on 12 June 1927, *SGA/CIVSEC/File 17.A.2.6.*

Note by Legal Secretary, 21 May 1939, *SGA/File CS/SC/11.4.*

Note on Legal Education by Legal Secretary, Khartoum, 14 April 1928, *SGA/DAKHLIA/17/2, File 17.A.23.*

Note on Legal Education, 3 February 1929, *SGA/DAKHLIA/17/2, File 17.A.23.*

Note on Legal Education, 1 December 1934, *SGA/DAKHLIA/17/2 File 17.A.23.*

Note on Publication of De La Warr and Garem's Reports, Khartoum, 27 November 1937, *SGA/CIVSEC/File 17.3.1.*

Note on the Case for the Vernacular, *SGA/Equatoria/File EP/17.*

Petition on Omdurman Mahad Ilmi, 26 April 1939, *SGA/File LS/SC/11.4.*

Petition to the Governor-General, January 1931, *SGA/CIVSEC/File/ 1.P.13, vol. II.*

Progress Report on Higher Schools submitted by the Director of Education to Governor-General's Council Meeting on 5 September 1942, *SGA/ GENCO/3/49.*

Southern Sudan Policy, Memorandum by the Civil Secretary, Khartoum, 1 September 1931, *SGA.*

Williams, C. W., Report on Education in the Southern Sudan, 9 February 1936, *SGA/Equatoria/File EP/SCR/17.A.3.*

IV   University of Khartoum Archives, Khartoum.

Hodgkin, T., Report on Extra-Mural Work, Khartoum, 1948, *UKA.*

Gordon Memorial College Fund, List of Donations, Legacies, etc., from 28 November 1898 to 9 February 1920, *UKA.*

Letter from Tothill, J. D., to Christopher Cox, 29 October 1945, *UKA.*

Minutes of the Council of University College, Khartoum, 1953–5, *UKA.*

Minutes of the Gordon Memorial College Council Meeting on 15 November 1944, *UKA.*

Minutes of the thirteenth Meeting of Higher Schools Advisory Committee, January 1944, *UKA.*

Notes on the Kitchener Memorial Medical School, *UKA.*

Wingate, F. R., Notes on the Warden's Report 1933, *UKA.*

Report on Higher Education in the Colonies, *UKA/File OMC/14.*

C   Unpublished theses

Abdu, O. M. Osman, 'The Development of Transport and Economic Growth in the Sudan 1898–1958', Ph.D. thesis submitted to the University of London, 1960.

Maqar, Nasim, 'Ahwal al-Sudan al Iqtisadiah Qubail al-fath al Misri al-Awal', M.A. thesis submitted to Cairo University 1956 (Arabic text).

Osman, M. K., 'Education and Social Change in the Sudan 1900–1958', M.A. thesis, University of London, 1965.

Rahim, A. W. A., 'An Economic History of the Sudan 1899–1956', thesis submitted for M.A. degree, University of Manchester, 1963.

Sanderson, L. M., 'A History of Education in the Sudan with special reference to Girls' Schools', M.A. thesis, University of London, 1962.

D   Other sources

Letters from G. C. Scott to his mother, 31 July 1935 and 14 August 1935.

Note by the Graduates Congress on Education in the Sudan, July 1939 (typescript), University of Khartoum Library.

Personal information from: Sir Christopher Cox (Director of Education Sudan, 1937–9), G. C. Scott (Chief Inspector of Education 1930–5, Warden Gordon Memorial College 1936–46), Mirghani Hamza (Minister of Education, Khartoum, 1954–5), L. C. Wilcher (Principal University College, Khartoum, 1947–56), S. Santandrea (The Verona Fathers, Rome), and V. L. Griffiths (Principal Institute of Education, Bakht er Ruda 1934–49).

2   Published Sources

A   Annual reports

The Gordon Memorial College at Khartoum, *Annual Reports and Accounts 1901–50*, and the University College of Khartoum, *Annual Reports and Accounts 1951–1956*.

The Kitchener School of Medicine, Khartoum, *Annual Reports 1924–1951*.

The Reports by H.M. Agent and Consul-General on the Finances, Administration and Conditions of Egypt and the Soudan from 1898 to 1913 (H.M.S.O. London), *The Reports by H.M.'s High Commissioner on the Finances, Administration and Conditions of Egypt and the Soudan from 1914 to 1920* (H.M.S.O. London), and *The Reports on the Finances, Administration and Conditions of the Soudan (Sudan from 1923) from 1921 to 1952* (H.M.S.O. London).

Sudan Government, *Annual Budgets, 1900–1956*.

Sudan Government, *Annual Reports of the Education Department, 1904 to 1914 and 1928 to 1948*, and *Annual Reports of the Ministry of Education, 1949–1956*.

B   Books and articles

Abdin, A. M., *Tarikh al-Thaqafa al-Arabia fi al-Sudan*, Cairo 1953 (Arabic text).

Abdul Magid, A. A., *al Tarbia, fi al Sudan fi al-Qarn al Tasia-Ashar* (3 vols), Cairo 1949 (Arabic text).

Abu Salim, M. T., 'Marakiz al Thaqafa fi al-Mahdia', *Al Khartoum*, January 1968, pp. 6–9.

Advisory Committee on Native Education in British Tropical African Dependencies, *Memorandum on Educational Policy in British Tropical Africa*, Cmnd. 2374, H.M.S.O., London 1925.

Advisory Committee on Education in the Colonies, *Memorandum on the Education of African Communities, Colonial No. 103*, H.M.S.O., London 1935.

Advisory Committee on Education in the Colonies, *Mass Education in African Society, Colonial No. 186*, H.M.S.O., London 1943.

Al Fajr magazine, Khartoum: vol. i, no. 11, November 1934, pp. 471–7; vol. i, no. 12, 16 November 1934, pp. 533–7; vol. i, no. 15, 1 January 1935, pp. 659–64; vol. i, no. 21, 1 June 1935, pp. 1018–19; vol. i, no. 22, 16 June 1935, pp. 1065–6.

Ali, Nasr el Hag, *Education in the Northern Sudan, Report to the Institute of Education*, University of London 1951.

Al Moayed newspaper, Cairo, no. 5043, 17 December 1906.

Al Nil newspaper, Khartoum, 5 October 1937, 20 January 1940 and 21 December 1964.

The Anglo-Egyptian Sudan, H.M.S.O., no. 98, London 1920.

Al Shial, J., *Rufaa Rafia al Tahtawi*, Cairo 1958.

Al Sudan newspaper, Khartoum, 19 October 1937, 25 December 1936.

Al Tunial, Mohamed Ibu Omer, *Voyage au Darfur*, translated by A. Perron, ed. Jomard, E. F., Paris 1840.

Annual Reports of the Church Missionary Society, London, 1901–2, 1904–5.

Arkell, A. J., *A History of the Sudan from the Earliest Times to 1821*. London 1955.

Arnold, T., *The Preaching of Islam*, London 1935.

Atiyah, E., *An Arab Tells His Story*, London 1946.

Beshir, M. O., *The Southern Sudan*, London 1968.

Bowman, H., *Middle East Window*, London 1942.

Browne, W. G., *Travels in Africa, Egypt and Syria, 1792 to 1799*, London 1806.

Bruce, J., *Travels to Discover the Sources of the Nile in the Years 1768, 1769, 1770, 1771, 1772 and 1773*, Edinburgh 1790.

Burckhardt, J. L., *Travels in Nubia*, London 1819.

Carr-Saunders, A. M., *New Universities Overseas*, London 1961.

Cash, W. W., *The Changing Sudan*, London 1930.

——, *The Nuba Mountains*, Church Missionary Society, London 1930.

Chirol, V., *Indian Unrest*, London 1910.

Christian Education in Africa, Conference at High Leigh, 8–13 September, London 1924.

College at Khartoum, Macmillan's Magazine, lxxxiii (1900), 272–9.

Contemporary Review, no. 422 (June 1899), pp. 854–68.

Cook, Sir Albert, *Uganda Memoirs*, Kampala 1945.

Crawford, O. G. S., *The Funj Kingdom of Sennar*, Gloucester 1951.

Cromer, Earl of, *Ancient and Modern Imperialism*, London 1910.

——, *Modern Egypt*, 2 vols., London 1908.

Crosby, E. S. and the Education Division Staff, *Sudanese Manpower 1956–1965*, U.S.O.M. to the Sudan, Khartoum 1960.

Crowfoot, J. W., 'Some Red Sea Ports', *Geographical Journal*, xxxvii (1911), 523–58.

Currie, James, 'The Educational Experiment in the Anglo-Egyptian Sudan 1900–33', *Journal of the Royal African Society*, xxxiii, no. 133 (October 1934), 351–71, and xxxiv, no. 134 (January 1935), 41–60.

Dempsey, J., *Mission on the Nile*, London 1955.

Fabian Society, *The Sudan, The Road Ahead*, London 1945.

Foster, J. F., *Education and Social Change in Ghana*, London 1965.

Furnivall, J. S., *Colonial Policy and Practice*, Cambridge 1948.

'General Gordon and Education in the Sudan', *Missionary Review of the World*, xxxi (1908), 360–4.

Gillan, J. A., *Some Aspects of Nuba Administration*, Sudan No. 1, 1931.

Gray, R., *A History of the Southern Sudan, 1839–1889*, London 1961.

Griffiths, V. L., 'A Teacher Training and Research Centre in the Sudan', *Overseas Education*, xvi, no. 1 (October 1944), 1–6.

——, *An Experiment in Education*, London 1953.

Groves, S. P., *The Planting of Christianity in Africa* (4 vols.), London 1948–58.

Hadarat al Sudan newspaper, Khartoum, 24 April 1921.

Halim, M. A., The Sudan Civil Service, *The Proceedings of the Conference on Tradition and Change*, Khartoum 1960.

Harper, J., Report on Work at Suakin 16 October 1890, *The Anti-Slavery Society Papers*, Rhodes House, Oxford, MSS. British Empire 522/A25.

Henderson, K. D. D., *The Making of the Modern Sudan*, London 1953.

—— *The Sudan Republic*, London 1965.

Heyworth-Dunne, J., *An Introduction to the History of Education in Modern Egypt*, London 1938.

Hill, R., *Egypt in the Sudan 1820–1881*, London 1959.

—— *Slatin Pasha*, London 1965.

—— 'Government and Christian Missions in the Anglo-Egyptian Sudan, 1899–1914', *Middle Eastern Studies* (London School of Economics), i, no. 2 (January 1965), 113–34.

Hillelson, S., 'Tabaqat Waddayfalla', *Sudan Notes and Records*, vi, no. 1923.

Holt, P. M., *A Modern History of the Sudan*, London 1961.

—— *The Mahdist State in the Sudan 1881–1898*, Oxford 1958.

Ibn Khaldoun, *Muqadima*, Beirut 1961 (Arabic text).

Jackson, H. C., *Pastor on the Nile*, London 1960.

Katb al Shuna, Ahmed, *Tarikh Muluk al Sudan*, ed. Mekki Shibeika, Khartoum 1947 (Arabic text).

Kinany, A. K., Islamic Schools and Universities, *The Year Book of Education*, London 1957, pp. 333-43.

Kirk-Green, A. H. M., *The Principles of Native Administration in Nigeria*, London 1965.

Lewis, L. J., *The Phelps Stokes Reports on Education in Africa*, London 1962.

Lugard, Sir F. D., *The Dual Mandate*, London 1922.

MacMichael, Sir H. A., *A History of the Arabs in the Sudan*, 2 vols., Cambridge 1922.

—— *The Anglo-Egyptian Sudan*, London 1934.

—— *The Sudan*, London 1954.

Magalat Hamiyat al Khartoum, no. 3, November 1960.

Magnus, P., *Kitchener, Portrait of an Imperialist*, London 1958.

Mahjob, M. A., 'Fi al Talim', *Al Fajr*, i, no. 11 (November 1934), 471-7.

Martin, P. F., *The Sudan in Evolution*, London 1921.

Maxwell, J. L., *Half a Century of Grace*, London 1953.

Mayhew, A., *Education in the Colonial Empire*, London 1938.

Ministry of Education, *Al Talim fi al Mudiria al Shamalia*, Khartoum 1962 (Arabic text).

—— *Al Talim fi Darfur*, Khartoum 1962 (Arabic text).

—— *A Report of the Sudan Educational Planning Committee*, Khartoum, June 1959.

Mudathir, Hassan, Madi al Mahad al Ilmi, *Magalat Mahad Omdurman*, 25 January 1963, pp. 31-8 (Arabic text).

Murray, A. V., 'Education under Indirect Rule', *Journal of the Royal African Society*, xxiv, no. 136 (July 1935).

Nadel, S. F., *The Nuba*, Oxford 1947.

Nadler, C. F., *The Two Sudans* (typescript), University of Khartoum Library.

Okeir, A. G., Education Among the Beja, *Overseas Education*, xxiii, no. 1 (October 1951), 194-6.

Oliver, R., *The Missionary Factor in East Africa*, London 1952.

Oliver, R. and Fage, J. D., *A Short History of Africa*, London 1962.

Poncet, C. J., *A Voyage to Ethiopia made in the Years 1698, 1699 and 1700*, London 1709.

Report of the Special Mission to Egypt, Cmd. 1131, H.M.S.O. London, 1921.

Republic of the Sudan, *Educational Statistics for the Academic Year 1959-1960*, Ministry of Education, Khartoum, April 1961.

—— *Educational Statistics for the Academic Year 1958-1959*, Ministry of Education, Khartoum 1959.

Republic of the Sudan, *Southern Sudan Disturbances*, Khartoum 1956.
—— *The Ten-Year Plan of Economic and Social Development 1961/62–1970/71*, Khartoum 1962.
—— *First Population Census of the Sudan, 21 Facts about the Sudanese*, Austria 1958.
Said, Beshir Mohamed, *The Sudan, Crossroads of Africa*, London 1965.
Sanderson, L., 'Some Aspects of the Development of Girls' Education in the Sudan', *Sudan Notes and Records*, xlii (1961).
—— 'A Survey of Material available for the Study of Educational Development in the Modern Sudan, 1900–63', *Sudan Notes and Records*, xliv (1963), 69–81.
—— 'Educational Development in the Southern Sudan 1900–1948' *Sudan Notes and Records*, xliii (1962).
—— 'Educational Development and Administrative Control in the Nuba Mountains region of the Sudan', *Journal of African History*, iv, 2 (1963) 233, 247.
Schmidt, P. W., 'The Use of the Vernacular', *Africa* iii, no. 2 (April 1930), 138–45.
Shalaby, A., *A History of Moslem Education*, Beirut 1954.
Shils, E., Political Development in the New States, *Comparative Studies in Society and History*, ii (1960), 281–2.
Shoqair, N., *Tarikh al Sudan al Qadim wal Hadith wa Jughrafiatuh*, Cairo 1903 (Arabic text).
Squires, H. C., *The Sudan Medical Service*, London 1958.
Stone, J., *The Finance of Government Economic Development in the Sudan 1899–1913*, Monograph in the Library of the Institute of Commonwealth Studies, Oxford.
Symes, Sir Stewart, *Tour of Duty*, London 1946.
Sudan Diocesan Review, Croydon, Surrey, England, viii, no. 1 (15 January 1929).
Sudan Government, *Annual Budgets 1899–1956*.
—— *Gazette No. 8*, November 1902.
—— *Gazette No. 44*, February 1903.
—— *Laws of the Sudan*, vol. iii, Khartoum 1941.
—— Legislative Assembly, *Weekly Digest of Proceedings, 1949–1951*, Khartoum.
—— *Memorandum on the Financial Relations between Egypt and the Sudan*, Cairo 1910.
—— *Note by Director of Education on the Government Plan for Educational Development in the Northern Sudan for the next Ten Years*, Khartoum 1946.
—— Plan for Educational Development in the Northern Sudan 1946–1956, *Proceedings of the Fifth Session of the Advisory Council for the Northern Sudan*.
—— *Proceedings of the Advisory Council for the Northern Sudan, 1944–1948*.

—— *Proceedings of the Legislative Assembly 18 November 1949 and 20 November 1950.*

—— *Proceedings of the Seventh Session of the Advisory Council for the Northern Sudan, May 1947,* and *Proceedings of the Sixth Session, January 1945.*

—— *Proposals for the Expansion and Improvement of the Educational System in the Northern Provinces, 1949–1956,* Khartoum.

—— *Proposals for the Expansion and Improvement of the Educational System in the Southern Provinces, 1951–1956,* Khartoum.

—— *Regulations and Syllabuses of Studies for Elementary Vernacular Schools under the Sudan Government Education Department, 1929.*

—— *Report of a Commission of Inspection on the Gordon Memorial College,* Khartoum, February 1929.

—— *Report of Ali Bey el Jarem on the Teaching of Arabic and the Training of Arabic Teachers in the Sudan,* 28 December 1937, Khartoum.

—— *Reports of Governors of Provinces,* Khartoum, 1925.

—— *Report of Lord De La Warr Educational Commission,* Khartoum 1937.

—— *Report of the Aliens Committee,* Cairo 1916.

—— *Report of the Committee on the Sudanization of the Civil Service,* Khartoum 1948.

—— *Report of the International Education Commission on Secondary Education,* Khartoum, February 1955.

—— Legal Department, *The Omdurman Mahad Ilmi,* Khartoum 1946.

—— *The Rejaf Language Conference 1928,* London 1928.

—— *Weekly Digest of Proceedings of Senate, Second Session,* Khartoum 1954.

The Scotsman (Edinburgh), 21 June 1910.

The Southern Sudan, Now and Then, Church Missionary Society, London 1950.

The Times, 30 November 1898, 16 April 1900.

Toniolo, E. F., 'The First Centenary of the Roman Catholic Mission to Central Africa', *Sudan Notes and Records,* xxvii (1946), pp. 98–126.

—— *Dawr al Irsaliat al Katholikia fi Harkat al Kashf al-Goghrafi wa ihm al Agnas al-Basharia bi al Sudan,* Khartoum 1958 (Arabic text).

Trimingham, J. S., *Islam in the Sudan,* London 1949.

—— *The Christian Approach to Islam in the Sudan,* Oxford University Press, 1948.

Tucker, A. N., 'The Linguistic Situation in the Southern Sudan', *Africa,* vii, no. 1 (January 1934), 28–38.

Udal, N. R., Education in the Northern Sudan, *Espratto Dagliatti dell' VIII Conegnotea l'Africa,* Rome, 11 October 1938, xvi.

United Nations, *Population and Manpower in the Sudan,* Department of Economic Affairs, Population Studies, no. 37, New York 1964.

United Nations Educational, Scientific and Cultural Organization, *Educational Investment Programming Mission, Sudan,* Paris 1963.

Wad Daifalla, Mohamed Al Nur, *Kitab al Tabaqat*, ed. Ibrahim Sidiq Ahmed, Cairo 1930 (Arabic text).

Waddington, G. and Hanbury, B., *Journal of a Visit to Some Parts of Ethiopia*, London 1822.

Watson, C. R., 'Missionary Conditions in the Egyptian Sudan,' *Missionary Review of the World*, xxviii (1905), 85–93.

White, A. S., *The Expansion of Egypt*, London 1899.

Wilson, J., *Education and Changing West African Culture*, New York 1963.

Wingate, F. R., The Story of the Gordon College and its Work; *The Story of the Cape to Cairo Railway and River Route 1887–1922*, ed. Weinthal, L., London 1923, part I, pp. 563–611.

—— *Wingate of the Sudan*, London 1955.

Zetland, Marquess of, *Lord Cromer*, London 1932.

INDEX

Abdel Qawi Pasha, 160, 161
Abdel Fatah Al Magrabi, 155
Abdul Majid Ahmed, 151
Abdul Rahman Abu Fag, 11
Abdul Rahman El Mahdi, 82
Abu-Haraz, 20
Abu Rikba, 62
Abu Sineina, 11
Abu Surur Al Fadhli, 11
Abul Gasim Ahmed Hashim, Sheikh, 48
Abwong, 147
accountancy, 84, 109
administration, educational, 61-2, 98, 100, 178
adult education, 98, 115, 135, 136-7, 234-5
Advisory Committee on Education in the Colonies, 136, 143, 164, 165
Advisory Committee on Native Education, 65
Advisory Council for Education in Northern Sudan, 163, 166, 171, 176
African languages, 186
African Languages and Culture, International Institute of, 70
Agricultural education, 14, 16, 24, 46, 81, 90, 95, 97, 99, 103, 104, 109, 114, 116, 138, 141, 149, 161, 190, 191, 232-3, 243, 244, 246
Ahfad schools, 87, 150, 165
Ahlia schools, 87, 156, 157, 165, 206
Ahmed Hashim al Baghdadi, 82
Ahmed Mohamed Salih, 151
Ainley, Miss N. E., 145
Aisha bint Al Gadal, 11
Akrawi Committee, 190, 191-2
Al Azhar, 5, 13, 14, 42, 48, 118, 154, 161
Al Bandari, 11
Al Dabah, 10
Al Damar, 171
Al Fajr, 149, 150
Al Hussain al Zahra, 22
Al Masalami, 11
Al Mudawi al Masri, 11
Al Nil, 158
Al Sudan, 127, 158
Ali Abdul Latif, 78

Ali Bey El Garem, 117, 118, 240, 247
Ali el Berair, 160
Alkawa, 15
Alliri, 73
American Presbyterian Mission, 32, 34, 42, 49, 51, 74, 86, 127, 151, 174, 232
Anglo-Egyptian Treaty (1936), 111, 118, 122, 158, 178
ankylostomiasis, 216
Annuak, 7
anthropology, 186
Apostolic Vicariate of Central Africa, 18
Arab Revolt (1916), 77
Arabic, 4, 9, 10, 15, 16, 37, 44, 52, 69-70, 71, 73, 103, 116, 117, 118, 120, 129, 146, 152, 172, 175, 183, 191, 234, 239, 240, 247, 252
archaeology, 186
architecture, 106, 186
arithmetic, 103, 239
army, 16, 29, 43, 78, 146
arts, 141, 240
Asquith Commission, 117, 144
Association of the Good Shepherd, 20
Atbara, 50, 156, 157, 233
Austria, Emperor Franz Joseph of, 18
Awad al Karim al Masalam, 22
Az Amru, 6
Azande, 145

Bahr Al Ghazal, 71, 72, 120, 147
Bakht er Ruda, 101-2, 103, 104, 106, 113, 116, 118, 131, 133, 134, 135, 136, 138, 170, 177, 179, 239, 240, 242, 243
Baluchistan, 56
Bara, 135
Bari, 70-1
Babiker Bedri, 46, 85, 87
Beirut, American University, 101, 149
Beja, 4, 11, 62
Belgian Congo, 70
Berber, 10, 15, 21, 76, 233
Bible Churchmen's Society, 127
bilharziasis, 216
Blue Nile Province, 135, 216, 244

Social Service Club, 150
'Society for the Defence of the Faith in the Sudan', 77
'Society for the Deliverance of the Country', 77
'Sons of the Nile', 77
Southern Sudan
  education policy in, 63, 116, 119, 122; Williams report, 122-4, 131, 144; plan, 148, 154, 172, 173, 174, 177, 187, 190, 232
  elementary education, 119, 120, 124, 147, 252
  Equatorial Corps mutiny, 187
  girls education, 145, 146
  government policy, 68, 128, 147, 174, 175, 252
  Islam, 5, 33, 127, 187
  language groups, 70, 119-20, 183, 252
  missionaries in, 51, 66-7, 69, 116, 119, 121, 123, 126, 127, 145, 152, 204-5, 252
  Muslim schools, 178
  Northerners in, 152, 252
  Southerners in north, 178
  teacher training, 147
  technical education, 16, 75
  tribal education, 51, 145
sphere system, 33, 121, 124
Stack Memorial School, 69, 71
Suakin, 15, 21, 32, 40, 44, 45
sub-grade schools, 132, 133, 156, 171, 190, 242
Sudan Cultural Centre, 140, 141
Sudan Defence Force, 178, 187
Sudan Mohammedan Law Courts Ordinance, 40
Sudan Plantation Syndicate, 82, 233, 236
Sudan Schools Club, 82
Sudan Schools Graduates' Club, 150
Sudan United Mission Society, 73, 127, 128, 130
Sudan United Tribes Society, 77
Sudanese Movement for National Liberation, 180
Sudanization, 168, 176, 178, 187
Sufis, 5, 6, 8, 21
Sukot, 9
Sultania library, 43
Sunday, 63
Syrians, 29, 80, 82, 227

Tabaqat, al, 12
Tahir Tatai, 22
Tangasi, 9
teacher training, 37, 45, 55, 61, 83, 85, 97, 98, 99, 116, 117, 118, 132, 133, 134-5, 138, 174, 179, 182, 230-1, 235, 240, 242, 243, 247; girls, 248-9
technical education, 16, 45, 89, 94, 108, 112, 114, 127, 144, 147, 161, 168, 176, 226, 233, 234, 250-1, 253
Technical Education Committee, 176-7
Tegali, 135
Tendelti, 135
Tengasi, 171
Tirinkitat, 81
Tokar, 11
Tokat, 220
Tong, 147
Tothill, Dr. J. D., 142
Trade Unions, 180
Translation and Publication Bureau, 137
tribal education, 51
Turco-Egyptian régime, 12, 17, 31, 35, 40
Turkey, Sultan of, 18
Turkish, 15
Turung, 9
Tuti, 6, 11

Uganda, 57, 66, 70, 145, 175, 237
Ulama, 7, 12, 21, 47, 48, 154, 171
Um Gerr, 136, 138
unemployment, 235-6
Unesco, 190
Unity High School, 86
University College, 116, 142, 144, 153, 179, 180, 181, 182-3, 186, 203, 248
  Council and Senate, 183
  Department of Education, 182
  Special Relation Scheme, 183-4
University College of Khartoum Ordinance (1951), 184
University of Khartoum, 116, 189
University of London, 116, 144, 183-4
Upper Nile Province, 16, 147, 174

Vatican, 126
venereal diseases, 138, 211
Verona Fathers Mission, 31, 49, 52, 146